THE PITCHBOOK

THE PITCHBOOK

A Banking Analyst's Tale of
Markets, Millions, and Mayhem

Vedran Vuk

This book is a work of fiction. Names, characters, organizations, places, events, and incidents either are the product of the author's imagination or are used fictitiously. Any resemblance to actual persons, living or dead, events, or locales is entirely coincidental. This book does use the proper names of certain long-established corporate entities and well-known personalities, but the characters involved with them and the events surrounding those entities and persons are wholly imaginary.

For information about permission to reproduce selections from this book or to contact the author, write to thepitchbook@gmail.com

Book design by nskvsky at Fiverr

ISBN: 9798515891961

Contents

THE PITCHBOOK

CHAPTER 1

GETTING THE SHADE RIGHT

Cocaine. Robert McClure had never seen it on Wall Street. Hollywood had promised him an investment banking career full of debauchery and endless excess, but that's hardly how it turned out. Where was Charlie Sheen doing coke in the back of a limo or the Wolf of Wall Street surrounded by wild and attractive women? In Robert's world, they were nowhere to be seen. Rather, his life was filled with the daily drudgery of the financial sector. His reality was a never-ending procession of long nights, Excel models, and PowerPoint pitchbooks. When his team finished one pitchbook, it was followed by the next, and then another, followed by the next again.

By title, Robert was an "investment banker" at Latham, Schroeder & Holt, which sounds impressive at Christmas parties to people who don't know any better. Specifically, he was an analyst in the oil and gas division, which ranked him among the lowest level of pond scum in Wall Street's hierarchy. While technically still in high finance, an analyst does not even really analyze anything. He does not bank anyone, and he neither negotiates nor affects a deal in any way whatsoever. Instead, the analyst, a lowly peon, cranks out presentation after presentation in PowerPoint. The actual job is closer to a graphic designer or an administrative assistant than that of a banker. The only real difference is that most graphic designers were not working 80 to 115 hours per week, every week. The monotony was only broken by occasional modeling work in Excel, which was just as miserable as the pitchbooks, if not more. On top of it all, Robert and his fellow analysts were always on call and were obliged to fulfill the most trivial whims of their managing director. If the MD wanted to change the presentation's color scheme from light blue to baby blue at 11 p.m., Robert and the other analysts would stay in the office until 4 a.m. doing just that. If the MD changed his mind to navy blue in the early morning, the analysts would have it done by 9 a.m. without protest.

Investment banking hours are enough to drive a person mad, but what truly turns the bright-eyed analyst into a raving lunatic in just a few years is the meticulous nature of an investment banking pitchbook. Everything about a pitchbook aspires to perfection. Every title uses the same custom font; every bullet is at the same height on every page; and every color is custom-selected from aesthetically pleasing palettes. Missing a period on a footnote was enough to warrant a pitchbook sent flying in your direction. No text is displayed in plain bullets, but must be adorned with graphics to make it more pleasing to the eye. The numbers must always match, add, and calculate, and they must always be correct. An obsessive-compulsive disorder is a great asset in this line of work rather than a hindrance.

The perfectionism was not without reason. Pitchbooks are the primary talking materials between an investment bank's managing director and the CEO or CFO of a company. With the pitchbook, the MD could point to graphs showing trends in the industry, financial metrics of the company, and of course, potential acquisition or divestiture ideas. However, pitchbooks are much more than just useful and practical presentation aides – they are the peacocks of the banking world. Their immaculate, brightly colored feathers parade and posture the supremacy of one bank over another. The more elaborate and detailed the presentation, the grander the display of prowess. Subconsciously, an absolutely flawless pitchbook conveys that a billion-dollar transaction will be equally executed with impeccable precision and perfection. Unfortunately for Robert McClure and his fellow analysts, that perfection was more often than not achieved on the backs of their labor in the early hours of the morning.

On his first day at Latham, Schroeder & Holt, Robert had entered through the clear double doors of the seventeenth floor with exhilaration. Back then he looked very sharp, standing a little over six feet tall with a toned physique. He was an athlete in high school and managed to stay in shape in college. Banking would change all of that in a few months' time. His flowing and curly brown hair was tamed by slicked hair gel and his green eyes shined with excitement. Dressed in a brand new Jos. A. Bank suit, Robert was ready to conquer the financial world and begin a fabled career. As he walked toward his new desk with a human resources assistant leading the way, Robert did not think of the job ahead. Instead, he daydreamed about reflecting upon this moment years in the future as a successful managing director. The bank was vibrant with energy. Hurried and nervous people rushed about the open floor shuffling papers, analyzing screens, and speaking financial lingo across international phone lines. He couldn't wait to join them. As he came closer and closer to the mergers and acquisitions desk, Robert snapped out of his daydream and tension began jolting throughout his body. This was not the first day jitters, but instead a slow, driving panic which would rule his life in mergers and acquisitions from here on.

Robert recognized the faces and names on the team from his multiple interviews for the position. While they had all been very pleasant then, not a single smile greeted him. John Granton, the team's associate, escorted him to his desk. As an associate, John was one notch above an analyst in the bank's hierarchy. An associate's role is part taskmaster and part drill sergeant. Their primary purpose is to execute the half-brained ideas from higher up in the hierarchy. Their secondary, and perhaps more important purpose, is to train, haze, embarrass and belittle the incoming analysts. If any semblance of an analyst's self-esteem survived the first few weeks of employment, the associate had failed miserably in his job. This behavior was not unique to Latham, Schroeder & Holt – the wrath of associates and their thirst for cruelty are institutionalized and ingrained traditions within any serious investment bank.

John was a few inches shorter than Robert, with a solid frame and a slightly protruding stomach that suggested both weight training and an unrelenting appetite for cheeseburgers. His black hair was slicked and neatly combed over to the side, stylish but not so much so as to alert too much attention to himself. His suit and grooming were immaculate and his shoes shined with new polish. John loved dressing the part of the banker each morning and relished in his role as the team's taskmaster. In the last few weeks, he had been counting down the days until the new class of analysts arrived to be placed under his command.

For his first task, John asked Robert to create a slide with a few bullet points on the recent history of mergers and acquisitions in the oilfield services sector. With no previous experience, Robert stumbled around the bank's various databases to collect information on various deals and their respective values. This process took him several hours as he was yet to become an idiot savant of his assigned sector of the global economy. While the Coca-Colas, Kraft Foods, and Exxon Mobils of the world are recognized by anyone, most regular people are clueless about multi-billion dollar giants such as Nabors, Baker Hughes, Schlumberger, and Technip. But then again, most people don't spend much time shopping for oil and gas pipe, valves, and drilling rigs. And since Robert had never replaced a blowout preventer either, the names behind the mergers were as alien as distant galaxies. The learning curve was beyond drinking from a fire hose – it was more like drinking from an anti-riot water cannon. As the hours went by, he knew the assignment was taking him longer than expected. John intermittently sent unsatisfied glances in his direction throughout the day which only heightened Robert's anxiety. When Robert finally wrapped up the bulleted list, he was rather proud of the end product. In fact, as he sent the slide to John for review, Robert smiled to himself, anticipating compliments on his first completed task. However, that was not the case, nor would it ever be at Latham, Schroeder, & Holt. John examined the slide, rolled his eyes, and released a deep sigh. This was not a natural sigh, but instead one purposefully loud enough for everyone on the desk to hear, including the other analysts, associates, vice presidents, and even the managing director. John snarled, "This is all wrong. Do it again like our presentation from last week. Make the boxes light blue."

"Sorry, I didn't know what the right format was."

"I told you that it was saved in the share drive under 'Templates'," replied John in feigned yet believable frustration. Of course, he had done no such thing. Nonetheless, Robert obediently returned to his desk and searched for the older presentation. In every detail, he copied the older presentation's exact format and placed the bullets in the same light peach-colored boxes. Next, he carefully centered the boxes on the slide at the exact levels and heights as the previous presentation. After several more careful reviews, everything looked good; so he sent the slide back to John again. Robert watched him from the corner of his eye as the e-mail was opened.

"What the fuck…come over here!" said John, again just loud enough for the whole team to hear. "Ok, watch me fix this."

First, John toyed with the text of each bullet. The first sentence read "In 2009, Baker Hughes acquired BJ Services for $5.5 billion". John first put the 2009 at the end of the sentence. Then, he changed "acquired" to "bought". Then, he added "Inc." to "Baker Hughes". With each revision, he shook his head and grunted…very audibly. He then reverted "bought" back to "acquired" and returned the date back to its original place. He grunted again.

"Does it look OK now?" inquired Robert sheepishly.

John did not respond or even look at him. So, Robert asked a second time.

No response.

John just stared at the screen for the next five minutes without even acknowledging Robert's existence. He moved his cursor to the next sentence. The cursor hovered above a sentence, but nothing was changed. Nonetheless, he still moaned with disapproval as if Robert had spilled red wine on an invaluable hand-woven carpet. The third bullet received the same detailed examination. Despite providing no input during the review, Robert was compelled to stand by John's desk like a new cadet at attention. Almost an hour later, John was done with the wording with hardly a change made to the bullets. This was only the start of it for the slide. He then began playing with the boxes and rectangles surrounding the text. John grimaced, "Why are the box outlines in dark blue?"

"That's the color in the old presentation saved under 'Templates'," answered Robert.

"No," said John, "the summaries are always in medium blue, but I already told you that." Robert knew for certain that the boxes were not medium blue in the old presentation, but he dared not talk back. John also knew that the boxes were not medium blue in the old presentation. However, this was all part of the tutorial's two-fold mission. The first part was to show the new analyst who was boss in the office. If an associate said that the sky was azure and not medium blue today, then that is exactly what it was. If an associate said that the sky was purple, a wise analyst would agree. The second purpose of the tutorial was to establish the incoming analyst as a clueless idiot in front of the entire team. After all, investment banks do hire the best and brightest – a smart analyst can become competition. By throwing him under the bus right away, it would be much easier to throw him under the bus again later when it served John's purposes. Furthermore, in the eyes of his superiors, it was also useful to paint himself as a mentor to the new analysts, albeit a disciplined and strict one who upheld the standards of the bank.

John clicked his mouse and the rectangle was altered to medium blue. Then, he changed his mind and began experimenting with three different shades of blue before settling on something other than medium blue. Seeing this, Robert felt like a patient with Locked-In Syndrome – every part of his body wanted to punch John straight out of his chair and call him on his bullshit, but his face could not move from the pleasant-new-employee smile that had been stuck in position since entering the analyst bull pen. John continued with his ingenious changes to the slide. He moved the boxes around millimeter by millimeter. First up, then down, then up again, left, left, more left, right, up, up, up, down, right, left. He stopped and stared at the boxes for about five minutes and then resumed moving them around again. When he was finally satisfied, he instructed Robert to insert green arrows connecting the boxes to emphasize the points within them.

By now, Robert understood the game…or so he thought. Returning to his computer, he exactly copied the arrow style from the older presentation. Perhaps John was done making his point. Satisfied that it looked very sharp, he again sent the presentation for his review. Within minutes, John was standing over Robert's desk.

"Open the presentation." More dissatisfied grunts and orders followed. "Make the arrows bigger…

"Wait, no, smaller…

"That's too small.

"No, too big.

"Not narrow enough."

John Granton issued his orders with a tone of life-or-death urgency, as if the whole investment bank would collapse without a properly shaped arrow. Nothing about his tone indicated that this was a joke. By now, Robert had almost lost his wits, and they hadn't even begun to debate the appropriate shade of green. On this slide alone, several hours had already been wasted, and this was slide one of approximately forty more in the pitchbook which all required reviews from John, the Vice President, and eventually the MD. And this was just day one of the two-year-long hell agreed upon in his employment contract.

On that first day, Robert thought that John was just a single insane aberration on their team, but he was wrong. This approach to pitchbooks was the de facto norm of the investment banking world. In fact, some associates and vice presidents were even worse. As one clawed his way higher up the bank's corporate ladder, sanity lost its grip on reality, and bankers placed even more emphasis on correct shades and properly aligned boxes. However, despite the madness of the process, the efficiency of the final product was difficult to argue with. When a CEO flipped through the presentation, he could easily absorb the condensed and well-organized information in less than fifteen minutes. While a single pitchbook could take hundreds of man hours of work, the end result was a perfect presentation boiled down to the minutes in a meeting between a company's management team and the bank.

That said, often those hundreds of man hours didn't translate into a single minute of review by a management team. Sometimes, the CEOs didn't even look at the pitchbooks. If the conversation strayed to deer hunting in south Texas or the managing director never managed to delve into the details of a potential transaction, the pitchbook might not be opened at all. As some executives have quipped, the presentations are accurately named "pitchbooks" as they are rapidly pitched into the trash after the bankers leave. This was the rhythm and dance of investment banking…and it was hardly the models and bottles most folks on Main Street imagined it to be, and it was a world that Robert McClure grew tired of at a most rapid pace…

CHAPTER 2

ALL ROADS LEAD TO HOUSTON

Robert McClure tightly knotted the bass lure to the fishing line. He knew that the lake before him didn't actually have any bass, and hence using a bass lure would seem foolhardy to any regular fisherman, but Robert knew better. This wasn't just any lake…it was the one four houses down from his parents' home in Laurel, Mississippi, and it was solidly packed with catfish, which under any normal circumstances should not and would not chase a bass lure. But lazy summer after lazy summer had taught Robert different. Mr. Charles, their neighbor, would feed the catfish every Sunday morning. Before throwing out the floating bits of food, he would rev up the engine of his early 70s Ford truck. At the rough sound of the engine, the fish would begin to surface and swarm at the shore nearest to the truck in a peculiar ritual learned by the fish. Mr. Charles would then toss handfuls of food to the eager subsurface crowd. The key was fishing on a Friday or Saturday. Within the enclosed ecosystem of the small lake, the catfish could not survive without good ole Mr. Charles. Toward the end of the week, the catfish would become so ravenous with hunger that even a bass lure would draw them out of the depths. These weren't small catfish but rather gargantuans too big for their small lake, with the average fish stretching from a few inches above the knee to the ground. In those days, Robert had not even heard the words "investment banking" spoken in his small town. Back then, the most important things in life were a good fishing hole, the right dirt road, and the best clearing in the woods for a summertime bonfire.

But eventually, life came calling, and he needed a plan. The standard options for a kid in his position were attending Mississippi State or Ole Miss. However, unless your daddy was the town accountant, a business degree from either was not going to do much for you in Laurel. And the only thing Robert's daddy was accounting in Jones County was the miles on his truck route logged religiously into his daily ledger. Furthermore, a degree with the word, "Mississippi" on it was worth the paper that it was written on in the business world outside a handful of surrounding states. Robert did not have a perfect map of the future, but even then he knew that the first steps had to be getting out of Mississippi and getting into a good business school. Realistically, there was no chance of him making it into an Ivy League school, let alone being able to afford the tuition. Vanderbilt was out of the question for the same reason. So instead, he applied to the University of Texas. It had a solid top 20 business program, and unbeknownst to him at the time, it was a feeder program for oil and gas investment banking. His acceptance letter had arrived a few days ago, but he was still waiting to hear about a scholarship that would make or break his decision.

Robert turned his attention back to the lake before him and the tiniest ripples on top of the water. The teenage Robert McClure didn't look all that much different other than being a little lankier and more suntanned from a summer largely spent in the outdoors. His wild, dark brown hair blew in the light breeze and his concentrated green eyes gazed out onto the small island in the middle of the lake. All was quiet and still except for a few floating turtles peaking their heads above the surface. As his fishing pole swung back to cast the line, he noticed a dip into the water from the small island – it was black and dark, a water moccasin, the natural enemy of every Mississippi boy. He urgently dropped his fishing pole, which partially splashed into the water, and grabbed the BB gun next to him. Robert began to pump it as fast as he could as the snake slid closer across the water. He aimed the gun carefully and wondered whether the quick six pumps were enough to break its skin. The gun let out a shot. The moccasin submerged below the surface. Did he get it? There was no way to know. The boy patiently waited for it to reappear, but the moccasin was nowhere in sight. Seeing one moccasin meant there were others, but for now, it was time to fish. He cast out his first line of the day and dragged it along the edge of the shore. Two-thirds of the way back to his reel – there it was! "YEEEESHHH!!" The line pulled abruptly with a monster catfish battling on the other end.

****

Mark Edwards inspected the pile of crisp and golden catfish with suspicion and bemoaned the lack of a sushi option today. He rapidly passed the fried fish and followed the sizzling sounds of the nearby hamburger station. Mark brushed aside his wavy blond hair from his darkly tanned face as he reached into his pocket for his wallet. The lady at the register was lost for a second in his dazzling green eyes and his youthful, charming looks, which were a peculiar rarity in the Latham Schroder cafeteria. Yanking out a ten-dollar bill, he looked back to see Robert stacking his plate with crispy golden fillets, which were virtually untouched by the lunchtime crowd. He walked over to a white square table encircled by colorful and curvy futuristic chairs in the middle of the dining area. The cafeteria was surely the creation of some en-vogue designer tasked with the duty of melding chic modernism with cold corporate practicality. The walls were decorated with bits of different colored pastel glass which occasionally twinkled in the sunlight, yet the squareness and uniformity of the tables evoked rigid order and conformity. As he moved toward the empty table, Mark Edwards stared at the spectacular view outside the floor to ceiling glass panels. Several months had passed since the fresh analyst class had begun its tour of duty at Latham, Schroeder & Holt, yet the view still caught his attention every day. It was late July 2014, and the price of crude oil was $101.57 per barrel, which promised the young analysts a bright future. From twenty-three stories high, all of Houston lay before them with building crane after building crane in the distance. The commodity boom had funded skyline expansions across Houston's city centers, and the fastest growing center was here in the Galleria where several half-built skyscrapers were reaching steadily skyward. Real estate in the city was booming, particularly within the 610 loop where houses received multiple bidders within one listing day. In fact, the IT department at Latham Schroeder was forced to block various real estate listing websites as employees spent far too much time house hunting rather than attending to the bank's business. The price of crude oil projected its warm rays like a sun god pouring down prosperity onto the city. The crude price touched everything and everyone: the waitress receiving big tips, the roughnecks earning close to six figures in the field and, of course, the bankers who benefited most of all. Even as 23-year-old graduates, the young analysts' salaries surpassed those of most grown men. An investment banking analyst earned $75,000 per year with an expected bonus of $50,000 to $60,000 if the deal flow was good. Sure, it wasn't enough to buy a Porsche, but it was sufficient to buy a used BMW and drinks for all your friends at the bar, which is what they imagined they might do if a night off would ever present itself. With the youngest analysts earning this much, it was no exaggeration to say that the city was minting new millionaires like clockwork in banking and the oil business. People were moving to Houston in droves from across the southeast and the rest of the country. Apartment blocks and townhouses were being built at an even faster pace than the skyscrapers to welcome the new arrivals. Crude oil smiled with admiration upon its creation. It was joyful and gleefully embraced the progress of its loyal subjects as it shined down upon them. Mark turned from the view of the growing city and the afternoon sun and got down to the business of chomping into his burger.

Soon, Robert joined him, balancing bottles of hot sauce and tartar sauce on his tray. Mark pointed to the fish. "What is that?"

"Catfish, my friend, catfish," replied Robert. "It's the first time for me to see it in the cafeteria."

"What's it taste like?" inquired Mark. While this may have seemed like a peculiar question in Houston, TX, Latham Schroeder & Holt wasn't really in Houston other than strictly in the geographic sense. The culture was pure New York City. The Houston office was simply a satellite of a vast Wall Street fiefdom that had seen the advantages of capitalizing on the growing shale oil revolution. To New York, the Houston office was their lunar landing module on the planet of Texas, a strange, uncouth, and uncivilized place in their eyes. Latham, Schroder & Holt was hardly the only bank attempting to nudge its way into the oil and gas sector. The city was crowded with banks headquartered from California to Canada to France and Switzerland. Several unique characteristics of oil and gas drew investment banking capital from across the world. Unlike most industries, oil and gas companies can easily spend more in capital in any given year than their annual revenue. As a result, the industry always needs to raise or borrow additional capital. Furthermore, land speculation and a wild rush to seize the best shale acreage across the United States guaranteed an endless pipeline of mergers and acquisition activity. And these acquisitions meant more fees earned and more equity and debt raised to finance those purchases. The combination of these factors made oil and gas one of the most lucrative industries to bank and an investment banking paradise. Everyone wanted in, and as a result, Houston saw an increasing influx of new residents like Mark Edwards, who had never known the pleasures of fried catfish, but now found himself encountering the fish for the first time on a plate.

"Here, have a piece."

Mark grabbed the catfish nugget from his co-worker and bit it with caution. "Hmmm…it's ok, I guess."

Robert shrugged. "What would you Californians know about good catfish? Hell, you guys don't even cook the fish half the time over there."

"Alright, take it easy with the California jokes. You'll wear yourself out if you start too early in the day."

"Ha, I've already told you, Mark. After maybe ten or fifteen years and after you start saying 'ya'll' for a solid five years, I'll consider giving you some slack on the California jokes. And if you become a fan of Texas A&M or UT football, I will even consider reducing this probation period to a maximum of three years."

"Don't worry man," responded Mark. "It'll be a cold day in hell if I'm still here in three years doing this shit. In three sweet years, I'll be back to surfing and sun," said Mark with a smile on his face.

"Yeah, I can see you now, man," retorted Robert teasingly. "You're driving down the highway with a brand new surfboard strapped to the back of your magenta Prius. You've got a car full of hot dudes because you know, you're finally using your film degree, if you want know what I mean. Yeah, seems like a really good time, bro – you'll have to invite me out."

"Fuck you, man!" chuckled Mark in good fun, "Don't make me rip into you with Mississippi jokes bro. You don't wanna go there – it's not too early in the day to start talking about your kissing cousins. Don't you push me, man. Don't do it."

Lunch was about only time that the guys could be themselves away from their masters. It was a welcome break in the monotony. Mark honestly was counting down each remaining day in Houston. This city was never part of his plan, but considering his poor choice of a college major, it's hard to say that he ever planned much other than hanging out on the beach. After years of preaching to his parents about his passion for film, he tucked his tail between his legs and asked for a favor. His dad was an executive at Occidental Petroleum in Los Angeles. One month later, Mark was on a plane to Houston with an offer from Latham, Schroeder & Holt and a promise to himself that this would only be temporary. He cringed to consider what his college buddies would think of his career choice. After two years of investment banking, he could land a job at a hedge fund back in California – maybe L.A. but more likely San Francisco as tech start-ups fueled hedge funds and asset managers in the Bay Area. Just two more years of this crap and he would be driving down Highway 1 with the top down…and not in a frickin' Prius…

As the two launched into their meal, Lenny Lee, the last member of the analyst team, rushed to join them, almost tripping over a chair on his way to their table. Lenny was dressed in a stylish, tightly fitted suit with a skinny tie, not quite European in fashion but almost there. He had short-trimmed black hair that matched his professional black-rimmed hipster glasses. For a nerdy Asian guy, Lenny was pretty stylish and perhaps overly so for an investment banker. Of the three, his suit was the nicest by far and was always dry-cleaned, crisp, and immaculate.

"Hey what's up Lenny? What'd you do this weekend?" asked Mark.

"Not much…watched *X-Men Days of Future Past*."

This was not an atypical response from Lenny. At least this time he didn't give them the details of his latest dungeon raid in World of Warcraft. Mark and Robert really don't know what to think of Lenny. The other guys didn't have much in common with him, but at the end of the day, Lenny was a fellow analyst and hence a comrade-in-arms. And, most of the time, he didn't say much which made him a pretty easy guy to get along with.

"Oh yeah, how was the movie?"

"Alright."

"How was your weekend, Mark? Any luck at the Anvil?" inquired Robert.

"Luck! Are you serious? As if I rely on luck. I went out with Troy and Sam from Houlihan…you know those guys, right? And yeah, so we met up with Katy, Kelly, and Charlotte. You remember them from like a month back? Well, we started with mixed drinks at the Anvil which turned to kamikazes at the Poison Girl which turned into me not knowing my own name at Boots and Shoots. Which then, of course, led to me hooking up with Kelly at my place, because I'm awesome. So, you know, overall a pretty good night," said Mark with a broad smile.

"Bulllllllshitttt," said Robert, turning to Lenny. "He did not hook up with Kelly. I can guarantee that. You are a fucking liar, Mark."

"Believe what you want dude, but I'm a gentleman – I can say no more."

"Oh you can say no more because there is nothing to say. You went home and passed out on your *Toy Story 3* sheets crying yourself to sleep. That's the real story," said Robert, biting into a piece of catfish.

Lenny stared blankly, not reacting to the conversation as the two continued their exchange. His mind was elsewhere, in particular on cell X357 of the input assumptions tab in the Excel model. He might have hardcoded it by accident. Lenny always double-checked everything and left nothing to chance. This had been true at every point in his life up until this very minute. He had dreamed of this job since junior high, earned the right grades in high school, and began studying for the SAT as a freshman. In college at Rice University, he double majored in Finance and Economics while taking leadership roles on the Student Council, the Chess Club, the Investment Team, and the Economics Club. His life was so spotless that even the most ardent tabloid journalist would be hard-pressed to find a wrinkle in Lenny's past. Despite this, his parents constantly badgered him on his decision to pursue investment banking rather than a more "respectable" career like medicine or engineering. In the Lee household, he was a rebel.

During his senior year of college, Lenny easily secured several investment banking offers, in part thanks to his talent and a part thanks to Rice University. While most US college graduates send out dozens of resumes to prospective employers, the best and brightest to some degree get their jobs on a silver platter. By graduating from an Ivy League or other prestigious institution such as Rice University, the applicants are essentially pre-screened for Wall Street. In fact, the banks come on campus to recruit – there is no need for faceless applications. Banks assess the candidates' interest in finance and their willingness to work the long hours, and provided these qualities are present an Ivy League graduate needs little more to find a way into the prestigious profession. Given his mathematical genius, expert proficiency in Excel, and encyclopedic knowledge of the oil and gas industry, Lenny had his choice of banks, turning down Jefferies, Morgan Stanley, and Citigroup for Latham, Schroder & Holt. He was driven and ambitious, an ideal workhorse for senior bankers.

"Hey, Lenny so do you ever go out?" asked Mark.

"Naw, not really. I'm usually just catching up on sleep on our off days. And Rice wasn't exactly a party school so I guess that I did get into it that much."

"Bro, you gotta go out with us some time. It'll be fun, dude."

"Alright, maybe next time. I'll see. No promises though."

"I need promises, bro. Don't leave me like that, Lenny."

"Well guys," said Robert, "I guess that we better get back to it. I'm sure that John has a whole pile of crap ready for us to scoop."

"You're probably right," groaned Mark. The guys jammed the last of their food into their mouths and dumped the rest into the garbage cans. They walked through the glass doors to the elevator landing and then descended to the seventeenth floor where the rectangles, numbers, and shades of blue awaited these ambitious young masters of the universe.

CHAPTER 3

OUR LORD AND SAVIOR, WARREN BUFFETT

Across the entire open office floor plan there was only a single smiling face at Latham, Schroeder & Holt – it belonged to Erik Schatzker, the newscaster from Bloomberg news beaming down from the overhead TVs. Everyone else was adjusting to the day's first wave of stress as they reviewed their inboxes filled with requests from clients and managing directors alike. The office layout was typical for an investment bank. Each chair had three screens in front of it comprised of a small laptop in the middle hooked into two larger screens above it. Row after row of screens sat on top of glossy tables reminiscent of Ikea furniture but more expensive. Nothing separated one worker from the next and nothing divided the ranks and compensation levels either. The penniless intern sat shoulder to shoulder with MDs pulling in a million per year. Unfortunately, rather than promoting an egalitarian environment, this layout made sure that the subordinates were constantly under the watchful eye of authority. The designers of the open floor format claimed that it helped facilitate communication between teams by removing the boundaries between them. However, in the age of smart phones, instant messengers, and e-mails, immediate proximity to your team is hardly necessary for communication. The real purpose and source of the efficiency gain was keeping up the pressure. With the open plan, managers could instantaneously spot someone resting for a moment to check their personal e-mail or Facebook. At the same time, low-level analysts could see exactly how many times per day their MDs checked the latest news on ESPN…which was often.

At one end of the floor were the commodity traders, boxed off in their own section behind a translucent glass door and wall. The traders each had six screens in front them which constantly flashed red and green like a string of Christmas lights struck by lightning. Some traders had even more screens, as in their world the total number of screens was considered directly proportional to one's importance and trading prowess. At the other end of the floor, mergers and acquisitions similarly had a frosted glass wall which separated it from the rest of investment banking. Were it not for a particularly silly SEC regulation, the floor would be completely open. According to compliance, these walls were necessary to separate the flow of inside information from one part of the bank to the other. However, no one could explain how these walls prevented anyone from opening the door to talk with someone from another group. But the rules were the rules, according to the government. The symbolism of the translucent glass walls did not escape Robert, and he wondered whether a particularly clever architect had intended them that way. Returning to his PowerPoint presentation, he tried to ignore Eric Schatzker and his warm smile on the flat screen directly above him. Robert turned his full focus on positioning an arrow to point out an oil well on a map of Midland County, Texas. He chose light green, the company's color for the arrow, dark blue for the outline of the text box identifying the well, and light grey for the box's background. John Granton continued to make his life hell, but Robert was catching on. After doing this fifty times per day for three months, the color codes were now second nature to him. He had memorized the three number custom color mixes for the entire Latham, Schroeder & Holt presentation palette which included approximately twenty specific colors to be used in separate specific cases. For example, a dark blue outline was always chosen for a text box calling out a well result on a map, while a light blue outline was used to summarize text in the overview section of the pitchbook. Besides mastering pitchbooks, Robert had also completed the arduous licensing exams required by FINRA. After almost six hours of testing, an intensive criminal background check, and even fingerprinting, he successfully passed the FINRA Series 79, the Investment Banking Representative Examination, and the Series 63, the Uniform Securities State Law Examination. The process of fingerprinting the applicants and memorizing regulatory rules as a fresh-faced analyst seemed strange to him. It was almost as if the financial regulators found him and his colleagues in the world of finance guilty until proven innocent.

His thoughts returned from regulatory scrutiny to the important task of perfectly aligning the PowerPoint objects in front of him. As he moved to the next arrow to point out another well result, something in the corner of his eye caught his attention – it was a flash of grey on the flat screen above him. A chubby, grey-haired man appeared on Bloomberg ready to be interviewed by Erik Schatzker and a group of other Bloomberg newscasters. The analysts immediately stopped in their tracks and turned upward toward the screen in reverence. It was as if an angel of finance had appeared before them and had struck them to the ground on the road to Damascus. There was nothing purer, nothing more brilliant than the power before them. They could no longer ignore the TV screens despite their workload and were in complete thrall to the grey-haired man's words. The celestial being smiled down upon them from the flat screen, “Hi, Erik, glad to be on the show again,” said Warren Buffett to his host.

“Warren, glad to have you back on the show as always,” said Erik Schatzker. “I know that your time is very precious so let’s get right to it. With the turbulence in world markets and central banks primed to raise rates, where do you see the market going now?”

“Well, I think the US economy is fundamentally strong. This is still a great country to do business in, and we will make it out of this rough patch.”

“Warren that’s a pretty optimistic view given how lots of market participants feel out there – so what are you investing in today?”

“Coca-Cola – you have to invest in what you know and then you’ve got to have the patience to hold it forever and see it through.”

John Granton was standing right behind Mark with his eyes peeled to the screen. “God, he’s a genius! What I wouldn’t give to be like that guy or to even work for him.”

“Oh, I don’t need to work for Warren Buffett. I can beat those bear markets year after year by myself” said Mark, “Just give me half a billion dollars, and I promise that I’ll prove it to you.”

“I wouldn’t give you two quarters to get me a drink from the Coke machine. You are a fucking retard,” replied John with utter sincerity in his voice.

“How do you think he does it?” asked Robert to the group as he rolled back in his chair. “I mean there are plenty of smart fund managers out there, yet no one can touch Buffett.”

“Well, you buy and hold forever, right?” said Lenny. “That’s the Warren Buffett way,”

“Dude, I could totally do that,” said Mark. “But how he does it isn’t the important question, it’s what you would do with Warren Buffett money.

Come on Lenny, you first, what car would you get?" inquired Mark Edwards as he swished a balled-up paper perfectly into the wastebasket.

Lenny took his fingers off the keyboard to think…

"Porsche 911, cherry red."

"Cherry red – weak Lenny, really weak," teased Mark. "You gotta go for yellow. Everyone knows that."

"And what about you, hotshot?" prodded Robert.

"Well, I don't know how you guys might feel about it with us being in oil and gas and all," said Mark, "but I'd get a Tesla – that and a Lambo of course for my Saturday drive."

"Of course, I mean the Lambo goes without saying, but I gotta knock you on one point here. Teslas are cool, but they're not even in the same league as a Lambo, not even close. We're talking Warren Buffett money here, not dentist in the suburbs money."

"Well, if you're such an expert, what's your car, Robert?" asked Mark.

"For my everyday car, I'd probably get a tricked out F-150, but if I was like a really liberal gay guy from California who likes surfing and stuff, which I'm not, but I'm just speaking for people who might be like that, then I'd go for a BMW i8. Tesla is weak, man, compared to the i8."

"Fuck you," said Mark, throwing another paper wad straight at Robert rather than the garbage can. "This guy just can't help himself."

"Hey Mark, it's cool. Latham Schroeder is an equal opportunity employment workplace. We are accepting of your lifestyle," responded Robert. "What you and another man do in the privacy of your Tesla is completely between you and that man. We support you."

"You guys are dumb as shit," added John, butting into the conversation with his commentary and protruding belly. "If you had Warren Buffett money, a Ferrari is your day car. Here's my list: Lambo, Ferrari, Porsche,

Jag XF, and an Alfa Romeo that I would just crash for fun. You boys aren't thinking big enough – have I taught you nothing?"

"Well, that's like a whole wish list of cars," pointed out Mark. "You gotta narrow it down. That's the whole point here."

"No shit, dumbass, but we're talking Warren Buffet money – you get the whole wish list. You drive one car per day if that floats your boat," retorted John, angry that his input had been met by anything other than adoration of his genius.

"Hey, come check this out." Robert had opened the BMW webpage to the i8 model and was spinning it with a 360-degree view.

Mark rolled his chair over to Robert's computer. "Oh man, that's really sick. Change the color to white pearl with blue highlights."

Robert did so, flipping the option from "sophisto grey"' to "white pearl" with blue highlights. Mark ran his hands through his sandy blond hair. "Oh that's fucking sick…that is fucking sick, man! Alright, I get what you're saying now about the i8."

John interrupted their sports car fantasies. "I can't believe it…I just can't fucking believe it!"

"What?" said Lenny, confused. He searched John's face for a clue as to what was going on. John was staring at the far end of the open floor plan – they all turned their heads simultaneously. "Oh shit, it's Sarah!" exclaimed Lenny.

Approaching from the elevator was Sarah from Human Resources. She wore a grey skirt that tightly hugged her body and a slightly sheer button-up white shirt. While technically professional, the outfit seemed two sizes too small and pushed the boundaries of "appropriate business attire" to its limits. As she moved down the floor casually swinging her hips, the four of them lost all sense of time and place as they stared in her direction.

"Can you be any more fucking obvious?" muttered John under his breath. Everyone flipped their heads back at once. Lenny, shocked back to Earth, spun in his chair and knocked a financial calculator and several pens off his desk. "Jesus Christ!" said John, momentarily burying his head in his palm. "You guys are the dumbest analyst class I've seen yet."

As Sarah arrived at their section of the floor, John stood up and threw a pitchbook in front of Mark and Robert with perfect timing. "Hey, I wanted to talk with you guys about the model." Sarah was close enough to hear John. "Go to cell X134 and AB139, fix that formula and link it to the hardcoded cell on the control panel. Mark, re-do all the formatting back to how it used to be. You guys are doing a great job – you're really catching on to all the stuff that I've been teaching you. Keep up the good work," said John, acting the part of a wise and helpful mentor. These were the first positive words ever to have escaped his mouth in relation to their work. He even went so far as to give Mark a pat on the back. Right as Sarah passed their desk, John glanced upward, pretending to just notice her presence. "Oh hey, Sarah. What brings you down to the seventeenth floor?" said John with a big friendly smile on his face.

"Hi John, we just have some new hires in operations on the other side of the floor. How are your new analysts settling in?"

"Just great. It's the best team that we've had in a long time – just an amazing group of guys," John smiled at the three of them like the proud coach of a Little League team.

"Well, I'm glad that you are getting along so well." Sarah continued walking down the hall and turned a corner. With each step, John mentally undressed her as he salaciously followed every move of her body. Lenny and Mark were similarly enraptured.

"Man, what I wouldn't do for a piece of that," said John. "I think I've got a shot as an associate…but then again she's probably too dumb to know what that means."

"You know…just a thought, but I don't know if it's the smartest thing in the world to have an infatuation for HR. That's a good way to go from banker to janitor," pointed out Robert.

"Ha, didn't think about that!" said Mark. "Hey, totally random thought here, but do you think Warren Buffett gets ass like that?"

The whole team was caught off guard as Ronald Lufkin, their managing director, walked up to them with a thick pitchbook in his hands. "Oh, you bet he does. I bet Buffett gets even better ass than that. That old bastard is probably putting Viagra in his Cheerios every morning. And by the way, that HR girl isn't even hot – I've had way hotter chicks. I can't believe my team has such low standards."

Ronald Lufkin's statement was hard to believe at this point. At fifty years old, his hairline was rapidly receding and his skin was pale and splotchy from years of investment banking and a consequent lack of sunlight. Though as a managing director his schedule was easier now, he still put in a solid sixty to seventy hours per week. However, the lighter workload couldn't reverse the years of physical damage done by the grunt work of his analyst days. Ron was short for a MD, standing at 5'9", but his presence immediately exuded an aura of authority and respect, even if you didn't know him, his job title, or even his industry.

"When I was an associate at JP Morgan London, we were crazy. Our team got laid all the time. You guys would have loved London back in '96. Hottest and easiest girls you've ever seen if you were a banker. Also, it didn't hurt that our bonuses were better than what they pay associates today. Too bad, you missed the boat on that."

"Sounds awesome," said a wide-eyed Mark.

"Look, I don't have time to talk with you kids about banking in the 90s right now. You need to fix this dogshit pitchbook. It's all fucked up and the meeting with Wellco Solutions is tomorrow," Ron tossed the pitchbook at Robert – it smacked him across his chest and fell in front of him. Ron's lips twitched slightly – he hadn't intended to hit Robert with the pitchbook, but he certainly wasn't going to apologize for doing so either. Robert flipped through the presentation and saw red marks riddling the fifty or so pages.

"Make all of those changes in red and then throw out slides fourteen to thirty-five. I don't like any of that crap. We don't need any charts on drilling or fishing tools. Just stay focused on the pressure pumping market. I'm not sure what I want in there, but have ten slides covering it by tomorrow morning, and they better be good. Let's not have any last minute changes because the slides look like shit." Ron walked over to his desk just a few seats down from them and picked up his phone ready to dial. "Oh yeah, one more thing, I don't like those light green arrows. Make them all a darker green in the whole presentation. I never want to see light green arrows in our presentations again. Do you understand?" The analysts nodded. "I didn't hear you," remarked Ron.

"Yes sir," said Robert nervously.

"Yes of course," uttered Mark.

Lenny was too nervous to say anything at all.

As Ron began his phone call, the three analysts exchanged tense, terrified glances. Robert stared up at the clock – it was 5:30 p.m. He had hoped for an early night for once, but Ron had just given his relaxing evening the kiss of death. Robert opened the presentation file from the share drive and changed the color of the first three arrows on the second slide. It was going to be a long night.

CHAPTER 4

DOWN TO THE MINUTE

Robert stared up at the vast, star-speckled Mississippi sky. Jenny Durmeyer sat next to him on the tailgate of his beat-up brown Chevy. Just behind them was a cooler half full of Milwaukee's Best cans along with Jenny and Emily's six pack of Bacardi Ice. Josh, Bo and Parker, his best buds from high school, were about ten yards away stacking logs for the bonfire. Emily carefully watched the boys from a safe distance. They placed several larger logs in the middle and then built a tepee of sticks and branches over them. Robert teased the guys from the truck as the structure toppled over for the third time. Josh and Bo had started plenty of fires before, but after ten beers, the task became increasingly difficult. With the help of some lighter fluid and after a few more mishaps, they finally got the mound ablaze. The accomplishment was celebrated with another round of cold ones.

Jenny and Robert kept cracking jokes at the guys and laughed the night away. Together, they watched the stars until it felt as if they were sinking into eternity. Everything around them breathed with the sounds of the countryside; a chorus of crickets, the crackle of a fire, the sound of footsteps bending tall dry grass, and the laughing of friends.

****

It was 2:37 a.m., and the team had reviewed the Wellco Solutions presentation for the last time, catching a final light green arrow that had previously eluded them. Other than the fluorescent motion-sensor lights above them, the office floor was dark and empty. The equity capital markets team had stuck around until about 8 p.m. The accounting team had been there until 11:30 p.m., but only because it was the end of the quarter. John had gone home just past midnight, leaving only the three analysts and hours more of work.

In the silent office, Robert recalled that night with Jenny. How had he gone from carelessly having fun around a bonfire a few years ago to this misery? But could he really complain? Growing up in Mississippi, you inevitably found yourself in one of two tribes, those who wanted to stay there forever and those who couldn't wait to get out. He chose the move-away tribe and then investment banking – this wasn't some sort of strange accident. When he arrived at the University of Texas and found out about investment banking in Houston, he left the fishing poles behind and jumped head first into making himself the most competitive candidate possible. Nobody forced him to read investment books and *The Wall Street Journal* like religious texts. If Robert had other opportunities, maybe things would have gone differently. The last that he had heard, Parker, his old friend, was working for his dad's tax firm. The guy who couldn't even get a bonfire started now had one of the only white-collar jobs in Laurel, just by the luck of the draw.

However, if Robert was honest with himself, he would have left anyway. Being an investment banker sounded a lot better than being the local tax accountant in Laurel, Mississippi. Robert had always wanted to be a big fish in a big pond rather than a minnow in a puddle. Furthermore, banking seemed like a meritocratic way to climb the ladder – the eighty-hour work weeks actually attracted him to the business and the dog-eat-dog world where the smartest hedge fund wins seemed exciting and in some ways even fair. It was a different world from Mississippi where your family and connections determined your success and social stratum. Wall Street and investment banking looked like freedom. Despite the painful days, in many ways, this was a dream come true for a Mississippi kid whose family had mostly been farmers since time immemorial. The rest of his tribe found their way to Houston as well. The city became the place to be for Southern kids who wanted something better, just like Atlanta had been in the previous two decades. College grads from Alabama, Mississippi, and Louisiana swarmed the city.

He had played these thoughts through his head a hundred times and knew this was the right decision. However, at this moment in the early a.m. hours, he was reconsidering his choices. His friends back home were probably drinking beer this weekend after a hunting trip, not much different than during his high school days. Was that so bad after all? Sure, he was "getting ahead," whatever that meant, but it certainly didn't feel like it tonight. Robert was dead tired, and this wouldn't be the last night like it in the week.

With the office so dark, it was easier to see Houston's other skyscrapers around them. Robert walked over to the large windows and looked out at the Galleria. In the neighboring towers a couple of lights had been left haphazardly on, but the offices were empty. Only one illuminated box two buildings away still showed any signs of activity. From his vantage point, Robert could see three or four guys frantically reviewing something on a table full of laptops and papers. He wondered which investment bank was in that building. Robert turned his head upward to the sky, but saw only blackness as the city's glow drowned out every star except for the North Star, which was barely peeking through the night. This was certainly not the star-filled night sky that he had gazed upon with Jenny Durmeyer by his side. The lone star stared back down at him and shared a moment of silence before Robert returned to his desk to clear the paper coffee cups which had accumulated over the evening. Mark and Lenny were packing up too. With a seventeen-hour day behind them, one would think that the guys would have rushed out the door, but they were too beat. They sluggishly folded their laptops for the night.

The pressure pumping market slides were done. A few days ago, they had known almost nothing about this sector of the oilfield services market, but after collectively reading several hundred pages of equity research reports, they now knew enough to assemble a basic industry overview on the key players and various geographies. Some presentations in the oilfield services market were easier than others, given their less technical nature. For example, the concept of fishing tools is a no-brainer. When something gets stuck down hole or a rig hand drops something in the well-bore, it naturally has to be…fished out. Pressure pumping was one of the more complex segments of the oilfield market and also one of the most important. To most people it is known as "fracking," which is actually spelled in the industry as "fracing" or "frac" since it is short for "fracturing." Clearly, there is no "K" in fracturing, but somewhere along the way, environmentalists who understood little to nothing about the industry began to spell it with a "K," in turn altering the lexicon for the average person. That says a lot about activists who are ready to save the planet, but can't even correctly spell basic industry terminology. In a frac job, an oilfield services company pumps millions of gallons of water and millions of pounds of sand into a horizontal well bore to crack the rock. This technology is what revolutionized the oil and gas industry in the 2000s. In very simplified terms, you need two things to get oil out of the ground, porosity and permeability. Porosity means that the rock in question can hold oil. Permeability means that the oil can flow through the rock. So before the shale revolution, oil companies had to find rock that had both porosity and permeability – a pretty difficult task and hence the continual decline in U.S. oil production until the shale revolution. For decades, every geologist in the U.S. understood that there were vast areas on the continent where the rock had great porosity but poor permeability. This rock held a lot of oil, but if you drilled down to it, only a small trickle would flow through the formation and come out of the well given the low permeability. Shale formations fit this exact combination of high porosity but low permeability. After nearly a hundred years of struggling with this conundrum, the industry finally found a solution. If the rock isn't permeable, you can make it permeable by creating cracks in the rock so that the oil can flow out. Hence, you fracture the rock by pumping water at a high pressure, and you also pump sand in with the water to help prop open the cracks, allowing the oil and natural gas to flow more easily.

In a matter of a few years, whole new fields became open to development. Fields hitherto thought to be worthless were suddenly on the market for as much as $60,000 per net acre, and the shale revolution was born. This naturally resulted in a wave of land grabs and acquisitions in the newfound basins which in turn fueled the mergers and acquisitions industry, and as a result, the shale revolution led to enormous demand for banking services to fund and execute those deals. Strange as it may seem, finding a new way to fracture rock was the reason that Robert, Mark, and Lenny were stuck in the office at 2:37 a.m. working on a pitchbook. The competition for M&A advisory services and capital markets business was intense, and no one was going to get any sleep while there were deals to be closed.

The final Wellco Solutions presentation draft looked pretty good to them and struck a good balance between the different sections. The trick to any pitchbook is including enough detail to impress a CEO without getting too deep into the weeds. Your managing director needs to look smart, but at the same time, you don't want so much detail in the pitchbook that a CEO might ask a very specific engineering question. The challenge with this pitchbook was marrying those two concepts. While the basics of a frac job are relatively simple, there are many different formulas such as slickwater fracs, gel fracs, hybrid fracs, and the list goes on. You could write a small book entirely devoted to just the types of sand used in the process, from Wisconsin white to Texas brown to ceramics and resin-coated options. As a banker, you don't want to wind up in a conversation on any of those topics as that's a sure way to make yourself look stupid in front of a seasoned petroleum engineer. The Wellco Solutions presentation was a minefield of technical lingo and concepts for the rookie analysts. They wouldn't know for sure whether they had stepped on any mines until Ron's review in the morning.

After sending him the final version, the three walked to the elevator without saying much to each other. They made small talk with the security guards in the building's lobby, who were always happy to see the M&A team as there was seldom anyone else around during the night shift. The team walked to their cars, scattered across a barren parking garage. Robert got into his Toyota and cranked it up. He drove to his apartment complex through a valley of glass skyscrapers. While the office buildings were now all empty, the highway was still filled with a decent number of cars for 3 a.m. Robert eyed the other drivers with suspicion. He was just getting off work, but what was everyone else doing on the road at this time on a weeknight? Were they also half dead after finishing a seventeen-hour shift, or had they been up all night smoking crystal meth? Either possibility was a serious road hazard, and Robert was certainly a hazard himself. The car seemed to park itself in another garage resembling the one which he had just left. Exhaustion took him over, and Robert felt as if his consciousness was staring down at his own body as it went through the motions of exiting the vehicle. He trudged to his apartment unit and finally entered it at 3:20 a.m. From the freezer, a bottle of Glenfiddich twelve-year emerged and filled an exquisite tumbler, neat and half full. He turned on Netflix and flipped through the options while taking mighty gulps. Five minutes later, he was asleep.

****

BEEP….BURR….BEEP….BURR….BEEP….BEEP…BURRRRR. Robert woke to the sound of his cell phone alarm and its equally loud vibrations at 6:30 a.m. The alarm was set early so that he could check his e-mail before deciding whether to sleep a little longer. His hopes of sleep evaporated upon scrolling through his inbox which was already infested with four e-mails from Ron. There was no point in even reading them – Ron doesn't send four e-mails unless something is wrong or, worse yet, several new additions to the presentation came to him overnight. It was time to get off the couch. He read the messages in between brushing his teeth and putting on his suit and tie.

The first e-mail was a good one. It said that the presentation was great except for page twelve where the data should be turned into a pie chart and page thirty-three where the data should be made into a bar chart. Ron also listed a number of other minor changes. Robert smiled – this wasn't so bad. He could make those changes in thirty minutes.

Unfortunately, the second e-mail turned for the worse. Ron had changed his mind. He didn't like half of the new slides after all. He wanted a slide devoted to plotting the average lateral lengths of wells in various basins and a second slide with a map of all drilled but uncompleted wells across the United States.

Terror swept Robert's body. The map alone could take half the day or more. The third e-mail listed yet more graphs and new wording for bullet points throughout the pitchbook, including sections Ron had already approved several days ago. Ron also requested a new slide tallying the horsepower for all drilling rigs in the Midland Basin of Texas.

The final e-mail simply said, "The meeting is at 11 a.m. today. When can you have the changes done and sent to print?"

"Oh shit," Robert said to himself. He was turning on the shower while dialing Lenny with his other hand.

After six rings, Lenny finally picked up. "Whaaaa…Robert…what… what's up?"

"Check your e-mail, man – we're screwed. We are so screwed – get in the office now!" Robert could hear Lenny groggily pulling himself out of bed and then silence as Lenny perused his e-mails.

"Oh fuck. OK, will be there asap. I'll get started on finding the data for the Midland Basin horsepower slide and the drilled but uncompleted well count. Can you take care of the chart reformatting?"

"Will do, thanks Lenny. You're a hero. See you in a little bit." Before jumping into the shower, he tried Mark's number. After ten rings, there was no answer. Under the scalding water, Robert did his best to enjoy the last minutes of the day which he knew would be his own and not part of the shit-show unfolding in his inbox. Stepping out of the shower and still soaking wet, he reluctantly dialed John Granton and laid out the situation.

"You fucking idiots! I knew that I shouldn't have let you dumbshits finish the presentation. Get in the fucking office. I'll see you there in thirty minutes. I'll take care of rewording the bullet points."

Robert arrived at his desk at 7:15 a.m. The office was half full already as market timing forced sales and trading to arrive earlier than investment banking and the coverage bankers. Lenny Lee was also at the desk, nervously punching away at the keyboard. His suit was for the most part still neatly pressed, but his shirt was clearly the same wrinkled one from yesterday and his tie was missing. The strong scent of cologne suggested that Lenny had no time for a shower. Either that or he was trying to cover up the smell of fear, but whatever the cologne could cover up, his eyes gave away, reflecting absolute panic.

John showed up at 8 a.m. in even worse shape than Lenny. While his suit and attire were perfectly in order, his eyes were bloodshot, and his speech was slurred.

"I just finished slide twenty-four – I'm jumping to thirty-seven and thirty-eight," yelled Robert

"Awesome, just got done with twenty-six and twenty-seven," answered Lenny across the desk.

"Wait what, you did twenty-six and twenty-seven? I just started working on those?" mumbled John who was clearly recovering from the night before and not as sharp as he needed to be in this moment.

"Don't worry about it John, we took care of it. Just work on slide forty-four," said Robert handing him one of the easier sections.

"Thanks, bud."

While John was not one to take orders from analysts or to say thanks, he knew that this was an emergency and if things fell through, some of the blame would fall on him as their immediate supervisor. He went to slide forty-four, happy to see just a few color changes were required according to Ron's precise e-mail instructions.

At 8:30 am, they received a text from Mark, who had just woken up and was only beginning to realize the gravity of the situation. About thirty minutes later, he arrived in the office, disheveled and distraught. "Hey guys, I'm really sorry. I'm so sorry. I thought that I was going to get a few extra hours of sleep with the project done and all."

"Don't worry about it", muttered Robert while clenching his teeth. Everyone was on edge, but they needed to keep their cool to pull this off. "Grab the intro slides one through five and make sure all of the contact information and titles are correct."

"OK, I'm on it man. Thanks, Robert."

At 9:15 a.m., Ronald Lufkin casually graced the seventeenth floor with his presence and threw his jacket around the back of his chair as his cuff links flashed in the light. "Where's my presentation guys? You should have finished it fifteen minutes ago."

"We're almost there" replied John, "I've got Robert and Lenny finishing up the last two slides."

"It better not take much longer. The meeting is at eleven, and I have to leave here by 10:30 to head for downtown. So, I need the pitchbook by 10:15," stated Ron sternly.

There was a small detail that John left out. Those two last slides were the map of the drilled and uncompleted wells and the one about horsepower in the Midland Basin – the most time-intensive slides. Thankfully, Lenny had managed to download the data and organize it into a graphics shape file. What he was managing within this short period of time surely put him only one miracle away from beatification at the Vatican.

"Am I glad that we have an Asian guy on our team or what," said Mark. "That would have taken me two days." Short on time, they split the geographies in four parts with each of them parsing the enormous dataset to map the drilled but uncompleted locations in their respective areas.

"I've got the DJ Basin in Colorado and the Uinta in Utah done," shouted Robert.

"Got the Delaware Basin in West Texas and New Mexico done," exclaimed Lenny.

"Almost finished with the Utica/Marcellus in Ohio and West Virginia," added Mark.

John was incorporating the pieces into a single map. The final touches were done by 9:45 a.m. and the pitchbooks were sent to the printers. Even with heavy industrial printers, it would take a while to print more than a dozen fifty-page books loaded with multi-colored charts, maps, and graphs. As the copies came out, the analysts formed an assembly line next to the printer. Robert was splitting apart the pages which had stuck together in the hot printer; Lenny was punching spiral holes in the copies; and Mark was placing an opaque sheet on the back cover and a clear glossy sheet on the front. He then passed the printed pages through the binding machine, which pulled back the elastic spirals and tightened them again through the punched holes.

With the Wellco Solutions pitchbooks complete at ten minutes after ten, they ran back to their desks with the presentations in hand. The pitchbooks were then separated into three equal piles among the analysts. "Alright, let's compare," said Robert. They each took the first pitchbook in their piles and simultaneously began flipping each page to ensure no printer errors. In unison, they flipped the fifty pages and then did it again for three more pitchbooks. This was done five more times until all the pitchbooks could be confirmed to be error-free and identical on every single slide. Although 99% of the time there were no printer errors, this was yet another strange ritual of investment banking which demanded perfection.

The time was 10:16 a.m. on the dot when Mark handed Ron a copy.

"Let me take one last look," said Ron. He flipped about five pages into it and then stopped for a few seconds and handed the book back to them. "Who did slide five here with our contact info?"

Almost shaking, Mark spoke up, "That...that was me."

"Well, Mark. You left out Irv Goldsmith from the contact page, the relationship banker for Wellco Solutions. So yeah that's kind of important. Also, you left out a letter in my e-mail address. Throw all of these pitchbooks away. Lenny, fix the presentation and then call the FedEx downtown. Tell them to print fifteen copies asap and we'll pick them up on our way to the meeting. Mark, we're going to have a talk later."

The team was defeated. John was using the limits of his will and self-control to resist throwing a pitchbook at Mark's face. He stared him down like a death row convict spotting his next prey. They had messed up big time, and Ron was not going to forget it.

CHAPTER 5

THE PITCHBOOK

At almost every client meeting, Ron selected John as his aide de camp in case anything in the presentation necessitated further clarification or explanation. Basically, the analysts did all the work and research while John took all the credit in the meetings. With Ron already up from his chair, John furiously gathered his folders for the Wellco Solutions meeting, but before he could get fully organized, Ron poured cold water on his plans.

"You're not going, John. We've got a meeting with Noble Energy on Wednesday. I need a presentation on the Marcellus Shale in exactly thirty-six hours from now. I need you to stay back and make sure it gets done right this time. Besides, all of you look like dogshit this morning. I wouldn't dream of putting you in front of a client."

"But," mumbled Granton completely caught off guard.

"Robert, you've got a tie on. Do you know this presentation inside and out?"

"Uh…umm…yes of course."

"Good, because I don't. You're coming with me. Don't just stand there, come on."

At the sound of these words, John was boiling with anger and already planning a pile of shitwork upon Robert's return. He would make sure that this unlucky analyst never saw daylight outside of the office again.

Robert haphazardly grabbed a few folders from his desk and rushed for the elevator without even looking back at his colleagues. He walked briskly alongside his managing director. Neither said a word to each other. The tension in the air was thick and a couple of colleagues from other desks curiously peeked over their screens to see what was going on, but to their dissatisfaction, there was nothing to hear, only an expression of utter rage on Ron's face and utter fear on Robert's.

They exited the lobby and hopped into the taxi waiting for them. "Do you have the address?"

"Nnnnno, I'll get it right away." Robert pulled out his phone and searched through his e-mail. "Got it! It's the Allen Center, twenty-third floor."

"And who am I meeting?"

"George Gardner, Chief Financial Officer, Mark Wallis, Treasurer, and Joe Stevens, Head of Corporate Development."

"Rick Stephens, the CEO isn't going to be there? I can't believe Irv. All this guy is supposed to do is play golf and have dinner with the C-Suite, and he can't even get us a meeting with the fucking CEO. Unbelievable."

The taxi took Memorial Drive en route to downtown, the closest thing to a scenic route in Houston winding its way through Memorial Park. Robert gazed enviously at the fit and healthy joggers of his age running through the pine trees mid-day on a Tuesday. His envy was much more than a desire for their open and relaxed schedules. At this point, just feeling the sun on his skin for a full day was an exhilarating thought – he yearned for a sunburn. Even when he had a chance to exercise, it was more often than not late at night in his apartment's gym. His life was movement from one indoor space to another indoor space with occasional exercise on a treadmill in front of yet another digital screen.

"I'm gonna drop you off at the FedEx, and I'll be waiting at the Starbucks at the bottom of the Allen Center, alright?' said Ron, finally breaking the silence of the long cab ride.

"You got it, Ron!"

The taxi made a few more turns and dropped Robert in front of the FedEx. He ran for the door and hoped for the best. The FedEx staff next to Latham Schroeder's office knew Robert, Mark and Lenny intimately from similar last-minute emergencies and would do the guys a favor on a tight deadline, but this office was a risk. Upon entering the FedEx, a nightmare scenario confronted him with almost a dozen people in line. To his dismay, he also didn't see a stack of bound pitchbooks behind the counter. Lenny had phoned the order, but with the morning rush, they might still be printing. In the line, Robert kept nervously checking his phone when he noticed something else which catapulted his situation from bad to worse. The three young guys directly ahead of him looked all too familiar – in their early twenties, nice suits, perfectly slicked back and gelled hair. They were talking about transaction comps and how their associate was a huge asshole. They had to be fellow investment banking analysts – God only knew what they needed to get done here.

It was 10:42 a.m. The three analysts finally reached the counter, and Robert froze in terror as the words came out of the first analyst's mouth, "Hi Jay, we all came down today because we're really really screwed. I mean we're gonna get killed if this presentation isn't printed in the next fifteen minutes. Can you help us out, bro? It's just ten pitchbooks."

Jay, the middle-aged FedEx manager, looked perfectly annoyed, "You guys are always coming down here with an emergency. You told me the same story last week".

"Please, Jay" said another one. "Please, man! You gotta save us!"

"Alright, alright, but this is the last time. You have to start sending this stuff in early."

Robert knew that he was completely screwed now. How could he beg the FedEx worker to speed up the process if these guys had just asked for the same favor? This Jay character would have to be some sort of FedEx Mother Theresa to listen to his pleas. Simple begging would not work. Robert said the Lord's Prayer inside his head. It was his turn in line.

"Hi Jay, do you have an order ready for Latham Schroeder & Holt? It might have been placed in the name of John Granton or Lenny Lee?" said Robert, clearly catching the ears of the three other young analysts waiting for their order.

"Well, I just finished printing them, but I haven't got them bound yet. We're pretty tied up so it'll probably take me another thirty minutes until I can get to them."

"I don't have thirty minutes," said Robert in desperation. He had never done something like this before, but he reached for his wallet and pulled out a twenty-dollar bill, "I'll give you twenty bucks if you can put it at the front of the line. Please, sir!" The other analysts' jaws dropped at the sight of someone even more desperate than them.

"I'm sorry that's against company policy. I can't do that"

"I'll make it forty, and I'll bind them myself!" said Robert pulling out another twenty from his wallet and slapping it on the table. Before Jay could respond, Robert lifted the gate at the counter and headed for the binding machine. The customers stared with bewilderment.

Jay didn't know what to say. He finally muttered, "Well…OK," took the money, hastily crammed it into his pocket, and then loudly yelled, "Next customer!" The following person in line stood there dumbfounded before realizing that it was their turn. Robert worked the binding machine like a pro and had the fifteen presentations bound in no time. He sprinted out of the FedEx, accidentally hitting one of the other analysts on the shoulder on the way out.

"Hey, man, what the hell!" yelled his competitor.

Robert didn't turn around even for a second to acknowledge any wrongdoing. The Starbucks was a full five blocks away. He ran the first block in full sprint, but then remembered to check his phone at a traffic light. There was already a message from Ron impatiently inquiring about his whereabouts. He wrote back, "Got them. On my way." It was 10:53 a.m. Thankfully, unlike other major urban centers downtown Houston is mostly free of pedestrians, which allowed Robert to continue his mad dash with minimal embarrassment. He ran as fast as possible with the stack of pitchbooks in his hand, but not so fast as to warrant a strong sweat, which could be just as embarrassing as being late to a C-suite meeting. Achieving this balance was no easy task in the Houston humidity and the July heat.

The Starbucks finally came in sight at 10:57 a.m., and he slowed to a brisk walk. Ron immediately spotted him from inside and met him out front. "Alright, let's go. We're gonna be late," he said sternly to Robert, who was still catching his breath. Ron led the way, taking long, powerful strides toward the Allen Center, and Robert followed closely behind. While Ron's movements around the office were typically the slowest and most relaxed on the team, here he took each step with strength and determination as he marched ever closer to his client. The much younger Robert, exhausted from his sprint through downtown Houston, was the one desperately trying to keep up with his managing director's pace. They entered the lobby. With several groups of business types leisurely crowding the escalator to the next floor, Ron opted for the stairs running alongside. On the third to last step, Robert tripped in his hurry and went flying. His shin hit the sharp edge of the very last step, and his body spilled across the polished granite floor. Almost everyone in the lobby turned to see what was happening as he let out an extremely painful yelp. Several people came over to help him up. Miraculously, he had managed to hold onto the pitchbooks tightly, like a wide receiver in the end zone. He politely refused the strangers' help and began to hobble back to his feet, grasping his shin to check if it was bleeding, as it certainly felt like the skin had been broken. Ron had not even glanced backward – his stare was squarely focused on the elevators as he quickened his pace.

"Hey, hold up a second!" Robert managed to shout.

His managing director was already in the elevator as Robert raced for the closing doors. He shot out his hand in the sliver of an opening and managed to stop the elevator in time. Ron turned to him as he again pressed the button for the twenty-third floor. "Are the presentations OK?"

"Yeah, they're fine. I managed to hold onto them."

"Good. Now look, don't say anything unless I ask you to or it looks like I need some back up, alright?" said Ron.

"OK, I got it," replied Robert.

The elevator doors opened onto the landing of Wellco Solutions. The company's name was spelled out in large white three-dimensional blocks illuminated by a blue light beneath them. The color scheme was familiar given the dozens of slides created last night using the same palette. They pushed back the two glass doors and checked in with the receptionist. It was 11:01 a.m. sharp.

"Mr. Lufkin and Mr. McClure, please have a seat. Mr. Gardner is in a meeting and will be with you momentarily," said the receptionist robotically.

The two sat in the lobby's plush brown leather chairs. Next to them was a shelf filled with various minerals in their raw uncut states: a brilliant geode, a piece of oil-stained shale, and even a large chunk of quartz flaked with gold. Next to the rocks and minerals was a vast collection of lucite deal toys, basically trophies of mergers and acquisitions as well as debt and equity raised through various investment banks. The deal toys told a story of acquisition after acquisition in the past decade totaling to more than a dozen swallowed companies. There was likely a broom closet elsewhere filled with even older deal toys commemorating transactions the market had long forgotten. Between the leather chairs were two small tables covered with various trade publications, *The Wall Street Journal*, and *Fortune* magazine.

Ron picked up a copy of the *WSJ* next to him. Without any real interest, he flipped through the issue and then threw it back on the table. As the newspaper landed back in the pile, Ron noticed a spiral-bound book with a clear plastic cover underneath the magazines. "Hey Robert, put this in your folder," Ron said softly as he handed him the find.

Robert couldn't believe his eyes – it was a pitchbook from Barclays. He flipped the first few pages before hiding it away – it was clearly a pitch for a divestiture for Weatherton, stock ticker "WNT" to be precise. A hedge fund would kill to get their hands on this. He hid the pitchbook with perfect timing as George Gardner entered the reception area with his executive entourage.

"Hi Ron, good to see you again."

Ron got up and shook George's hand with a big smile. "This is Robert McClure, one of our newest analysts and probably one of the brightest that we've had in a long time."

"Pleased to meet you, Robert."

Robert shook his hand and introduced himself to the rest of the team, making the customary exchange of business cards.

"How have things been? Irv told me that you and Rick went out to Pebble Beach a few weeks back," Ron said brightly with his face showing none of the anger and disgust which had gripped him moments earlier in the elevator ride up to the twenty-third floor.

"Sure did, it was terrific. I just love Pebble Beach. I never want to leave when the weekend is over. It's so relaxing and so much fun." The group walked into a conference room with a large table in the middle. George Gardner and his group all sat on one side and Ron and Robert sat on the other with no one at the head of the table. Robert laid out their business cards in front of him in the order of who sat where so as to not mistake anyone's name, a nice trick learned in his early corporate meetings at the bank.

"So, what do you got for me today, Ron?" asked Gardner.

"Well, we've been talking with a few smaller pressure pumping companies that I think are ready to sell. Not all of these are going to pull the trigger tomorrow, but a few would be interesting enough for Wellco to start a conversation."

Ron was at his best walking the Wellco Solutions team through the various acquisition possibilities and name dropping his relationships with potential takeout candidates. He made sure to get sidetracked with stories of hunting or watching football with the respective CEOs and CFOs. Ron was smiling, laughing, and seemed to be having an all-around good time. From this meeting, one would think that Ron was the nicest, most warm-hearted, and genuine person ever to walk the Earth. Robert kept smiling as well and tried to stay engaged in the meeting, but his mind kept drifting to the pitchbook from the lobby. He couldn't wait to get back to the office to crack it open. How big was this deal? Could it move the stock? Was it a stale transaction or something that could happen any day?

Ron called on him to answer a question, which nearly caught him off guard as he was already fantasizing about the riches the Weatherton insider information could yield for the imaginary hedge fund in his mind. He quickly snapped out of it and began explaining the calculations and figures in the Wellco presentation like a trained parakeet. He listed stats about the pressure pumping market, went through the increasing trend of longer horizontal lateral wells, and laid out the horsepower of the drilling fleet in the Midland Basin. In the past forty-eight hours, he had lived, ate, and slept this information and could cite any fact, forwards and backwards, even with his mind a million miles away. As the meeting wrapped up and the final handshakes were made, Ron was already planning a follow up meeting with Rick Stephens, the CEO, and strategizing about how to get him involved in the conversation next time. Robert was thinking about none of those things and was instead looking at his phone – WNT had opened today at $23.87 per share.

CHAPTER 6

THE ANATOMY OF A PITCHBOOK

As soon as he returned to the office, Robert grabbed an empty conference room and began flipping through the Barclays pitchbook. He was familiar with Weatherton; they were one of the biggest players in the oilfield services sector and Latham Schroeder had done deals with them in the past, but nothing in the last few years. The company had recently been on a rocky road and was more likely than not to sell assets to shore up its balance sheet. Following this line of thought, the Barclays pitchbook focused on a potential divestiture of the company's drilling rigs in Venezuela and its workover rigs in Russia. This would explain what the pitchbook was doing in the offices of Wellco Solutions. It was a difficult sale, especially for a package deal. Very few buyers needed both Russian and Venezuelan rigs at the same time. Even divesting each geographic segment separately would be a feat. If the Barclays bankers could pull this off, the market would definitely be surprised. No one on the Street was baking in any value for these assets as they were barely breaking even. If Weatherton monetized the worthless assets for cold hard cash, the stock price would jump. For a $17 billion firm like Weatherton, this might be only a 4% or 5% spike in the share price, but that would still be enough to make a very leveraged bet pay off. Of course, timing a highly leveraged position like this was nearly impossible…unless one had inside information. As he turned each page, Robert prayed the pitchbook had enough key facts to make such a bet. Most importantly, he needed dates of a potential transaction.

The organization of a pitchbook is a pretty simple thing. The introductory five or six pages are known as the credentials. These pages represent the investment bank's dick measuring highlights. They show the number of billion-dollar transactions closed by the bank, its rankings in the industry, as well as case studies of particularly important deals closed. In this section, the pitchbook may further detail the size of the team across continents, name key prestigious clients, and provide contact information for the banking team. In case the client isn't sufficiently impressed at this point, some pitchbooks even list everyone's academic degrees on the deal team, which would typically cover an assortment of Ivy League and top tier universities. In short, the first few pages are meant to communicate that "Yes, I can close your $3 billion acquisition, and yes my dick is at least ten inches long."

The next section, known as the industry overview, can be more insightful. Basically, it has a bunch of charts showing general industry trends such as the rig count, capital budgets, and movement in crude oil and natural gas prices. The executive team across the table should already be familiar with these trends, but nonetheless, the charts are provided as reference points. After this section comes the company overview, a summation of the company's key financial metrics such as revenue growth, production volumes, and debt metrics. The CEO very likely knows all of this information as well; however, the section is useful for discussing an acquisition and how it could impact debt metrics and the production profile of the firm. As this is all publicly available information, these sections were not at all useful to Robert.

The opportunities section is where things get interesting. In a buy-side pitchbook, the bank shows a couple of proposed acquisition targets that are early in the sales process or may be willing to sell soon. In these pitchbooks, the bank represents the client as the buyer of the potential transactions. In a sell-side pitchbook, the presentation jumps almost immediately to detailing an asset for sale. This was the case here: Barclays was representing Weatherton as the seller of the Russian and Venezuelan rigs.

The neatly laid-out pages of this section is where investment bankers add value to management teams in their often murky role as advisors. On paper, a banker's job is to offer sound advice regarding debt structure, capital raises, and acquisitions. Much more importantly, bankers act as the town gossips of the industry. They know who is having a tough time, who is thinking of raising money, and who is divesting assets – all very useful information, particularly if another client is in the market to buy assets, for example. Bankers also know who is retiring, or getting a divorce, or who's ready to roll the dice again on a new acreage package. While the pitchbook may not spell it out, this industry gossip is the real value brought to the table by a knowledgeable investment banker. If a potential buyer can get a first crack at buying an asset before everyone else gets a chance, the advantage can be worth hundreds of millions of dollars under the right circumstances. The advantage is not much different than the same situation in real estate. If you can make an offer on a house before it hits the market next week, you're in way better shape than being in a competitive process against several bidders after the first open house. Of course, there is also a benefit to the seller. Making a quick transaction is advantageous as the seller can avoid a burdensome and extended sales process which includes allowing potential bidders (aka competitors) to poke around the company's books, assets, and operations. So, while the gossip may seem unethical on the surface, in reality, it serves to benefit both buyers and the sellers and naturally the banker in between the two.

The Weatherton pitchbook was off to a good start. It was more or less an extended teaser document. In a teaser, an investment bank details an asset early in the sale process. The teaser gives just enough information to get an interested potential bidder to sign a non-disclosure agreement. After that, the potential bidder is given another pitchbook known as an information memorandum which shows the asset for sale in more detail. Then, serious bidders are invited into an online data room that holds piles of information on the asset. Companies try to be selective on who is allowed into the data room so as to avoid divulging too many trade secrets, especially if the sales process falls apart. After several weeks of due diligence, the bidders finally place their bids and are then typically narrowed to a second round. From those, the company chooses the winner.

Thankfully, this teaser had the treasure map that Robert was looking for. Or in this case, it should perhaps be called the "treasure calendar". One of the final pages laid out a calendar with dates highlighted for signing the non-disclosure agreements, opening the data room, and the first round of bidding on July 14th, 2014. With this information in hand, a hedge fund could make a pretty good guess on the sale announcement date as it was likely to happen within three or four days of signing the purchase and sale agreement, which happens shortly after the final bids. While the exact date would still be difficult to pin down, a few weeks as a margin of error on a major acquisition is still pretty good.

Nonetheless, there were two main obstacles to profiting from a trade based on the Weatherton pitchbook. First, despite working like a dog, most of Robert's payoff as an investment banking analyst came in the form of the year-end bonus. Meaning that after paying his exorbitantly high rent inside the Loop, his student loans, and car payment, there were only a couple of thousand bucks saved up in his account. It wasn't much to show for the 80-hour work weeks. With the help of the inside information, good timing, and excessive leverage on this trade, Robert could maybe turn the $5,000 in his brokerage account into a whopping $8,000. A 60% return is nice, but with so little to put down in the first place it wasn't going to get him far, certainly not to a life of freedom and piña coladas on the beach. If he was going to make the most of this, he needed more cash. For an institution with more resources like a hedge fund, a 60% return could be worth tens of millions, if not more.

The second conundrum was the margin of error. Despite the details in the pitchbook, the close date of this particular deal remained quite murky. Sure, the pitchbook labeled the first bid date, but the second bid date was undisclosed in the calendar. Today was already July 29th, meaning that the first round of bidding was over and the second round was likely done by now as well, yet there had been no announcement in the news. Either this deal was happening any second or something had gone wrong, which was entirely possible given the difficulty of divesting Venezuelan rigs. Other possibilities further added to the uncertainty. Suppose the due diligence simply took longer than expected or market conditions turned for the worse and Weatherton pulled the deal. Or worse yet, suppose the bids were simply not good enough, and Weatherton decided to shut down the deal process. These were all plausible outcomes.

In addition, even if the final bid date was clearer, one was still vulnerable to the vagaries of the market. What if the acquisition does happen within days of your estimate, but the price of crude oil takes a beating over the same time period? The stock price jumps 5% on the day of the acquisition but only after falling 10% in the preceding week as a result of oil prices. The longer you wait for the transaction to happen; the longer you are exposed to swings in the market. You can be completely right and still lose money with bad luck and oil prices against you. The trick to successful insider trading is to roll the dice as many times as possible when the odds are on your side. It is not one big secret trade upon which you can retire. It's something done over longer periods of time and obscured by numerous legitimate trades.

Robert closed the pitchbook and walked back to his seat across the open floor. The M&A desk was already abuzz with orders flying from John Granton. Before he could begin yelling new demands in his direction, Robert tossed the Weatherton pitchbook in front of him. "Hey, check this out…we found it in the lobby of Wellco Solutions today. It's a Barclays pitchbook for some Weatherton rigs."

"Nice find," said John, flipping it open with his eyes glued to the pages. Momentarily, he forgot the punishment that would soon be bestowed on his least favorite analyst, but only momentarily. He flipped the pages with enough force that each of the heavy glossy paper pages cracked like a whip, "I don't think this deal has a chance of happening – there's no way in hell. Rigs in Russia and Venezuela? You gotta be kidding me." John tossed the pitchbook aside with a level of disinterest that matched his initial excitement.

Lenny slid the pitchbook to his side of the table, and Mark peered over his shoulder to have a look as well. "I like their formatting. This light blue scheme is way better than ours, but I'm not so sure about their font choice," said Mark as Lenny flipped a few more pages forward. "Oh, I don't like their credentials and contacts page at all. Look how disorganized those boxes are."

"Yeah, you're right," said Lenny. "This is total crap." They turned to the next page. "That's nice. Check out their map and well call-outs. They must have a geologist on their banking team to put together this level of detail."

"Jesus Christ! You guys are a bunch of retards," said John. "Stop reading that pitchbook and get back to doing your fucking job."

****

Somehow, the team managed to complete the day's orders without more assignments immediately being dumped on them. For once, they had an early night, and the timing could not have been better. As soon as Robert returned to his apartment, he fired up his brokerage account to check the latest news on WNT and the stock price. This opportunity was simply too good to pass up. In some ways, Robert's edge was even better than that of a hedge fund. With such a small positon, there was no need to cover up the trade through a series of other legitimate trades. Would anyone at the SEC be watching the account of a twenty-three-year-old analyst with a $5,000 position in WNT? Hell, he could even buy short-term call options. In most cases, such a leveraged bet would ring alarm bells at the SEC, but how could they prove anything? Finding a confidential document by accident was the best insider trading cover of all time. Since Robert knew no one at Weatherton or the Barclays deal team, it was impossible to connect him with a source of the inside information. Only if the Feds broke into his apartment and found the pitchbook laying on his bed could they find proof and nail him. His brilliance and good luck would seem to be the only reasons for his investment in WNT to an outside observer. And even if the SEC caught him completely red-handed, would they really pursue someone over a $5,000 trade?

The stock price hadn't done much in the past few weeks and the front month call options looked cheap given the low-level of volatility. The set up was perfect, and Robert calculated the maximum number of options for his $5,000. Everything was ready, but there was one more thing to check before clicking the "buy" button. He logged onto the Latham, Schroder & Holt internal drive to check the latest postings on the compliance page. Every major bank has an internal compliance list which temporarily forbids trading in certain shares. While the list does not outright explain the reason for the trading halt, one can assume that the bank is involved in some sort of transaction involving inside information. For example, the debt capital markets team could be raising bonds for the company or the equity capital markets team could be helping the company issue stock. While only a few members of these individual teams may have access to the inside information, the trading restrictions cover a much larger range of employees who may potentially know or overhear details regarding a transaction, despite not directly participating on the debt or equity market teams. Not all of these deals are necessarily huge market movers. For example, if a company is doing something commonplace such as extending the term on its credit facility, the market would yawn at the news. So, the presence of a company on the list does not necessarily give anything away. Although the SEC may not have an interest in prosecuting someone like Robert McClure, the agency certainly wants to see proper maintenance of these restriction lists at a major bank. In addition, the bank itself is interested in tracking the trading activities of its employees. As is normal procedure, all employees must surrender their personal brokerage account information at onboarding, and their transactions are tracked thereafter to ensure compliance with the bank's policies and the restricted trading list.

Robert scrolled down the nearly endless number of securities. When reaching the W's, his heart sank in his chest. Robert pounded his fist into the table. Weatherton held a restriction on trading. "Who were the idiots working on a deal with Weatherton? Come the fuck on, guys," thought Robert. The mergers and acquisitions team was not certainly working on anything, maybe it was Irv and the damn relationship bankers. He flung the now useless pitchbook across the room and searched his phone for Chinese takeout. “Fuck my life, man…” He wasn’t going to be a ten-thousand-aire after all.

CHAPTER 7

LUNCH

In November, the team hit a particularly bad stretch. Robert had been in the office for three weeks straight without a day off as John's wrath had not subsided in the slightest since the Wellco Solutions meeting. After nineteen hours at the desk yesterday, Robert had decided to call it a night at 2 a.m. as his eyes could not proofread one more slide. Now, he was back early in the morning to finish the job. Other than the few traders already in the building, the floor was empty at 7 a.m. As he had done for months before starting the day, Robert scanned the news for anything on the Weatherton divestiture. There was still nothing. The compliance department's restriction had turned out to be a blessing in disguise as Weatherton's stock price continued to slide downward. Perhaps next time that such a pitchbook presented itself, the deal would be actionable and Robert could trade on it, but right now, there were more important things to think about rather than imaginary stock trading schemes. Thankfully, the pitchbook for Excursion Energy, their latest pitch, was looking good. At this point, he was catching only the slightest mistakes – things even John and Ronald Lufkin might miss – a box one millimeter too far to the left, a slightly too dark border on another page, and a few barely off center green arrows. After re-calculating the numbers for what seemed like the thousandth time, everything checked out.

Ron arrived to the office surprisingly early and threw his coat on the back of his chair, as was his custom every morning. "What are you doing here so early, Robert?"

"Nothing much, I finished up the Excursion pitchbook last night, and I'm going over the numbers to make sure everything foots."

"You know you guys don't need to pull crazy hours like this. Take it a little easier on yourself."

"It's no problem at all. I just wanted to make sure it's right," replied Robert. He hated this sort of bullshit, which came from every managing director on the Street. They were 100% responsible for the culture of their respective sweatshops, but they occasionally needed to say things like this to make themselves feel better about over-working their analysts. What did he expect Robert to say, "Oh, you're right Ron. I'm just going back to bed now, and I'll wrap up this pitchbook in a few days."

"So how's it looking?" inquired Ron, getting back to business. "Will it be done by nine? The meeting is next week so I need the final version today."

The doublespeak was unbearable, but the only possible response was a polite smile. "Yeah, no problem at all. I'm just about done. I'll have it to you in thirty minutes."

"Sounds good. By the way, I really haven't had the chance to look through Excursion's financials yet. I've been too tied up with the Wellco Solutions talks and the Halliburton mandate. Wanna go to lunch today and run me through it?"

"Sure, no problem. I would love to. Thank you, sir "

"No need to call me sir. You're not a caddie."

Robert went over the presentation for the last time and handed it to Ron. "Thanks Robert, I'll review this now."

John had just come into the office and was turning on his computer. He began clearing out his early morning inbox. "Ron, tell me if there's anything wrong with the pitchbook, and I'll check it myself," stated John sternly with his eye contact on Robert rather than Ron, to whom the comment was directed.

"I'll let you know," answered Ron.

The pitchbook review almost pushed Robert's nerves over the edge as he watched the process from the corner of his eye. His right leg bounced up and down incessantly from the stress. Ron's red pen hovered above each page. The pen lowered as if to make a correction and then returned to its original position. He flipped to the next page. The pen again swept downward and again retreated once more. On the following slide, he wasn't so lucky. The pen circled something and then made another mark. With the pen's every move, Robert's leg shook ever more violently. Ron then became transfixed on a certain page, spending a full five minutes on the slide. The pen did not move. What could possibly be keeping him there? What slide warranted such close examination? Robert was frozen, staring blankly at his computer screen as the examination continued. When Ron finally turned the page, Robert made a soft sigh of relief.

After another excruciating fifteen minutes, the pitchbook was returned. "It's pretty good. I just caught a couple of small mistakes, and I need one page taken out, but it's pretty good work."

"Thanks!" Robert smiled, only to catch an envious and hateful glance from John. The weight of two metric tons lifted from his shoulders. A little before noon, the pitchbook was final, and two copies were printed for their lunch.

Ron got up from his chair. “Robert, come on, let’s go. Bring the books.” Robert scrambled from his desk and made his way to the elevator with Ron. Mark and Lenny looked at each other, perplexed. Robert was absolutely jubilant at the opportunity to have lunch with the big boss. Maybe this was his chance to stand out.

As the two rode down the elevator, Robert wanted to avoid the awkward silence of their last trip, but what should he say? It had to be something intriguing or something smart. Talking about SEC football was a good fallback, but that wouldn’t set him apart from any of the other jock analysts to have passed through the halls of Latham, Schroeder & Holt. “So, do you think that we have a chance of getting the mandate on the Excursion deal?”

“There’s always a chance – that’s why we do this. Even if it’s a one in a hundred chance, which is about right for Excursion.”

“But why not focus on just the deals where the chances are higher, like the Wellco Solutions deal?”

“Well, think about it this way. If we close a deal with Excursion, that could be a two or three million dollar fee for the bank. If you could buy a lottery ticket with a one in a hundred chances of hitting two or three million dollars, wouldn’t you buy it?”

“Of course, I would,” answered Robert, “That’s incredible odds for such a huge payout.”

“Exactly, and best of all, you don’t even have to pay for the lottery ticket. It literally costs me nothing to put together a pitchbook and go shake hands with the clients.” Robert looked away from Ron, resisting his body’s impulse to physically cringe as he recalled the hundreds of exhausting hours putting together those pitchbooks. “If I do it a hundred times, I’m almost guaranteed to land a deal somewhere along the way. Part of it is just a numbers game and staying in front of clients until they're finally ready to buy or sell something. It's just like Wellco. We've got a mandate there. That's not exactly my first time in their office."

"Right, of course. By the way, speaking of Wellco, you know that pitchbook that we found in their office?"

"Yeah, what about it?

"How often have you found a pitchbook like that?"

"A couple of times, actually. But most of the time it's a useless buy-side pitchbook. It's nice to see what the competition is doing, but it's really not that helpful at the end of the day unless you're lucky enough to find a perfect sell-side pitchbook. The Weatherton book was pretty close – were it only a better deal with a clearer final bid date, that would have been the ticket. But, with oil prices moving lower lately, that deal is going to be a hard sell. Yesterday, we were at $78.20 per barrel. In my opinion, all this oversupply talk is bullshit. Watch and see. We'll be back to a $100 or at least $90 per barrel by year end. Regardless, the current crude price is going to make any deal difficult to close. Why do you ask about that pitchbook?"

"Oh, no reason at all. Just wondering, you know."

"Well, it's an important lesson, if nothing else. Don't ever leave one of our pitchbooks sitting around and never talk about deals in public. Always keep the conversation ambiguous if you're at a restaurant or anything like that, and take a look around to see who might be listening. You never know who is over at the next table, especially if you're somewhere nice."

They crossed the parking lot of the garage and Ron tossed Robert the keys. "Here, you drive – I gotta answer some e-mails." Stunned and nervous, Robert clicked the key chain, which flashed the lights of a BMW 7 Series about five cars down from the elevator entrance. It had to be this year's or last year's model. They got in, and Robert turned the ignition. On the one hand, he was ecstatic to be driving a 7 Series, if only for a short ten-minute ride. On the other hand, dread gripped him with the thought of scratching the car or getting into an accident on the way to the restaurant. With this on his mind, he drove to Masraff's at the speed of a senior citizen, utilizing only a fraction of the horsepower under the hood. Fortunately, they arrived at their destination without incident and dropped off the car with the valet.

Ron asked the hostess for a quieter table toward the back and closely examined the contours of her hips as she led them there. The waiter arrived almost instantly the moment they sat down. Ron ordered a lump crab cake, a side salad and a filet mignon a la plancha. Robert had a Caesar salad and the burger.

"So," Ron started. "The debt metrics for Excursion don't look so bad post-transaction, right?"

Heeding his superior's recent advice, he peeked over at the nearby tables. With no obvious suits near them, he proceeded. "Yes, correct. After the proposed transaction, the net debt to EBITDAX will be 2.9 times. That's not terrible, but not great either," answered Robert. EBITDAX was banker shorthand for a closely followed metric in the oil and gas industry: Earnings Before Interest Taxes Depreciation Amortization and Exploration. While "exploration" clearly does not start with an X, the abbreviation was one of those quirks in the industry. Basically, the metric is a shorthand method for calculating cash flow.

"What are some of the better players running at now?"

"2.0 to 2.5 times – you start getting into trouble with bank covenants at 4.0 times net debt to EBITDAX and..."

Ron's cell phone rang midway through the sentence. "Hey, Erin. How's it going? Did you get that paperwork done?"

Pause.

"Great, great I'll get my mother to sign it this weekend. Now, do I have to get it signed at a notary to prove that she's competent?"

Pause.

"Alright great, great. Yeah, I don't think they would be able to tell that she's lost it anyway."

Pause.

"Alright, thanks again, Erin. I'll send the paperwork over when I get it signed. Bye!" Ron hung up and placed his phone back on the table. "Sorry about that, Robert. That was my attorney. You wouldn't believe the sort of shit that I have to put up with. I recently asked my lawyer to write up a will for my mother. The last thing that I want is a half and half split with my brother.

"I didn't know you had a brother. Is he in finance also?"

"Not exactly. He's a manager at McDonald's, just a complete loser. More or less, he's been a bum all of his life."

"I'm sorry to hear that, Ron."

"It took the guy seven years to make manager. I feel sorry for the high school kids who work under him. Imagine that…I'd go insane."

Yes, imagine working for someone terrible like that, thought Robert to himself.

"Does he get into trouble a lot or something like that?"

"No not all. He's never been to jail. Doesn't do drugs. To put it kindly, he's a little smarter than Forrest Gump. It's nothing diagnosed, not like he has Down's or something. Just dumb as a brick. He goes to his job and then this apartment to watch TV all day and that's all the jerk does. It's fucking ridiculous. My mom's 401K ran out three years ago, so now I'm the one paying $40K per year to take care of her. That's a lot of money."

"So what's in the will if she doesn't have any money left?"

"Well, she has her old house in West U. It's a complete teardown, but the land below it is easily worth $600K. As the will stands now, my brother and I would both get half when she passes. I mean do you think that's fucking fair? I'm here doing all this stuff for my mom like paying her retirement, and my brother isn't doing anything but he's going to keep half the cash. Is that fair?"

"Um…I guess not."

"Of course it's not fair. That's why I'm talking to my lawyer and re-writing the will to include a clawback provision. When the land eventually gets sold upon her death, I'll get my half plus whatever I paid for my mother's retirement expenses. I mean otherwise I'm not getting anything for helping her out. I'm just being fair. That's all."

"Yeah, guess that's right," said Robert barely getting the words out of his mouth.

"Anyways, enough about that. But speaking of money, did I tell you about my conversation with Karl Stevens, the Head of Investment Banking, about the bonus pool for this year?"

"No, you didn't!" said Robert, suddenly springing back to life.

"Well, Karl said that the bonus pool looks a little bigger than last year. And don't tell this to anyone but last year, I cleared over $1.1 million in total comp. So, I'm hoping to hit $1.5 this year."

"How much did the analysts make last year?"

"Forgot, but it really depends on how the bonus pool is split up. I don't know if John ran you through this, but the bonus pool doesn't work like commission. You don't close a deal and then get to keep 5% of the fee or something like that. Even though we've closed two deals this year, which is good, it doesn't guarantee anything. Basically, all the fees earned by everyone in the investment bank are thrown into a giant bonus pool. Then, Karl Stevens and the other big wigs decide how to divide the pool based on a number of factors. The primary one is performance, but a lot of it also has to do with retention. Suppose a guy who is a heavy hitter from debt capital markets just had a terrible year. Maybe the macro environment was against him, or maybe he was a little lazy, or whatever, it doesn't really matter. Because he was a heavy hitter in the past and could be one again in the future, they may pay him a big bonus to keep him on board even though he brought home almost no business this year. In fact, they can take some of the fees that we earned at M&A and give it to that debt capital markets asshole. Karl Stevens might decide that it's worth it to overpay him to keep him on board. If he doesn't get a good bonus or at least a decent bonus, the debt capital markets asshole will jump to another bank He'll weave some story to his new employer about how Latham Schroeder wasn't giving him the resources needed to get the job done and how the relationship bankers were terrible. He'll show them his old track record and will then jump ship. I've seen it a million times – and so has Karl. So, that's why Karl can dip into our bonuses when the DCM guy starts complaining. At your level, Robert, you don't see a lot of this, but at my level, you have to do two things to succeed: bring in revenue and play the bank's politics."

"Wow, I had no idea that's how it works."

Ron took a large bite of his crab cake and gave a little shrug, "And to be fair to the DCM guy, I would do the exact same thing if I were in his shoes. If I had some leverage on Karl Stevens to boost my bonus by carving out a piece of flesh from the rest of the group, I'd do it in a heartbeat. And I know what you're thinking, 'Oh I wouldn't do that.' Once you get higher in the ranks and have that opportunity, you absolutely will and should do the same. It takes a lot to make it to managing director Don't let someone else eat a slice of your pie – you eat their slice first. You're a smart kid. Hopefully, you get there one day and then these will be your problems."

"Thanks, Ron. I hope so too. But still, for this year I guess that we'll do alright then?"

"Yeah, don't worry about it, kid. You, Mark, and Lenny are working hard. I'm sure that they'll take care of you. I'll put in a good word. They know that you guys are burning the midnight oil at the office."

"Thanks, Ron. I really appreciate that!"

"Good," said Ron, clattering his cutlery down on his plate. "Now, let's get back to those debt metrics for Excursion..."

CHAPTER 8

COUNTDOWN TO BONUS TIME

Robert McClure was the third generation of his family to live in Mississippi. His grandfather had settled in the state as a young man, planting cotton at first and then switching to soybeans years later. He even had the foresight toward end of his life to plant acres and acres of pecan trees, which typically take ten years to reach full maturity. By now, the trees were fully grown, their branches extending out to the sky. If only his grandfather could see them. However, this was always how it was going to be. No old man plants pecans with the guarantee of seeing them fully grown. It would be nearly as foolish as planting an oak with the expectation of one day carving a desk from it. The trees were planted for the next generation, not him. Though his grandfather was no longer in this world, Robert and his father continued to take care of the family farm as best they could. When Robert left for college, the maintenance of the farm fell solely on his father. The pecans produced just enough to pay the laborers and to keep the farm going, but year after year, one misfortune or accident after another pushed the property further into the red. One year, it was the storm which snapped a tree branch right on top of the farmhouse. Another year, it was a deep frost that ruined the crop. And some years, the trees simply didn't produce as much as others.

Regardless of the latest misfortune, his father would always dig into his savings and make it work. Thankfully, he could do so thanks to what was a damn good job for those parts. He drove a local route truck, making $50,000 a year with health insurance and a small 401K. With a job like that, he could never let his guard down – not for a second. Folks in Jones County would kill for work like that. So, he woke up every morning and gave it his all, earning a reputation as a truck driver by which one could set their clock. A small house in town, the family farm, and a son in college, it was more than he could have possibly dreamed when he was a nineteen-year-old dad, scared and looking out into a cold world. With his son gone far away, Robert's father would often walk alone along the rows of pecan trees and reminisce. As a young boy, this same path led him and his own father to the fishing hole on the property to catch brim. Mr. McClure also recalled the hot punishing summer sun on his skin and his aching muscles toned by farm work. At the end of the day, his mother would almost always have a cool Dr. Pepper ready for him and chastisement for his father for overworking him in the heat – though he never listened. As the elder Mr. McClure walked down the rows of pecan trees, he wondered what his son was doing at this very hour….

****

Robert and the team had survived a long, cold winter, at least by Houston standards, not that weather matters at all for young investment banking analysts. Each day, they were in the office by nine and were out by 10 p.m., if they were lucky. More often than not, they were unlucky. Constantly inhabiting air-conditioned or heated environments, the seasons had no meaning other than on the rare weekend off. And even in those cases, they would get so hammered in mid-town as to hardly remember whether the night was cool or hot or windy or wet. The only season that mattered now was bonus season. By mid-February, the bonus announcements had already been postponed twice. The original date had been January 31st, but nothing happened. An excruciatingly slow week passed with no news again. Then, they were told February 10th, which seemed like eons away to the analysts counting down the days, nights, and minutes: 1:01 a.m.…1:02 a.m.…1:51 a.m.…2:46 a.m. The date was then delayed even further, to February 17th. To the bank's internal budgeting team, this probably seemed like only the smallest inconvenience. To the analysts and associates, and even the managing directors, who would never admit it openly, these delays were like nails screeching down a chalkboard which mysteriously grew in length each week.

The team had had a solid year, with four deals closed: one sizeable 65,000 net acre deal, two smaller ones, and the sale of a mid-sized pressure pumping company to Wellco Solutions – adding another deal toy to their reception lobby. For a small team, it was quite an accomplishment. Their fees easily put their group in the black by a few million bucks. In fact, Lenny was certain of this as he calculated the team's fees in a monthly presentation for Karl Stevens. And through Lenny, the other guys knew it too. This was going to be their first Wall Street bonus, and it was going to be a good one…or so they hoped. However, some other factors shook their confidence. In the past few months, oil prices had gone from bad to worse. OPEC had thrown everyone a Thanksgiving surprise by refusing to prop up the market any longer. Back in October 2014 when it was at $80 per barrel, no one in the business could believe that the price of crude could fall any further. As a result, almost no exploration and production companies had locked in commodity prices with hedges to protect themselves from another move to the downside. Half the industry was drowning in debt incurred from the boom and unable to drill economic wells below $50 per barrel where the price stood now. Oil no longer beamed its glowing rays across the city of Houston. Instead, it shook with fever – it felt strung out and worried – and no part of the city was safe from oil's convulsions. Its loyal subjects were laid off by the thousands. Everyone tried to reassure themselves that this was different from the 1980s when the price of crude was so low that Houston was on the verge of becoming the next Detroit. Robert, Mark, and Lenny tried to assure themselves of the same thing. They had closed four deals in the year – $50 per barrel or not, they had a good year. Surely, four deals would guarantee them a good bonus, and by next year, oil would be up again. After all, oil prices made a V-shaped recovery in 2009 and that was the worst market crash on record since the Great Depression. This was likely nothing other than a momentary downturn.

Robert looked across his desk at his fellow analysts. They had been employed at Latham, Schroeder & Holt for almost a year, and they were physically falling apart. Mark Edwards long ago lost his surfer tan and could now camouflage with a pack of polar bears. His sandy hair was wispy, its color faint. His eyes were always slightly reddish from the glaring screens and his youthful optimism, which had once seemed the driving characteristic of his personality, had been replaced by a somber realism.

Lenny Lee was in worse shape. He had gained about fifteen pounds in less than a year and had an emerging belly on top of his otherwise skinny frame. His suit didn't fit anymore, and he knew it. Lenny hoped to lose the weight somehow. Maybe if he woke up an hour early each morning, he could sweat off the pounds at the gym, but reducing his sleep from five hours per day to just four was easier said than done. To keep hope alive, he kept his wardrobe the same, despite its awkward, tight-fitting appearance. The only youthful thing left about Lenny was his outbursts of acne, which were plentiful since his face was always buried in his hands from hours of reviewing pitchbooks each day. As a result, his forehead had a constant greasy sheen underneath the fluorescent lights.

Robert McClure couldn't say that he was in much better condition either. His hands, particularly around the knuckles, had become flakey. It was some sort of strange psychosomatic reaction to the stress. On the toughest weeks, the chalk-like dryness would spread to the point where Robert was embarrassed to flip pitchbook pages at client meetings. Furthermore, his muscles had completely deteriorated – his legs became sore from the shortest of walks on his rare weekends off. When he did make it to the gym, he found himself lifting less every time rather than more. Coffee always roiled through his veins, and he felt as if every ounce of his energy was sapped from his body at all times. Only caffeine, adrenaline, and the fear of making a mistake on a pitchbook kept him going. Despite their physical ailments, all the suffering was behind them now. Today was February 17th, bonus day. It couldn't possibly be pushed back again. Today, all the work would be worth it.

By noon, no one had heard anything about the bonuses. Brett Hillsby, the Vice President, one rank above associate, was in the office, but there was no sign of Ron anywhere. Rumors and chitchat regarding the bonuses spread among the employees all morning. Finally, at 12:45 p.m., Ron walked through the doors of the seventeenth floor dressed in his best suit. As he removed his coat, his brightest gold cuff links shined brilliantly in the fluorescent lights. Ron was in a good mood, though not overly elated. "Brett, come with me to conference room 17C. And bring your notepad." Brett Hillsby, a barking Doberman most days, followed Ron to the room like a timid first-year analyst.

Twenty minutes later, Brett came back alone with a smile on his face. "Guys, Ron just had lunch with Karl Stevens this morning. He told me the bonus, and the rest of you are next. John, go to conference room 17C. Ron is waiting for you."

While this news should have been exciting, the analysts looked at each other only to see fear staring back at them. The room was absolutely silent and few keyboards clacked as everyone focused on the bonus conversation ahead. Robert checked his March Madness basketball brackets just to get his mind on something else before the final moment.

John Granton came back into the room, sat at his desk, and looked blankly at the screen. "Mark, you're next."

Mark departed for 17C. He returned in less than ten minutes looking defeated, with his shoulders slumped low and his eyes avoiding contact with anyone. Robert now felt alarm. Brett seemed happy with his bonus, John seemed alright although not ecstatic, but the first analyst was crushed after the news. Maybe, it would still be OK? After all, Mark was not the hardest working analyst and had made a fair number of serious screw-ups during the year.

"Lenny, you're next," said Mark, passing the Olympic torch of bonus discussions. Lenny Lee looked nervous. His tenure in the conference room was longer than Mark, perhaps fifteen minutes more. Upon his return, his demeanor was not crushed but it certainly was not good either. Robert and Lenny were neck and neck for the top analyst spot, with Lenny likely in the lead. If Lenny didn't get good news, there was little hope for him unless he managed to take the honor of top bucket analyst for the year. Robert stood up and made his way to the conference room, not needing Lenny to tell him the obvious as he was the last to be called.

In room 17C, Robert McClure found Ron sitting at the end of a sixteen-chair conference table. He didn't look unhappy but had an air of professionalism to his posture, another bad sign. "Robert, come sit over here." By the tone of his voice, Robert knew almost for certain that the worst was coming. "Robert, you've done an excellent job this year. I mean really amazing. You're constantly going above and beyond. You've mastered the pitchbooks, the models, and you're good with clients as well. In my many years of investment banking, you are definitely in the top 20% of new analysts. I want you to keep up the good work."

What was this? Robert couldn't believe it. From the depths of his personal abyss, his spirits were lifted with every word. He started to guess the possible bonus…$60K, $70K, maybe even $80K…the models and bottles were finally here. It was all worth it. His first taste of success was… "But, unfortunately, the bonus pool this year had only a small portion reserved for junior employees. The total pool was bigger than expected, but we hired a couple of new MDs in 2014 who had locked-in bonuses. Also, a couple of managing directors and executive directors from equity capital markets threatened to leave, so the bank threw them a bigger slice. For this year, your bonus is $35,000. I know that it's not what you expected, but I promise you that I will take care of you next year and will go to bat for you, Lenny, and Mark. I'll talk to Karl Stevens personally, and we'll get you the bonus that you deserve. There just wasn't enough to go around for everyone this time, especially with the commodity price environment. Do you have any questions?"

"No, sir," said Robert, attempting his best to show no emotion and wondering if his eyes betrayed the despair he felt on the inside. Ron slid him a check across the table made out for $35,000. Robert felt a wave of confused emotions. In his hands was the biggest check of his life. At the same time, Robert was a banker and could do the math quickly. At eighty hours per week and a total all-in comp of $110,000, this was equivalent to $55,000 for a forty-hour work week, which was not exactly models and bottles. According to the Bureau of Labor Statistics salary data, the median elementary and middle school teacher in the U.S. earns $58,000 per year and that's with a whole summer of vacation. Librarians made $59,000. Plumbers and electricians earn $55,000 per year. While everyone back home thought that Robert had the golden ticket, this didn't feel like it. His hourly compensation was not much better than some guy plunging a toilet or installing electrical wire. Hell, if a plumber or electrician put in an extra forty hours of overtime and worked an eighty-hour week, he or she would actually earn $137,500 per year with overtime pay – a whole $27,500 more than Robert's "prestigious" job. Overtime in banking was nonexistent, and analysts earned not one additional cent for each hour over forty.

Ron got up and patted Robert on the shoulder. "Keep up the good work, pal. Now let's wrap up the Pioneer Natural Resources pitchbook, I need it by 7 a.m." Robert sat paralyzed for a few moments and then followed Ron back to the mergers and acquisitions desk.

Ron gave a few words to the M&A team. "Hey guys, I'm going to call it a day, but I want you all to know what a great job this team has done. This has been an incredible year for Latham Schroeder, and you made it happen. Also, in two weeks, Sally and I are having a little party at the house, and I want the whole team to come. Set your calendars, alright? Thank you again for all of your hard work this year."

Almost every other group in the bank was released early given that it was bonus day. By four o'clock, the usually hectic floor was a ghost town – other than the small group of M&A analysts still there and a couple of essential back office operations people. A janitor walked by in confusion, not knowing where everyone had gone and stared at the remaining analysts, unable to work out why they alone remained, before returning to his duties. Their all-important task this time around was pitching Pioneer Natural Resources the sale of their Eagle Ford assets. Given that anyone could see the dwindling importance of the Eagle Ford in Pioneer's acreage portfolio, their pitchbook would likely be the fifth or sixth pitch from a major bank regarding the exact same acreage position. Their chances of actually winning this mandate were practically nonexistent. The day drifted into the night as the three plotted charts and calculated figures. Each hour dragged on forever given that their spirits were even more depressed and beaten down than usual. After what seemed like a millennium crammed into ten hours, it was 2 a.m. yet again and time to shut out the lights and head home. The final presentation was sent to Ron. The guys packed their laptops into their bags just in case any additional requests arrived in the early morning before they could reach the office.

"Fuck this!" yelled Mark out of nowhere, "Fuck! Fuck! Fuck!" He threw a stack of pitchbooks from his desk at the computer screen. It toppled over and the glossy pages flew everywhere. The next targets of his wrath were a coffee mug full of pens, which he splashed across the desk and a rolling chair he kicked ten yards across the floor. Robert and Lenny stared in disbelief at the sudden outburst. Given the late hour, they had been nearly lulled into sleep, but were now fully awake and not sure how to respond to Mark's outrage.

"Damn it guys, they totally screwed me on the bonus. I mean totally screwed me." No one had talked about their bonus up until this point. It was a major taboo in the banking industry, but from the miserable look on Robert's and Lenny's faces throughout the day, Mark knew that they hadn't done well either. This wasn't just about the money. In fact, for someone from a wealthy family like Mark, the money was actually the least part of it. Mark Edwards didn't have to worry about scrounging for his next meal or paying student loans. It was the simple idea of being misled with countless promises and giving everything to the bank only to find out that in return, you were screwed. It was the feeling of being used – not tricked once for a few bucks, but screwed over the course of an entire year, for over four thousand hours of your life, and for what? The bonus check was simply a measure of how deep the dagger had gone into their backs. Here they were working until 2 a.m. again with no end in sight. And all that they had to look forward to was next year's bonus, a full twelve months away, and trust that the same employer, who had screwed them this time, would treat them better next time. This evening was the first ten hours of the four thousand, one hundred and sixty more work hours estimated for the next year.

"Hey Mark, it's gonna be alright, man," said Lenny. "I know that this sucks, but we'll get our exit-op one of these days. Just stick it out. You'll see. I got screwed too. It'll be alright."

The term "exit-op" was young banker slang for "exit opportunity." It is the fabled dream of every analyst, the next major career step. The two most common exit-ops are the buy-side, either a private equity firm, which purchases private companies in order to resell them or take them public, or a hedge fund, which trades public stock. Other possibilities include working in corporate development for a publicly traded company, essentially a corporate in-house mergers and acquisitions team. Or, lastly and least desirable, after three years of being an analyst, you could get promoted to associate, essentially John Granton's position. An associate worked about seventy hours a week and was paid between $150K to the $200Ks. The compensation at least made the promotion tolerable, but it was still a lot of grunt work with little improvement in the lifestyle.

"Lenny, we're not even a year into being analysts, and I can't take this shit anymore. We still have at least another year or two before we can make it to an exit-op. And it doesn't help that oil prices keep tanking. We're at $53.24 per barrel as of yesterday. There's no exit-ops for us man. We're just fucking screwed," said Mark tersely.

"He does have a point about the oil price," said Robert. "Unless Saudi goes back to managing the oil market tomorrow, we'll end up being a generation of analysts that did all the work and never got the reward. Keep your fucking fingers crossed on that exit-op, Lenny."

"You're exactly right," added Mark. "What private equity firm is going to hire when they're losing billions on their books? And even if the market was better, exit-ops are complete bullshit anyway. What are you gonna do, Lenny? Move to a private equity fund where you work seventy hours a week instead of eighty or to a hedge fund like Citadel where they'll grind you even worse than here. Or take a look at John – he's our boss, and honestly, his life is shit. What's he get…maybe eight or nine more hours of sleep per week? He's been an analyst for three years and now he's gotta do another three or four years to even have a shot at VP. And I do mean just a shot at it. If there isn't space for him, they'll just show him the door and thank him for his six years of service. It would serve that prick right, but that's beside the point. They'll just replace him with one of us and not think twice about it."

"Come on, man. It's not that bad," replied Lenny. "We're still investment bankers. That's gotta mean something."

"Maybe it means something to your 'tiger mom', but it doesn't mean shit to me."

"Ouch, that was a little harsh Mark," said Robert. 'Take it easy."

Mark paced back and forth in front of their computers, "I just don't see the point anymore. We're not making money; we're just working for the faint hope of one day making that big exit-op. Give up the seven best years of your life from twenty-three to thirty and hope for the best. All of my friends in California are having a blast right now! They work forty hours a week, go to bars, hit on girls, and have actual hobbies. I'm sick of their fucking surfing photos on Facebook. And what do I have? I'm here, stuck in this fucking glass cube. Even if I had the time, I couldn't catch a wave in Galveston to save my life. The only waves that I'm seeing is the up and down of oil prices and the sharks in this business like Ron, that piece of shit. And what's it all for? No, really, why the hell are we doing this? Just so we can get a scratch-off lottery ticket to some fantastical, easy lifestyle way over the other side of a giant hill. After it's all said and done, I might just find out that my ticket doesn't have the winning numbers. I'll be fat, probably bald and talking about the good old days in college because the last ten years of my life just passed me by in this fucking office in this piece of shit of a city. That's what's happening guys – clear as day."

They said nothing to each other until Robert broke the silence. "Hey, man just chill. Let's wrap up for today. Just cool down and try not to think about all this stuff. It's only bringing you down. It's 2:20 a.m. on bonus day. We've done enough. Let's go home."

"Alright, cool man. I'm sorry for all this, guys. It just fucking sucks, man."

"I know…but Robert's right. It's all gonna be OK," said Lenny, offering a second consolation.

CHAPTER 9

A LIFE OF MONEY, FAST CARS, AND MANSIONS – JUST NOT YOURS

On the night of Ron's party, the team got out of the office at 7 p.m. for the first time in over a month. While this would seem like a gift, the event felt more like a work function than a break. After all, who wants to spend more time with their co-workers and bosses after countless sleepless nights with them? The team carpooled together to Ron's house in West University, a neighborhood nestled perfectly between the Medical Center, Downtown, and the Galleria, capturing three prime areas of high net worth employment within a fifteen-minute commute. Hence, the neighborhood was composed of a mixture of all the city's wealthiest individuals: doctors, lawyers, oilmen, and financiers. The only group missing was the old money, still nestled securely in River Oaks.

Ronald Lufkin's house was like many in the neighborhood, a large recent build replacing the old 1950s ranch homes once standard in the area. A few of the ranch homes still stood, cast into the shadows of the new mansions that towered above them. Ron's house, built in a contemporary

Tuscan style, was clearly oversized for its lot, as is the unfortunate trend of much real estate in Houston. With five bedrooms and around seven thousand square feet, the house spewed its mass over a lot which could comfortably fit a four thousand square foot home. Ron didn't have any kids, so the size of the house was certainly not out of necessity. It was rather a physical manifestation of his pride and success. The front entrance was an exquisitely carved door with an oval top, flanked on each side by gas lanterns. However, it was neither the splendid entrance nor the house itself that stood out to Robert and the guys. Rather, it was the car parked in the driveway. Surely enough, Ron's BMW 7 Series was there, but next to it was a brand new Porsche 911 Turbo S. The burgundy color left something to be desired, but nonetheless, the car was a sculpted work of beauty.

The analysts spilled out of Mark's old BMW 3 Series, a hand-me-down from his mom. "You guys see that, right?" asked Lenny. "That can't be Ron's car, can it? I mean the bonus was pretty bad this year for all of us, right?"

"No clue, but I know exactly what it's worth: $188,000," added Robert, having memorized the MSRP from his many visits to the Porsche website between editing pitchbooks and organizing transaction comps.

"That is sick, man. Very nice," said Mark, still gazing at the car as they walked toward the exquisite doorway of the house. Robert rang the doorbell and was soon greeted by their managing director dressed in a light cashmere sweater and jeans with a newly poured scotch on ice in his hands. He was nearly unrecognizable – none of them had ever seen him outside of his investment banker garb before.

"You guys like my new toy over there?" said Ron, nodding toward the Porsche.

"Oh yeah," replied Mark. "That is awesome! Congratulations, Ron." The rest of the team offered up their earnest, duty-bound congratulations to their boss as well.

"Come on in guys and fix yourself a drink. The bar is right over there."

The party had about twenty-five guests in all. The team recognized one or two as corporate development guys from pitches earlier in the year. Joe Marisco, Head of Commodities was there along with a couple of other familiar faces from the office. Intermixed with colleagues from work were a few non-alpha males whose stance gave them away as non-bankers. They were too relaxed, and although confident they lacked the oozing overconfidence of a high level managing director.

The analysts went straight for the bar and poured themselves highballs of Dewar's – Ron must have been hiding the good scotch for himself, an unsurprising tactic given the analysts' ungenerous bonus this year. Robert took a sip and went up to Ron and the small group of people surrounding him. "Thanks for having us over, Ron."

"No problem, kid. Have you met my wife, Sally?"

"No, sure haven't. Pleased to meet you." Sally was ten years younger than Ron. She must have been drop dead gorgeous in her twenties and probably well into her thirties. Sally had shoulder length blonde hair, potentially colored, blue eyes, possibly contacts, and a high probability of being from Dallas given those aesthetic tastes.

"You already know Kyle from corporate development at Caption Resources, and these are our longtime friends, Sandy and Joe." Sandy almost mirrored Sally with a nearly identical outfit, blond hair but green eyes.

"Hi, good to see you again Kyle. Good to meet the rest of you," said Robert, purposefully trying to hold back the "y'all" which was the first thing to come to his mind. He was after all an investment banker, and not a country boy any longer.

Sally picked up the thread of the conversation that Robert's arrival had interrupted. "So, like I was saying, Sandy. We finally got around to supporting some of the charities on our list. We gave $20,000 to UT like we do every year, half in my name and half in Ron's of course. You know, we met at UT when he was a MBA student, and I was studying English Lit. So, I guess we owe them everything. Hahaha! Then, we gave another $10,000 to MD Anderson Hospital – we know so many of the doctors there and their work is just a miracle. We also gave to the 'Colors for Life' charity for the first time. Ron wrote them a check for $30,000. Basically, it's a charity that offers professional college level water coloring lessons to inner city kids in Houston. I mean it's just wonderful. They really change lives."

While Robert tried to participate in the conversation as best as he could, he got his cue to leave when the theme switched to favorite holiday interior designers in town. Ron escaped the conversation with him and took the analysts aside. He instructed them to keep the clients entertained and drinking. Finally, orders that they were glad to follow.

Robert circled the party and made sure to chat briefly with the clients and anyone who was anyone at the bank. The goal of such events was to entertain and make the impression of being a fun person while at the same time retaining one's professional composure and not crossing the line of inebriation. Unfortunately, an hour into the party, Mark was failing to balance himself along this fine line. While he wasn't yet belligerently drunk, he was drowning in his conversation over EBITDAX multiples with one of the corporate dev guys and blatantly missing Lenny's cues to dial things back. Fortunately, his phone saved him from further embarrassment as a few new e-mails hit his inbox. "Lllleett me ccheck this." He looked down at his phone. "Aw shit."

"What is it?" said Lenny.

"Bloomberg just posted a story about Pioneer Natural Resources selling its assets in the Eagle Ford 'according to sources familiar with the matter'."

"Oh shit," said Lenny. The team had just finished the Pioneer pitchbook for the Eagle Ford assets. Their meeting with the management team was only two days away. Thankfully, they hadn't presented their idea yet, but that didn't change the fact that somebody a.k.a. Robert McClure, Lenny Lee, and Mark Edwards had to re-do the entire pitchbook and insert a new pitch.

"I'll tell Ron the bad news," said Robert.

The party guests stared at Robert as he walked over to Ron with a clear sense of urgency. In the short time it took to cross the room, his gait underwent an almost lycanthropic transformation from fun-loving young banker to the slave of a dreadful curse. He pulled Ron aside so the clients would not hear about the problem. "Ron, Bloomberg News just reported that Pioneer is selling the Eagle Ford. What do we do?"

"Yikes, oohh, well it's simple. Here's what you do. Take out all the Eagle Ford slides, add a couple more possible acquisition opportunities in the Midland Basin, and then find five or six sizeable acquisitions in the Delaware Basin. They haven't talked about doing anything over there, but why not?" answered Ron rather calmly. "You guys better get back to the office. Don't stay up all night. I'll have a look at the draft first thing in the morning."

Robert abruptly plucked the rest of the analysts away from their conversations and directed them toward the door. As the team exited the party, they could hear Ron laughing loudly at someone's joke. He turned to them as they shuffled out the door. "Hey guys, thanks for coming!"

"Thanks Ron!"

"Yeah thanks, it was a great time!"

"Alright, who is the most sober driver here?" inquired Lenny as they approached Mark's car.

"Not me," answered Mark raising his hand.

"I had two scotches," said Robert.

"Then, you are the winner," said Lenny, taking the keys dangling from Mark's index finger and handing them to Robert.

"Agreed, I'm definitely not letting the Asian guy drive after a few drinks."

"What the fuck, man? That's uncalled for," said Lenny, mildly bothered.

"I mean you can't handle your liquor bro. It's true. Don't get mad at Robert for speaking truth," added Mark laughing.

"Fuck you guys."

The three loaded themselves back into Mark's hand-me-down BMW. "This is complete bullshit," observed Mark as the car rolled away from the party and back toward the office in the Galleria. "Total bullshit."

"So, how are we gonna spilt up the work?" asked Lenny from the back seat.

"No clue, Lenny, but I got a plan," remarked Robert, abruptly pulling the car into the Valero gas station on Kirby Drive just outside of West University

"What are you stopping for?" asked Mark drunkenly.

Robert didn't say a thing as he stepped out of the car. Mark and Lenny watched in confusion as he entered the gas station and went to the back. They were still stupefied upon his return with a large paper sack in hand. "Here's to not giving a fuck," said Robert, pulling out a case of Miller Lite from the bag and placing it on the back seat next to Lenny.

"Hell, yeah man, hell yeah!" said Mark, giving him a high five. Robert also pulled out an eight-pack of Red Bull from the bag and handed it to Lenny. He then shuffled through the songs on his phone until he finally found what he was looking for, *C.R.E.A.M.* by the Wu-Tang Clan. He adjusted his Bluetooth to synch with the car and blasted at it at full volume – the deep bass shook the whole car as Old Dirty Bastard of the Wu-Tang Clan went straight into the chorus, "Cash Rules Everything Around Me…CREAM! Get the money. Dollar dollar bill y'all!" The car sped out of the parking lot. Mark smiled in the passenger seat and cracked open a beer.

"Hey Lenny, give me one from the back there, will you?" said Robert.

"You do know how illegal this is, right?" asked Lenny rhetorically in a concerned voice.

"Yeah, I do. Fuck it man. I'm not thinking about that right now. I'm just thinking about choking to death the person who did this to us. That's way more illegal than drinking this beer," said Robert before taking a giant gulp. "Like…how does Bloomberg even know that Pioneer is selling their Eagle Ford acreage? What the fuck does 'according to sources familiar with the matter' mean in the press release? Sounds pretty suspicious to me."

"I don't know…maybe a Bloomberg journalist is banging an analyst on the Pioneer deal team. Who knows?" answered Mark between sips of his Miller. They all laughed.

"I mean you're onto something here," added Lenny. "Who would be that stupid to hand over information like that to a reporter, and for what reason? Pioneer hasn't officially announced anything. For Bloomberg to run the story it can't be made up; it must come from a good source. I mean this is Bloomberg News, not an internet message board. There's gotta be a leak, but why leak the deal in the first place? It doesn't make sense. What incentive do any of us have to call up Bloomberg tomorrow and tell them that we're working on a new Wellco Solutions deal, for example?"

"Yeah, that's exactly what I was thinking," said Robert. "Who benefits… and how good is this source? Did they get a copy of the pitchbook or something like that? Did the VP tell someone about it while drunk for some stupid reason? Everyone hears rumors all the time in this business. We've heard a million of them in meetings with management teams and more than half of them never happen. So, it's got to be pretty convincing evidence of a deal to print on Bloomberg."

"For someone who doesn't give a shit about investment banking, you really sound like someone who gives too much of a shit," said Mark, taking another large swig.

"Ha!" said Robert, parking the car in the Latham, Schroeder & Holt garage. He finished his beer and reached into the back seat for another. He clanked beer cans with Mark. "Lenny, you ready for one?"

"Naw, someone's got to keep their head straight on this team."

"Suit yourself!"

The team walked past the security guards with the beers in hand and the full case in plain sight. The guards, who were used to seeing them leave the building in the a.m. hours, just smiled and chuckled, "How you boys doing?"

"We're doing great…couldn't be better! See you guys in a couple of hours," said Mark. By the time they arrived at their desk, it was already 10 p.m. and the entire floor was empty, a not unfamiliar sight at this point in their analyst careers. They split the work and got to researching new possible acquisition targets for Pioneer. About thirty minutes into the task, Lenny gave in to temptation and opened a beer and a Red Bull beside it.

"There you go buddy, hell yeah my brother!" announced Mark. "Hell yeah!" The gang reached across the desk and gave each other a cheers before returning to their slides. The hours flew by and the pitchbook was coming together much better than one would expect given the significant progress also made on the case of Miller Lite.

By 4:30 a.m., Lenny and Robert were packing for the night. Mark had volunteered to read the pitchbook one more time, print a couple of color copies, and clean up their late night party. Lenny and Robert called a cab. If the alcohol in their blood stream didn't get them into a wreck, the lack of sleep surely would. They waved goodbye to Mark, who would stay another thirty minutes, as they headed for the elevator. The same security guards watched in bewilderment as a cab pulled up and the two analysts got inside with Robert lighting a cigarette before getting in. He only smoked when he drank and tonight a smoke was certainly called for. Another pitchbook down.

Robert got to his apartment and slumped on his couch. After a moment he lifted his hand and stared at his watch as if it was a mysterious foreign object. It was just past 5 a.m. He tried to sleep but after fifteen minutes he was still awake, experiencing the restlessness that only people who have worked twenty-hour days understand – his mind was wired and continued to think frantically about the Pioneer pitchbook even as his body was shutting down. He grabbed the remote from his coffee table to turn on the TV and then noticed something in the corner against the wall. It was the Barclays pitchbook, still lying in the same spot where he had thrown it in a fit of rage all those months ago. That pitchbook had been so close to being the real deal. However, still to this day, no deal had ever been announced. The downturn in oil prices must have sunk it like Ron said. Good thing he didn't waste his meager savings on that trade.

And then, it suddenly struck him. Even if this pitchbook didn't work, maybe there was still a chance to make lemonade from lemons here. In fact, if he was right, this could still be the opportunity of a lifetime. He jumped on his computer and opened up PowerPoint. He worked furiously for another hour and a half, using all of the skills mastered over the past year to throw together a presentation at lightning speed. As the morning sun rose, Robert McClure put the finishing touches on his creation and smiled – the rest of the guys would see it when the time was right. This was their way out. This was it. Satisfied and now at ease, he finally fell asleep, managing to get at least a few hours of rest.

Ron walked into the office early to find Mark already there, passed out on his chair with several empty Miller Lite and Red Bull cans scattered across the analysts' desks. "Jesus Christ," exclaimed Ron as he wrapped his coat around the back of his chair. "Mark, get up. Where is that pitchbook?" Mark opened his eyes, not knowing where he was for a few seconds. When he figured it out, utter fear was his first emotion of the day.

"Oh my God, I'm sorry. I must have fallen asleep last night." Thankfully, less than a dozen people were already in the office. They were further away and didn't seem to be paying much attention to him yet. His face was turning red, but one thing saved him from complete embarrassment. Next to his very last beer from the previous night was a stack of printed pitchbooks. He got up from his chair and handed a copy to Ron before hastily clearing the table of beer cans and then rushing to the restroom.

"Great, this pitchbook is going to be a masterpiece," muttered Ron sarcastically.

The rest of the guys straggled into the office dead on their feet. Lenny opened the Pioneer Natural Resources presentation ready to make edits. Robert didn't follow suit. Instead, his first thought was to check the price of PXD, the ticker for Pioneer Natural Resources. On the Bloomberg rumor, PXD had already jumped 4.5%, which was an extraordinary leap for a stable large cap company.

Their taskmaster returned the pitchbook with the suggested edits around mid-afternoon. The crew was actually glad to have a thorough review from him – it gave them time to heal their hangovers and zone out. However, it also meant that it would be another long night correcting the pitchbook and satiating Ron's unquenchable thirst for new slides. The pitchbook was covered in red markups, but it could have been worse. While minor mistakes were plentiful, Ron actually liked the chosen acquisition targets and the general layout. The team had reached the point where they could do this half asleep or half-drunk, as had been the case last night. They knocked out the changes and left before midnight to catch up on some much needed rest.

CHAPTER 10

AN ESCAPE PLAN

The Pioneer Natural Resources meeting went extremely well, aside from Pioneer having no interest whatsoever in the Delaware Basin or in additional Midland Basin acreage either. The team's latest late night sacrifice was once again all for nothing. However, at least there was one point of interest to the meeting. According to Pioneer's management team, the company had no intention of selling its Eagle Ford assets. The Bloomberg newsflash that had pulled them out of Ron's party with such urgency was nothing more than an unsubstantiated rumor. In fact, the CEO was quite upset with Bloomberg, and the firm's investor relations department spent the whole week quelling the rumors. Although interesting to learn, this information did nothing to make the analysts feel better about being screwed with yet another dead-end presentation. They were just glad to be done with the pitch and relished their first free Friday in a long time. The rest of the week was relatively slow, which gave Robert some extra time to work on his secret side project. When Friday arrived, the team heard they would get out at 6 p.m. It was the perfect opportunity to finally reveal to them his escape plan from this soul-crushing business.

"Guys, you wanna hit the Anvil after work for an hour or two?" asked Robert.

"Sure, sounds good." said Mark, "Lenny, you in?"

"Yeah, let's do it."

"My man! Awesome Lenny!" exclaimed Mark.

"Hey, but don't tell John or Brett. I don't want anyone else from the office to come. I just wanna take it easy, you know what I mean," added Robert.

"Gotcha. Yeah, for sure."

When six o'clock rolled around, they were able to slip out of the office without any last minute emergencies and made their way to the Anvil. Unfortunately, the few tables and seats at the bar were already taken. While this was an early getaway for them, half of Houston had left their offices two hours ago. The young investment banking musketeers took full advantage of the expert bartenders, first with a round of Manhattans and then Sazeracs per Robert's suggestion. By drink two, a strong buzz pulsed through them, and the Anvil's refined cocktails were no longer going to cut it. They grabbed an Uber to Midtown for a crowd a little more their age. Shots of Fireball led to shots of Patron and an ever-growing bar tab which was further lengthened with the help of two Texas A&M girls taking full advantage of their well-padded bank accounts. After bar-hopping to several more establishments and proving to most of Midtown every poor stereotype of a young banker, the three retreated to Robert's apartment where they popped open a round of Bud Lights and Mark dialed up Domino's Pizza.

"Where do you guys think Domino's stands in the pizza league tables? If you're a delivery guy at Domino's is that like working in Middle Market at SunTrust Bank or something like that?" jested Mark.

"Totally bro, but who is the Goldman Sachs of the pizza world?" responded Robert.

"North Italia for sure. You know the one right next to Whole Foods near our office."

"That's good pizza dude, but totally not Goldman. It's too small to be Goldman. North Italia is more of a boutique like a Lazard or a Jefferies."

"Yeah that's a good point, but what's the best large corporate chain? Maybe Papa John's? There's really nothing in the pizza world on the Goldman level… it's kind of a poor analogy if you ask me," said Lenny.

"I'm gonna tell the next stuck-up Goldman kid that I meet that he works at the Papa John's of banking," said Robert, taking a swing of his beer.

"Hey man. They would probably agree. Better ingredients make better pizza. It's an Ivy-League thing."

Robert had hoped for a more serious topic than pizza rankings leading up to his big reveal, but after this many drinks that now seemed a slim possibility. It was now or never. They slumped into the sofas with beers in hand. Mark was ready to turn on the TV when Robert grabbed the Barclays pitchbook from the pile of financial magazines and papers on the coffee table.

"Hey, I wanted to talk to you guys about something. Do you remember this thing?"

"Yeah, of course, I didn't know you still had it." Lenny grabbed the pitchbook and began flipping through it again.

"But have you seen this before?" asked Robert, handing him a single sheet of glossy pitchbook paper from his desk. The sheet was a Barclays teaser for Pioneer's Eagle Ford position, essentially a one-page ad for an acreage sale with just enough information to tease someone into signing a non-disclosure agreement for further information. The teaser highlighted the most important aspects of a possible Eagle Ford sale with a map, some production and reserves data, and a few impressive recent well results.

"How the fuck did you get this Barclays teaser?" said Lenny, passing the copy to Mark, who looked at it, similarly stunned. "Pioneer just told us that the Bloomberg story wasn't real! I mean we were literally in their office this last week. Were they lying to us? Why would they do that? Wait until Ron sees this…he's going to freak out. I mean look…the footnote is dated as of just two days ago – this is gonna happen, and soon!"

Lenny passed the teaser to Mark. "Holy shit, man. This is amazing, did you grab it in their office or something?"

"They didn't lie to us about the Eagle Ford sale." Lenny and Mark looked at each other in confusion. "I didn't find this teaser," said Robert.

"What are you talking about, man?"

"I made it." Robert let the three words sink in. There was an awkward silence for a few seconds.

"Wait, what?" uttered Lenny. "You did what?"

"I took the Barclays pitchbook and copied their exact format. I picked a transaction that could actually happen, pulled well data from our database, and created the teaser."

"But, why?"

"Pretty simple, Lenny. I'll explain in a minute." He walked over to the kitchen cabinet and pulled out a bottle of Glenlivet 15-year French Oak Reserve and poured it into three highballs. "First, let me ask you guys something, and note that this whole conversation doesn't leave the room. Raise your hand if you checked the compliance list after finding the Weatherton pitchbook to see if you could buy the shares."

"Dude, guilty!" Mark laughed as his hand abruptly shot upward along with Robert's hand. They looked over at Lenny who was trying to avoid their eye contact. He timidly raised his hand as well.

"That's exactly my point. Anyone who found a pitchbook like that would use the information if they could. Well, at least anyone on Wall Street. So imagine for a second if someone found this teaser," said Robert, holding up the fake slide. "And imagine if that someone was a hedge fund analyst or a portfolio manager with billions of dollars in the market. He would act on the information without a doubt. This teaser is the perfect form of inside information. You didn't hear it from a friend, you didn't steal confidential information, you literally just found it on the street. There is no way that the SEC can trace your knowledge of an upcoming deal to any person or computer file. To them, you just look like a guy who got a little lucky taking a large position before a major acquisition. Absolutely nothing ties you to the teaser unless you don't dispose of it for some stupid reason. Sure, the SEC might be suspicious, but suspicion alone does not make a case. That Weatherton pitchbook was irresistible to us. To a hedge fund manager, it is free money – millions to be exact. It could make their year."

"But so what?" replied Mark. "We play a joke on a hedge fund guy and then run out of the bushes laughing like two kids who just set a bag of dogshit on fire outside his door. What's your point with all this?"

"It's our escape ticket, man. I want a way out of all this bullshit. I'm tired of Ron, the associates, and the mindless hours of busy work. I want our piece of the pie. I'm tired of watching someone else eat my slice right in front of me." Mark and Lenny took large gulps from their glasses. "I'm sick of being treated like an animal, of working on zero-chance pitches until 4 a.m. in the morning, of getting stiffed on our bonuses while our bosses buy Porsches and donate tens of thousands to save the fucking whales. And, I know how the deal is supposed to work. You gotta put in a few years of tough work, and then you can be the big swinging dick in the office. But that's all bullshit. Oil is down to $50 per barrel, and the whole industry is imploding around us. If we don't grab our slice of the pie now, there won't be one left after our three analyst years are over. This isn't the 1980s anymore – it's not even 2005 or 2006. The days of young guys working our tails off and getting to managing director are done. Forget about that fairytale and forget about getting a job at a hedge fund. The banks are getting smaller, the hedge funds are going out of business, and the bonus pools are dogshit compared to back in the day."

"You got a point," said Mark, raising his glass in a symbolic toast of agreement.

Robert continued getting more passionate and his speech grew more slurred given his losing battle against the effects of the alcohol. He took another gulp of Glenlivet. "You'rrrre damn right! They're goin' to work us to death and then maybe one of the three of us will get promoted to associate so that you can be worked to death some more. Or, we can use a fake pitchbook like this to make ourselves rich beyond our wildest dreams. We'd never have to work again."

"I don't know, Robert," said Lenny. "I'm OK with slugging it out a couple more years and getting to associate. I think I can do it. We're working hard, and Ron recognizes that more than you think. Also, I'm not exactly sure what you're getting at here."

"You're right, Lenny. I'm sure that Ron does see your work, but what are you going to do after reaching associate? You think they're going to promote an Asian guy to VP? Look around the office. How many Asian or Indian VPs or MDs do you see? Fucking ZERO is the answer. Sure, there are plenty of Asian analysts and associates slogging away and working like loyal pencil pushers, but do you see any getting promoted beyond that? And it's not just our bank, but the nearly the whole Street. I'm sorry man, but this isn't tech banking… I don't mean to be a jerk. Oil and gas banking groups want the all-American preppy football-watching guy as the face of their mergers and acquisitions team. That's who they think sells acreage over steak dinners with clients who have the exact same background and interests. Look, I'll give it to you, Lenny. You're the best analyst out of the three of us, but they'll promote Mark over you in a heartbeat just because he looks more like a Vice President to them."

Lenny sat there not saying a word, but he was clearly hurt. He wasn't hurt by Robert, only by the reality of his words. This was something that he had already felt but did not want it to be true. However, the fact that others noticed the injustice as well only validated the suspicions.

Mark moved to change the subject, "I mean it's a cool teaser and all, and it looks perfect. But like Lenny said, how is this supposed to get us out of this bullshit? Love the rant, man, but I'm still not getting it." He grabbed the Glenlivet bottle for a refill, first a tiny splash then followed by a solid pour. "When did you even have time to put this together?"

"No, no…I get it now, Mark." The look on Lenny's face began to change from desperation to exhilaration as the plot settled in. "It's genius…Robert, it's so fucking genius. We buy the shares first, and then we let the hedge funds drive up the share price based on a fake pitchbook." Robert's smiled broadened as Lenny continued, "What's even better is other than making the fake pitchbook, we don't even break the law here. We let someone else break the law for us by acting on 'inside information.'"

"Exactly!" said Robert. "You got it, Lenny. And take for example, PXD here. We buy call options on PXD. We then distribute fake PXD pitchbooks. We know that the hedge funds are going to use our fake inside information. So, they start bidding up the stock price in anticipation of a sale. Rumors of a deal start spreading even wider to their friends and contacts. That creates even more buying pressure, and the shares keep going up, but we are the first ones in the position. And right before the fake deal is supposed to be 'announced', we sell our options, cash in, and get out before anyone finds out that the deal is never going to happen. That's the plan, guys!"

"Oh shit," escaped Mark's lips and a devious smile formed on his face.

"And the best part is that no one will figure it out!" Robert continued, flying with excitement now. "Sometimes deals do fall apart; sometimes the bids aren't good enough or the financing doesn't come through. A bunch of hedge funds would lose money, but they wouldn't come looking for us even if they figured it out. What would a hedge fund say to the SEC 'Hi there Mr. SEC agent. My fund used inside information to bet on this stock, and we think that the inside information may have been fake. Can you go after these crooks?' said Robert in a mock cartoonish voice. "We just have to find a good way to distribute the pitchbooks. It shouldn't be too hard. I imagine we leave a few copies around different Starbucks in midtown Manhattan, maybe drop off a few at Dean and Deluca and wherever hedge fund bros might find them. In some ways, this is the oldest trick in the book. People have been running pump and dump schemes for ages with micro-cap stocks. The scammers buy shares of a thinly traded microcap with a market cap less than $50 million. Then, they fill message boards with bullshit stories about the company's impending acquisition, patent or FDA approval or whatever. Next, they send millions of bogus e-mails with the same message, and the stock starts climbing upward as suckers begin buying the shares. If enough mom and pop investors are dumb enough to buy it, the stock price skyrockets. That's a classic pump and dump. What's different in our case is that we're not trying to trick mom and pop investors and old widows. We're going to screw over the most sophisticated institutional investors in the market. And in our plan, there isn't a mile-long paper trail. In a classic pump and dump, there are millions of easily traceable e-mails and message board posts. Plus, it's not that hard to figure out who is manipulating the market in a $50 million market cap stock. For us, there's no paper trail and since we're only targeting large hedge funds, we can do this with way more liquid stocks where no one will even notice our tiny investment compared to the rest of the market. We don't need to aim for micro-caps. We can go much bigger."

"It's totally awesome," said Mark.

"And we're the only ones that can do this because we've been trained by those exact same investors – we know their world. Unless you've been slaving away on pitchbooks, you can't pull this off. An amateur would never make it look right. It's practically an inside job." Robert stood on top of the couch, practically yelling. "Guys, we CAN DO THIS! We can GET RICH! WE CAN MANIPULATE THE SHARE PRICES AND GET AWAY WITH IT! We're going to make SO MUCH FUCKING MONEY!"

Suddenly, there was a loud knock on the door. Robert lost his balance on the couch, falling face forward onto the floor and spilling his scotch everywhere. Mark dodged out of Robert's way and knocked over two empty Bud Lights, which shattered against a side table. Lenny screamed "Oh shit!" as he sprang up off the couch. There was another, more forceful knock from the outside. Lenny sprinted for the door and without thinking, swung it open. On the other side stood a 5'7" Asian kid with bleached blonde hair and saggy pants holding two pizzas. His eyes were wide with horror, and he stuttered out, "Dddomino's Ppppizza…did you guys order the large pepperoni and the mushroom and sausage with peppers?"

It took Lenny a moment to regain his composure. "Um yeah that's us. I mean, yes. We ordered the pizza…yeah a pepperoni mushroom. Here's forty bucks, keep the change!" Lenny slammed the door. "Holy shit guys, what the fuck!" he said as his heart rate slowly returned to a resting pace. "What the fuck."

CHAPTER 11

SATURDAY MORNING COMING DOWN

The team's collective hangover was barely wearing off on Saturday morning when their Blackberries began to buzz with e-mails from the office. Ron had been talking about an acquisition with the CEO of Ocean Management, an offshore oilfield services firm. While Ocean had been solely focused on drilling offshore for the past thirty-five years, Ron thought that it would be a good idea to pitch them a nearly bankrupt onshore 3-D seismic firm. It was a long shot, even by their usual standards, but that didn't matter to Ron, who wasn't doing the hard work of making the pitchbooks. From his home office, Ron called John Granton to relay precise instructions, which included a new slide deck packed with torturous graphics requiring extensive data collection. John called each of the analysts and summoned them to the office after their long night. The three dragged themselves into the seventeenth floor looking terrible and all carrying some sort of nursing aid, be it Gatorade or a bottle of 5-Hour Energy.

John was eager to dispense orders. “Alright ladies. Mark, take care of the introductory section. Put all of our oilfield services tombstones on the front. Put highlights around the offshore deals. Build a few case study slides of the most important deals. Lenny, do an offshore industry overview with at least ten slides. Also, Ron wants a map tracking the movements of every semi-submersible rig in the Gulf of Mexico. Robert, do the company overview and start another section on the competitive landscape for onshore 3-D seismic, and I’ll do my thing.”

The usual rhythm resumed, with John Granton barking orders and screaming at them over the most pointless details. While this pitch had zero chance of success, there was nevertheless one advantage to the deal. Ocean Management was one of the last offshore companies clinging to its headquarters in the former commercial capital of the South, New Orleans. If the team was lucky, this could mean a trip to the Big Easy. By lunchtime they had put together a decent shell of the presentation. They were now pretty good at throwing something together at the last minute, not that this fact made their job any easier. Being able to do a pitchbook in half the time only meant that the MD could get two pitchbooks done within the same timeframe. The hours saved were property of Latham, Schroeder, & Holt and not their own. Thankfully, since Ron was “working” from home, John decided to use this rare opportunity to take the day off himself. It was to be another weekend of just the analysts in an otherwise empty office.

Robert only waited five minutes after John had left to begin the next stage of his plan. He stopped typing and stood up. “Guys, everyone is gone. It’s just us. Remember what we talked about last night? This is our shot. Let’s make the pitchbook.”

“We’ve got a ton of work to do for the Ocean Management pitch. Are we really doing this, Robert?” said Lenny.

“Look, I know that I’m asking a lot here, but I can’t create a believable forty-page pitchbook without you. It’s just not possible. We’re a crack team. We can get both done. We’re already way ahead of schedule on the Ocean Management pitch.”

“You don’t have to tell me twice dude, I’m on board,” said Mark. “I’m ready. Stop being such a wuss, Lenny. So what’s the game plan? What company are we doing?”

“I’ve been doing some research, and I’m thinking Collins Petroleum. It’s a super realistic transaction. The Street has been speculating about it forever. Collins has great acreage right on top of RSP Permian and Diamondback who are both way bigger and have the capital to swallow Collins in one big bite. However, Collins is a family-run company – so no one believes that it will ever sell. And because it’s family-run, it trades at a discount to RSP Permian and Diamondback. The potential deal has been talked about forever – we’re just setting a calendar date for what the Street has been expecting for a long time.”

“I gotta say that it makes sense to me,” said Lenny. “It’s smart,” Lenny looked down at his desk, thinking. “Damn it...alright Robert, I’m in.”

“Awesome, Lenny!” said Robert, giving him a high five. “You know what to do. Mark, take care of the intro. Use the Bloomberg terminal to look up the historical upstream deals closed by Barclays. Highlight the ones in the Midland Basin. Build some case study slides around those. Lenny, take care of the company overview for Collins Petroleum, stock ticker CPO. I’ll take one of our previous industry overviews and re-do it in the Barclays format. I’ll also create the calendar, acreage layout, and the recent well result slides.”

The team switched tasks and pounded away at the fake Collins Petroleum pitchbook. Their window to work on the project was limited; there was no way they could put together a plausible pitchbook without the bank's resources. The Bloomberg terminal alone had an annual subscription price of more than $20,000, and without the opportunity of the empty office, they would never have the chance to use it – it would be hard to explain to a managing director why you're looking at Barclays transaction comps on the Bloomberg terminal. Ron would probably assume that you were interviewing with the competition and getting ready to jump ship – a reasonable assumption given this year's bonus season. After a few hours on the Collins presentation and a couple of boxes of Chinese takeout, they had to switch back to Ocean Management as Ron began demanding early drafts and additional slides via e-mail. For the next eight hours or so, they raced to make up for lost time and put their entire focus on Ron's pitch. At about 12:30 a.m., they had done enough for the night. Mark and Lenny were shutting down their computers and were mentally preparing for an early Sunday morning in the office. As they made their way toward to the exit, they looked back to see Robert still at his desk. "Hey man, you coming or what?" yelled Mark.

"Guys, it's 12:30, it's an early night. I'm going to stick around and do some formatting on the Collins pitchbook."

"Are you kidding me?" said Lenny.

"No, I'm not, but don't worry about it. You guys just go home. I'm going to put in another hour. I'm trying to match the exact light blue Barclays shade for their boxes. I've got it almost perfect."

Mark gave a big tired sigh. "Bro, fuck man…why do you have to be so crazy, Robert?" He ran his fingers through his wavy blond hair and threw his bag back on the desk. "Let's do this…let's do this for real."

"No really, it's cool man. I'm serious. I can do this part by myself," said Robert. "You don't have to stick around. You've already done enough today."

"Naw, man. We're not letting you suffer alone. I'm with you. That's what I promised and that's what's gonna happen." Mark stretched out his hand for a fist bump.

"God, banking has messed with our heads," said Lenny, laughing to himself. "What is wrong with us?" He groaned. "I'm staying too."

"Fuck yeah, man!" said Mark, giving him a fist bump as well.

The three sat back down at their desks with the entire open floor plan dark except for the motion sensor lights above their section. With the rest of the floor black, they could see the city of Houston clearly through the office windows. They worked through slide after slide, laughing as they edited, perfected and reviewed each detail, each shade, each box, over and over again. They had done this a million times before, but this time it didn't feel like such drudgery. This time, it wasn't about making money for someone else – it was for them.

On their way out, the security guards were confused to see the usually miserable analysts jubilant and trading jokes at 3:30 a.m. "Those bankers gotta be on drugs," said one of the guards to the other as the young analysts walked out. "Yeah, for sure," responded the other shaking his head in disbelief.

Robert drove to his solitary apartment, but tonight, somehow it didn't feel so desolate and cold. For the first time in a long while, he felt free and fell asleep with a smile on his face.

****

Sunday morning in Mississippi was the one day of the week where not much of anything would get done. Robert's grandpa would not work on the farm on Sundays, and his father would not lift a finger either, even in circumstances where he probably should have. While part of this was clearly observance of the Lord's Day, the other part was simply the fact that there was nothing else to do in Laurel. In addition, it was a time to reflect on the week. Even if the sanctimonious feeling did not last for the other six days of the week, it was better to reflect for one day than none at all. At church, his grandpa prayed devotedly in the pews like a Tibetan monk marooned in central Mississippi. His grandma always knelt close beside him, her hands tightly clasped, the essence of piety.

After the service, the whole family would gather at the Windmill Country Café. On any given Sunday, their table could extend from six seats to well over a dozen if they were joined by extended family and friends from church. As a boy, Robert spent most of the sermon dreaming of the Windmill's biscuits and gravy and the country fried steak. If Jesus was giving points for attendance, his report card was in good standing, but if it was graded by attention span, he was not doing so well. While surely a trick of his memory, Sundays in his mind were always in the middle of summer, cloudless and sunny, untouched by worry and unencumbered by the world.

****

Sundays at Latham, Schroeder & Holt were something altogether different. As standard practice, the analysts worked through Sunday to deliver a first draft for a pitch that would be taking place in three weeks. "First draft" was code for an immaculate presentation. While this made absolutely no sense, earlier was always better for Ron. He never held even a passing thought that this may cause any sort of inconvenience. Sunday was just another day for his analysts to maximize his bonus. The more pitches that he threw out there, the better the chances of securing a fee.

Of course, once upon a time, Ron had been an analyst himself. In his view, his approach was no different than his own treatment back in the day. Why, Robert, Mark, and Lenny should feel so lucky to be employed by him. Grinding analysts to bone was a time-honored tradition on Wall Street. It's just something that everyone has to go through. To give them a break would be to deprive them of an invaluable learning experience. And sure, the bonuses were bad this year, but tough luck. There were even worse managing directors out there, right?

For a mere second that morning, Ronald Lufkin had considered giving the analysts a day off next Saturday, but his thoughts quickly drifted to his recent Maserati test drive and what color would look best in his driveway. He parked his burgundy Porsche in the reserved parking spot and leisurely made his way to the office in khakis, a vineyard vines polo, and Italian loafers. The analysts, John Granton, and the Brett Hillsby were busy toiling away on the pitchbook. Occasionally, these in-person impromptu weekend office visits were necessary to keep the troops on their toes. Ron had picked up this tactic from his old managing director from his analyst days. In fact, his MD had been even worse and would call the office every night at 10 p.m. to get a progress report and more importantly to make sure that everyone was still there. Furthermore, at random intervals, the office would receive calls at 1 a.m. to see who was still in the trenches. Ron examined the draft, marking page after page. At noon, he demanded an extra fifteen slides without clear instructions and departed to meet a friend at the River Oaks Country Club, leaving the office just as quickly as he had arrived.

The rest of Sunday was spent on the pitchbook. John Granton and the Brett Hillsby left around 6:30 p.m. Shortly afterward, the analysts escaped to Kenny and Ziggy's to grab a couple of sandwiches for dinner – a pastrami for Robert, a roast beef for Mark, a gyro for Lenny and a round of Karbach beers for them all. "I'm paying for the sandwiches," said Robert to the rest of the guys crammed into the booth with him. "I can't thank you guys enough for doing the shell of the Collins pitchbook. It's starting to look really good."

"Dude, are you kidding me? What do you mean 'really good'? That fucking pitchbook is killer. The Barclays analyst team couldn't have done it any better themselves!" exclaimed Mark.

"No, you're right. Maybe, I'm being a little modest. It looks fucking awesome."

"You're damn right it does!"

"We got the pitchbook in good shape. We just need a little more time for the finishing touches. However, we've got another problem to figure out. Who is gonna make the trades in their account?" said Robert.

"We all can. Can't we?" garbled Mark with a mouthful of roast beef.

"No, not exactly. It would draw too much attention. Imagine if all three of us from the same M&A group bought short-term call options on the identical stock and then all sold at a similar time. That's definitely not a crime, but it would raise red flags, first with our compliance department and second with the SEC. In court, we probably wouldn't be found guilty of anything, but who wants to go under investigation in the first place. We've got to do this smarter."

"All good points," said Lenny. "It's way too suspicious. Also, we have to keep this to the group. Getting others involved is how everyone gets busted. You tell your cousin's friend to buy the shares for you and before you know it, you're behind bars. If you're gonna do that, you might as well go for old-fashioned insider trading and use confidential information from any of our deals at Latham Schroeder. The right way to do it is to keep this in our circle."

"Why does it have to be a circle, bro? I always envisioned us more like a triangle," stated Mark with a smirk.

"Sure fine, triangle it is for the Legend of Zelda fan in the group."

"Awesome."

"Circle or triangle, I can't make it work in my account. That's the first problem," said Robert. "I'm just not liquid enough. With that shitty bonus, the cost of living in the Inner Loop, and my student loan, I've got like $10,000 bucks in my trading account, and that's exaggerating to save face."

"I'm not much better either," said Lenny. "I've got $30K, but to be honest, I'm a little freaked out to pull the trigger from my account, you know. I mean…I'll help out with the pitchbooks and all, but actually doing the trades is more than I'm comfortable with."

They both turned to Mark who was continuing to stuff his face with the roast beef sandwich. "What? Why are you guys looking at me?"

"I don't mean to be blunt Mark, but if I had to guess who has the largest excess cash reserve here, I'd say it's you," stated Robert.

"Well yeah, what about it? It still doesn't mean that I'll do it. If shit hits the fan, I take the fall for sure. It's all traced back to me."

"Oh come on, man, don't be a pussy. You'll be like the top of the triangle," said Lenny with a smile.

"I was thinking more like an equilateral triangle. This changes things, maybe I want to go back to being a circle after all."

"Looks guys, there's no such thing as just dipping your toe in the water here. Circle, triangle, or rhombus, if the SEC gets wind of this, we're all going away for a long time," added Robert. "That said, whoever actually pulls the trigger from their brokerage account could feel more of the heat than the rest. It's a valid point, but what if I make you a deal? Mark, we use your account, but I'll volunteer to go up to New York and distribute the pitchbooks. That way, we're both taking risks. If someone is busted with a copy in hand, it'll be me."

"Well, that sounds kind of fair but what's Lenny gonna do? And what happens if our plan doesn't work or the market moves against us? Who covers my losses? It kind of sounds like I'm up shit creek, bro," rebutted Mark.

"I'll cover your losses," piped in Lenny unexpectedly. "That'll be my part. If the market turns against us, I'll cover your loss like insurance. I've got $30,000. So, for the first $30,000 of potential losses, I'll take the hit.

You guys lose nothing. Only after $30,000 do you start losing money pro-rata on the account. You guys are taking the bigger legal risk, but I'll hedge your financial risk."

"Well, that sounds pretty good. Man, fancy words there Lenny, 'pro-rata" and 'hedging,'" said Mark. "So how much scratch can we put in altogether? After I throw in another $50K or so, Robert adds his $10K, we have about $90,000 to play with."

"That should be more than enough to get us going," said Robert.

"What about the other end of it?" asked Mark. "If we do score big, how do we get the money out of my account? I can't exactly write you guys a check."

"First world problems...we'll figure that out when we get there. At this point, we're at the proof of concept stage. Let's prove that our strategy works," answered Robert. "There's also one other thing that we need to do. Start pulling out as many models and pitchbook templates as you can from the bank computer. If this really works, we're going to need them. Also, reach out to some of your buddies at other M&A teams. Don't make it weird, but if you can get copies of any of their old pitchbooks, that would be awesome. We need more formats to copy other than just Barclays. It doesn't have to be recent. Ask for something from like three years ago."

"Sounds like a plan," said Lenny. The three raised their bottles, clinked them, and drank down the cool beverages.

CHAPTER 12

NEW YORK

Robert was on the first Southwest flight of the morning to New York. He had partially convinced Ron and Brett Hillsby of a serious case of the flu. With only four days left before the Ocean Management meeting in New Orleans, every hand was needed back at the office and his absence during a critical time did not put him in the best light. Ron was almost certain that Robert was interviewing with another bank, but hopefully what Ron thought wouldn't matter soon, if their pitchbook was a success.

It took a few more late nights and a rare free weekend, but the Collins Petroleum pitchbook was done. In the past three weeks, they easily clocked a hundred hours of work per week with the combination of their regular duties and their extracurricular activities. At thirty pages in length, the pitchbook was on the short side, but it was enough to be convincing. Besides, the more pages in the pitchbook the greater the likelihood of mistakes, and in this instance flawless execution was more important than size. The Collins book was scrubbed clean to a level of perfection only achievable by a crack team of investment banking analysts.

In a proverbial sense, their heist was no longer a daydream: the dynamite had been purchased and the bank's blueprints were studied for dozens of hours. Everything was ready to be put in motion, and now Robert was in flight and ready to crack the bank's safe – or in this case, to defraud New York hedge funds. They were now invested in the scheme. If there was still a chance to walk way, it was fading with each mile the plane drew closer to New York.

With a hundred pitchbooks printed on glossy paper in the overhead compartment above him, the gravity of the plan began sinking in. This was actually going to happen. For the first time, he began thinking about the deeper moral implications of their pump and dump scheme. Robert McClure reassured himself that what they were doing was right, but at the same time, he remembered his economics lessons from school. There was no free lunch. Their gain would come at someone else's expense, but even then, he felt justified in his actions. After all, their plan wasn't your stereotypical pump and dump scheme. No widows and pensioners were going to get hurt, and yes, the hedge funds would get burned, but only because they chose to stick their hands in the honey pot. If the hedge funds were honest, they would simply return the lost pitchbook or even throw it away without acting on the information, but in this business, there was little chance of that happening. Was he to blame for their wrongdoing? No one was forcing them to act on the inside information from a discovered pitchbook.

In addition, Collins Petroleum would be just one bad trade in a year's performance. The investors would never even know that their returns could have been a percentage point or two higher were it not for the fake pitchbook. No one person would feel the loss, as the damage would be spread across a giant portfolio. Well, the portfolio manager's bonus would take a direct hit but who would shed a tear for their loss? It made him feel better that at least his ultimate victims were rich. Stealing from Wall Street was barely even a crime in most people's eyes after the 2008 crash. To Main Street, the banks and hedge funds were scum deserving of nothing less than a hangman's noose. In some ways, Robert could even stylize himself as a sort of Robin Hood taking from the rich and giving to the poor. However, that also didn't make much sense either as not one nickel of their proceeds would go to the poor. Robert, Mark, and Lenny were certainly over-worked, but hardly impoverished. Instead, this heist would be a perverse redistribution of wealth from the very rich and over-privileged titans of Wall Street to the barely rich and slightly over-privileged youth of Wall Street.

That was the simplistic view of what they were doing, but Robert was too smart for his own good. As he signaled to the flight attendant for another bottle of water, he couldn't help but look at his scheme from another perspective. Those hedge funds had investors. Thanks to his FINRA licensing exam, Robert knew that only accredited investors could put their money in a hedge fund, meaning individuals with incomes greater than $250,000 or at least $1,000,000 in net assets. Yes, that included a lot of rich assholes, but it also included plenty of successful small businessmen, school endowments, charities, and even things like the pension fund of the stewardess who had just handed him his water. While the damage would be minimal to those groups, it would still be done. What would his grandfather think of all this? It wouldn't be good, for sure. Hell, his grandpa probably thought the day-to-day work of an honest banker was already evil enough. Imagine if he knew about his grandson's scheme now. Maybe he did from somewhere up above. Robert shifted uncomfortably in his seat at the thought.

His mind switched to more pleasant daydreams. Robert envisioned his final day at Latham, Schroeder & Holt. He would not be quitting in order to open a cupcake shop or a coffee shop as some bankers do in an act of defiance against their soul-crushing industry. No, he would outsmart the Street at its own game and would show John Granton, Brett Hillsby, and Ronald Lufkin that he was smarter and better than them in every regard. On the Street, seniority didn't matter – the dollars in your bank account were the only measuring stick. They would leave Latham, Schroeder & Holt as market geniuses, not quitters – it was the ultimate triumph and the ultimate revenge. To exit the industry in any other manner was conceding a win to Ronald Lufkin and the other managing directors of this world. Models and bottles were just around the corner, but the resignation itself would be the sweetest reward of all.

The daydreams kept him occupied until the plane touched down in LaGuardia. What a shithole of an airport, Robert thought. It resembled a bus station more than the key terminal to America's most powerful city. Houston's Bush Intercontinental Airport and Hobby Airport were modern marvels compared to this dump.

He took a taxi to a snazzy boutique hotel in Hell's Kitchen, checked his bags at the front desk and then made his way out onto the street. Robert looked the part of a smart young investment banker on his way to the office in mid-town Manhattan. His brown hair was slicked back with so much gel that it almost looked black. His suit was immaculate and crisp and his green eyes look outward with determination like every other banker pacing toward their morning tasks. Only the satchel stuffed with pitchbooks appeared somewhat out of place. This was all part of the story. If someone saw him "accidentally" drop a pitchbook, his appearance needed to be as believable as the pitchbooks. One couldn't "accidentally" lose an investment banking pitchbook while wearing sweat pants. On his phone, he had charted a detailed map of coffee shops, bagel and breakfast places, and high-end hotels attracting business clientele. His first stops were several hotel lobbies away from tourist spots, particularly Times Square.

Next, he checked off a couple of the coffee shops from the list. After that, it was time for an experiment. At a Starbucks on his route, Robert ordered a grande cappuccino and sat down. He set a pitchbook on the table, took a few sips of his coffee, and then proceeded to switch tables, leaving behind the pitchbook. There it sat undisturbed…for a quarter of an hour. Customers avoided it like the plague, likely thinking that the table was taken. Finally, a Brooklyn hipster sat down, nudging the pitchbook toward the edge of the table. This wasn't exactly his target market, but for the experiment, the hipster would do. Surely, pure curiosity would compel him to examine the foreign object. However, the hipster didn't even glance at the glossy booklet right in front of him. Robert grew increasingly angry staring at the hipster's overflowing beard. In Mississippi, such a beard was not a fashion statement and suggested quite the opposite of a guaranteed vote for the Democratic Party. What was this hipster doing here anyway with a five-dollar coffee in hand and a two-thousand-dollar Mac computer? His slovenly outward appearance certainly did not suggest gainful employment. While the subsidized hipster man baby was the outlet for Robert's frustration, the real reason for his growing fury was the looming possibility in his mind that the whole plan was stupid and more than likely to fail. Mark and Lenny had gone along with his plans, and they had spent countless hours making the Collins pitchbook, but what if no one bothered to pick up one of their pitchbooks? The little time off in their schedules would have been wasted on this stupid adventure – they would never forgive him for it. Worse yet, what if they placed their call options and the stock price moved down instead? Lenny would be entirely justified in wanting to kill him.

He glared at the hipster and grew ever more furious upon seeing him loudly making a call with the latest iPhone. Jesus, even the hippies in this world are assholes these days, Robert thought. The pitchbook sat there untouched and unappreciated until the Mac, which had been butting against it for some time, finally pushed it over the edge of the table onto the ground.

Just as it fell, a sharply dressed businessman in his late thirties happened to walk by and crouched down to retrieve it. Robert's eyes lit up. The businessman reached out to the hipster with the pitchbook and asked, "Is this yours?"

"Nah, bro, I don't know whose that is. It was already here when I sat down."

"Oh OK, I guess that I'll just toss it," said the businessman. He glanced at the cover. Robert's heart was pounding. Surely this guy would recognize what he was holding. Instead, to Robert's dismay, the businessman walked over to the nearest trashcan and tossed the pitchbook before returning back to the Starbucks line. Robert's momentarily elated hopes sank into an abyss. If the hipster was a harbinger of doom, this was confirmation of the plan's failure. How many times today had this same scenario played out in hotel lobbies and coffee shops across the city?

The consequences of his new reality were settling in. There was no easy way out of the drudgery of investment banking. Robert would just have to work through another year and hope for the best on next year's bonus. At the same time, he would have to watch Ron trade up his Porsche for the latest model on the back of the analysts' labor. If he was lucky, there was the possibly of making it to associate or jumping to private equity where he could be a lifeless automaton for yet another master.

Of course, the third option was to quit altogether. But then all the abuse so far would have been for nothing, and Ronald Lufkin wins. His career felt like a vice squeezing him from two ends, with two separate pressures keeping him trapped in the same place. On one end of the vice, riches dangled in front of him, supposedly within reach. Maybe, if he just worked harder pushing the eighty-hour weeks to ninety-hour weeks, he too could become a managing director one day. The second end of the vice was the fear of quitting and giving up your chance, foregoing the possibility of ever getting that dangling carrot. Even if becoming a managing director is almost impossible, you still have a shot as long as you keep playing the game. If you quit, then you have zero chance of ever making it. This predicament has similarly tortured young bankers throughout the ages. In fact, the whole system is designed to create such a dilemma. What choice did he have but to continue? Next year, he would likely tell himself the same thing but with two years of indentured servitude under his belt. He did not want to continue, and at the same time, could not make himself give up.

His grande cappuccino had cooled enough to finally take a sip. As he did so, the plastic lid buckled over the edge of the paper cup and coffee spilled onto his shirt. “Ah shit!” exclaimed Robert and got up to retrieve napkins and a new lid from the counter. Why did this always happen? Maybe this was his way out – clearly there was a market for better plastic coffee lids. Greater fortunes have been made on stupider products. Perhaps he could make a pitchbook to raise money from private equity sponsors for a plastics company. Robert was wiping his shirt with the napkins when he turned around to see a well-dressed young man in his late twenties hovering over his table, staring directly at his stack of pitchbooks. The young man made quick, panicked eye contact. Why was this fellow banker type giving him such a strange look? All of a sudden, the young man grabbed the top pitchbook from the pile and darted for the door, knocking into another startled Starbucks’ guest.

“Hey!” screamed Robert. “That guy just stole my pitchbook!” Responding to a natural impulse, he pushed his way through the packed coffee shop, weaving left and right between the customers. "Hey, stop!" he yelled as he stepped out onto the crowded street. The thief was already three quarters of a block ahead of him. Robert pursued him, feeling his black dress shoes give way under this unexpected physical activity. The runner was gaining ground and after about a block, Robert let him get away as he grabbed his knees, panting heavily for such a short run. "Man, I gotta get back to the gym," he said to himself with a smile beginning to form on his face. His instincts and adrenaline gave way to reason as he realized what this meant. Robert started laughing to himself. Even a few New Yorkers, accustomed to just about anything on the street, stared out of the corners of their eyes at the young banker who was apparently losing his mind, but Robert continued to laugh. If this random young Wall Street analyst was willing to steal this pitchbook, that meant the other copies were sure to catch someone's attention. Robert walked back to the Starbucks to collect his bag and the stack of pitchbooks.

"Did you catch him?" asked the barista. "Want me to call the cops?"

"No, no that's quite alright," replied Robert with a chuckle and a big smile on his face. The barista appeared perplexed but returned to fixing a caramel frappucino. Robert exited the coffee shop and called Lenny. "You guys won't believe what just happened! Some investment banking-looking guy just stole our fucking pitchbook."

"What? You mean he picked up a copy?" answered Lenny.

"No, he didn't just pick it up. He stole it from a pile sitting on my table at Starbucks while I was getting a coffee lid. He saw what it was, and he stole it. I chased him for almost two blocks, but he got away. This is going to work, guys. It's going to fucking work!"

"Holy shit, Mark, someone just stole Robert's pitchbook," Lenny said to Mark, whose jaw dropped in astonishment. "Robert, that's amazing news! Keep it up! You're the fucking man!"

"What are you girls talking about?" said Ron, walking by next to them. "Is that Robert on the phone? I thought he was sick today. What's the good news…did Robert get the job?"

"Oh no Ron…nothing like that, it was just Robert saying that he's feeling a lot better and that he can make the New Orleans trip on Friday. I was just saying that he's the man for helping us out you know given that he's sick and everything."

"Great then," Ron said. "I've got another pitchbook for you to do before the Friday trip so we'll need all hands on deck. Thanks for the update, Lenny."

Robert went back to distributing the pitchbooks across midtown Manhattan with renewed determination. Given his new insight from the coffee shop experiment, he sought out nooks where someone would feel comfortable flipping through the pitchbook or even taking it. Added to his list were various lines on the subway. With a day pass, he peppered the most popular commuter routes with pitchbooks. Robert had been walking the streets of New York for nearly twelve hours straight and was beginning to look disheveled rather than sharp. He canvassed the hotels and coffee shops to the point of exhaustion. On his way back to the Hell's Kitchen hotel, he decided to take the edge off after a long day and stopped at a small family-run liquor store to buy a bottle of Glenlivet. In his room, he popped open the wooden top and poured the brown and translucent scotch into the hotel-provided highball. After consuming about a third of the bottle, he collapsed on top of the bed sheets.

****

In the morning, a luxury Uber arrived in time for the earliest flight out of LaGuardia so that he could walk straight into the office upon landing in Houston. His last several pitchbooks were saved for this ride, two of which were left in the Uber. The rest were "accidentally" abandoned around various seating areas at the airport while being careful as to not leave too many. The last thing that he needed was to alert the TSA of suspicious activity. However, he also didn't want to pass up this opportunity to diversify his drop locations.

On the plane, Wi-Fi enabled him to return to his day job i.e., the pitchbook Lenny and Mark had been working on all night. Before landing, he edited quite a few slides and then drove straight from the airport to the office. As he approached the M&A desk, he gave Lenny and Mark a small smile.

"Well, someone's happy," said Ron Lufkin, creeping up behind them.

Robert did his best to fake a cough. "Thanks Ron, I'm feeling much better. The day off really helped. I was in terrible shape."

"No problem at all, Robert. I don't want to work you guys to death or anything." Thankfully, Ron returned to his chair without any further assignments. Robert plugged his laptop into the docking station connected to the two screens in front of him. Before opening the latest pitchbook file, he checked the ticker CPO for Collins Petroleum on *Yahoo! Finance*. Nothing. The stock was completely flat. In fact, it was slightly lagging behind the sector, which was up half a percent today.

When they had a moment alone without the prying ears of superiors, he asked, "Hey Mark, did you execute the trades?"

"Yeah, sure did. I put the limit orders in last night and they were filled this morning. I bought $90,000 of one-month options. This better work."

"It's gonna work. Trust me."

"Well dude, it's not working so far. We're already down two percent on the options. With the leverage, the price moves are way more aggressive than the underlying stock."

"I know, man. Just keep cool. It'll work – I promise. Let's get back to wrapping up this pitchbook." The two returned to their task with their eyes darting back and forth scanning for errors in the Ocean Management presentation.

CHAPTER 13

LAGNIAPPE

Ron landed at Louis Armstrong Airport in New Orleans around two o'clock after a fifty-five minute direct flight from Houston. He texted Robert, Mark, and Lenny, letting them know of his arrival so that they could pick him up at the front. On a typical trip, only one associate along with a vice president or analyst was necessary. However, after their hard work over the past few days, Ron wanted to reward the guys; so he had invited them to join him on the Ocean Management trip to New Orleans with a single caveat – they would drive the whole way, as he wasn't about to expense three round-trip tickets. His entertainment budget, used for wining and dining clients, was approaching Latham, Schroeder & Holt's internal limits for the quarter, and given the state of the oil industry, it was unwise to cross the line this year. He was hardly going to waste the last of the budget on his analysts. His hotel was a suite at the Hotel Monteleone on Royal Street for three full days so that he could enjoy the weekend in the Quarter. The rest of team would check into the Best Western near the airport, a full thirty minutes from the French Quarter and with a checkout time first thing tomorrow morning.

After only a few hours of sleep following a typical night's work, the analysts met at the Houston office in the early morning and drove for nearly six hours to New Orleans, just in time to pick up Ron from the airport. Everyone was on edge during the long ride. In the past few days, oil had slid down almost three dollars and was trading in the mid-40s. Crude's most recent price tantrum dissipated any hopes of a short-lived depression in prices. The stress and pressure in the office was palpable as bankers no longer predicted a V-shaped recovery in prices but rather a U-shaped recovery. Some even considered the U-shaped recovery overly optimistic and suggested a "bathtub-shaped" recovery unless the Saudis returned to managing the market. Naturally, the shares of Collins declined in tandem with oil prices. Although not as bad as the rest of the sector, CPO was in the red and the leverage on their call options amplified the losses further still. Mark's account was down over 20%, or $18,000 in the hole. In their fake Collins pitchbook, the final bid deadline was next Wednesday, only three trading days away. If the scheme was working, the shares should have likely traded higher by now.

Mark was in a rotten mood, and for good reason. "Look guys, if we go down another 5%, I'm gonna close the position."

"I agree," said Lenny. "I'm done – I'm getting killed here covering the position."

"What the fuck, Lenny? What happened to the $30,000 that you were gonna use to help cover Mark's position?" remarked Robert angrily.

"Dude, things aren't going well. That was back before the losses started piling up. It's different when you start seeing red on the screen. I still got faith, man, but only for another grand or two. It's not exactly looking good for us right now."

"I don't see a reason for alarm bells yet, guys. We knew going into this that the market can turn on you just like this," said Robert angrily. "Reach down between your legs and hold onto your balls here for a second. I think someone is already buying the shares. WTI crude and XOP, the exploration and production ETF, are both down 6% while Collins is down just 2%. For a small cap company like Collins, the stock should be hit twice as hard as the index – it should be down around 10%. I'm telling you that someone out there is accumulating shares. There is no news, yet CPO is doing better than the whole sector."

"Yeah, easy for you to say with the least skin in the game. I'm getting killed here, man." shrieked Lenny. "We've burned through over a third of my bonus in a matter of days. And your theory is nice and everything Robert, but the game plan here isn't to lose less than the index. You can't pay rent with less-than-expected losses. Why did I get into this? First, I get a shitty bonus, and then I light my shitty bonus on fire with your stupid idea."

"Just stay the course and stop freaking out. We don't sell until the close of the market on Tuesday afternoon. I don't care if the stock goes down another 10%. By then, we should know if someone is pushing up the market or not. We're so close – now is not the time to back out. We've got see this thing through. We all agreed that we were up to it. Chill the fuck out. Hey, there's the exit to the airport." They pulled up to the curb where Ron was waiting for them. Mark jumped out of the shotgun seat and let Ron take it.

"Thanks for driving up here; I hope it wasn't too bad of a drive."

"No not all," replied Robert. While his tone gave the impression of honesty, his eyes, red and tired from a lack of sleep, told a different story.

"Great, do you have the address for Ocean Management?" inquired Ron. "It's somewhere in the CBD."

"Got it right here," said Lenny. "We've already punched it into the GPS."

From the airport, they drove through Metairie, the suburbs of New Orleans. If it weren't for the road signs indicating the locations just ahead, one would think that this could be the suburb of any city in the United States – however certainly not a prosperous one. What had once been a bright new subdivision, growing from the venerable French Quarter and Garden District, had begun to age, although much less gracefully than the latter parts of town. With its row after row of 1950s homes, perhaps there was not much charm to lose in the first place. In many cities, these kinds of neighborhoods had given way to the development of McMansions and cookie-cutter three story townhomes, but not in New Orleans – no one could afford them with the perpetually sliding local economy. The city, in some ways, is one massive conservation effort of yesteryear's grandeur and a long-gone-by era for the entertainment of the tourist crowd.

Past Metairie and adjacent to the French Quarter, the Central Business District was a sorry excuse for a downtown. It was a dying husk of an offshore oil industry that once existed here in strength. Over time, the jobs left in favor of a better business climate in Houston, leaving behind a tiny remnant of the industry. The local populist politics only hastened the move. Buildings, such as One Shell Square, retained their names, reminding the few people still working in the CBD of the business district's former glory. The company of its namesake, Shell, and the old Amoco were either almost gone or hardly hanging on in the city. Half the skyscrapers were empty, as were the streets for what was ostensibly a busy business day. New Orleans was night and day in comparison to NYC, still fresh on Robert's mind

"Dude, I'd love to work down here," said Mark. "Imagine, walking a few blocks to the French Quarter, pounding some drinks after work, and then catching a trolley home. That's the life."

"Glad you have your priorities straight, Mark. Grab the pitchbooks," said Ron. The four of them parked in a nearby garage and strolled to the building. After an awkwardly silent elevator ride, they arrived at Ocean Management's unimpressive lobby on the thirteenth floor. The furniture in the reception area had been beaten down by years of boom and bust cycles. Ocean Management long ago learned that excess in the boom led to disaster in the bust. As a result, an executive decision was made decades ago to avoid spending on frills such as furniture during the upticks in business. For that reason, among other cost-saving actions, Ocean Management was still in business in New Orleans while the competition had been whittled away, oil downturn after oil downturn and recession after recession. Nonetheless, a few items were worth spending on, such as the very sleek logo across the entrance, which stood in sharp contrast to the crummy furnishings.

"Would you like any water or a coffee?" asked the secretary.

"Yes please, water," answered two of them almost in unison. It was early March and already hot, even worse than usual for this time of year in New Orleans. The one-block stroll to the office in their suits had nearly brought them to a full sweat. They wore shades of grey, specifically for this trip, both for the practically of beating the heat as well as fitting in with local business fashions which often favored lighter shades when suits were absolutely necessary. The team was shown to a conference room with large floor to ceiling windows displaying an impressive view of city. From this vantage point, one could immediately understand New Orleans' significance to commercial trade as the Mississippi River snaked its way through town, hugging the French Quarter in the shape of a crescent.

The management team entered the room and traded business cards and handshakes. Their entourage was considerable, including the CFO, COO, Treasurer, and the Head of Corporate Development, quite a display for something as impractical as the acquisition of an onshore 3-D seismic business. Perhaps there was some genuine interest in the deal after all. When a firm simply wants to be polite to a banker, it sends the thirty-five-year-old Treasurer or some similarly aged and ranked person from Corp Dev. In this case, nearly the full C-suite was present with the exception of the CEO. The two sides exchanged pleasantries and talked about the humidity, a go-to small talk subject for out of town visitors. The conversation briefly touched on the few oil and gas finance conferences still taking place in New Orleans such as Johnson Rice and Scotia Howard Weil and then, they got down to business.

Ron flipped through the presentation and made his regular pitch about Latham, Schroeder & Holt's extensive relationships with both offshore and onshore oilfield services providers. The three analysts stared blankly at the executives across the table, too tired to process what was being said and counting down the minutes until their return to the hotel on the other side of town.

Just as Ron was moving into the company overview section of the presentation, their phones, which were faced down on the table, buzzed in perfect unison. They all ignored the vibrations. Whatever the important message, it didn't trump a one-on-one meeting between their managing director and a management team. The vibrating sound distracted the executives for a moment, but the conversation resumed. Ron jumped straight into the synergies associated with onshore seismic. Since Robert couldn't care less about this job anymore, he checked his phone anyway. The buzz was an alert from *Yahoo Finance!* on his closely followed stocks. The subject line of the e-mail read: "BLOOMBERG NEWS: COLLINS PETROLEUM, MIDLAND BASIN ASSET SALE EXPECTED".

With his hands twitching, he urgently opened the link, which included a short article from Bloomberg news. "According to sources familiar with the matter, Collins Petroleum has entered into a sales process of its Midland

Basin assets. An announcement of a deal is expected within the next week. The company did not comment on a potential transaction…" Robert checked the stock price. Collins's ticker, CPO, was up 7.32% and rising! The phone nearly fell out of his hands. He made eye contact with Lenny and Mark, and pointed feverishly at his screen. His awkward behavior attracted the attention of the Treasurer and the Head of Corp Dev. At this point, Robert didn't care about the client's reaction. Lenny was trying to avoid his eye contact and frantic motions as Robert kept pointing at the phone.

Ron turned toward Robert for a moment and gave him a gaze simultaneously communicating two messages: "What the FUCK are you doing!" and "We are going to have an unpleasant talk after this." Management was taken aback by the momentarily demonic expression on Ron's face as well as his quick transformation back to a smiling and pleasant demeanor as he continued the discussion on the potential deal.

Mark couldn't resist any longer and slowly reached for his phone – his eyes went wide. He nudged Lenny, who finally checked his phone as well. Ron grew increasingly irate as his three analysts had their faces buried in their phones instead of pretending to listen to the client, as was their expected role. Lenny's jaw dropped without volition as he read the Bloomberg article, making the situation even more peculiar.

The stock was now up 9.7%.

The discussion reached the slide tracking all recent movements of semi-submersibles in the Gulf of Mexico. "This is a very interesting slide, but I can tell you right now that it's missing some of our data. I'm pretty sure that we went out here with two rigs in June," said the Chief Operating Officer pointing to a mostly empty portion of the Gulf on the map.

"Robert, did you verify this correctly?' asked Ron, on the brink of exploding with anger.

"Yes, I did. Are you sure it was June? I tracked the movement of those two rigs to very late May so that's why they're not in the June data." Robert was certain that he was correct – he had no doubt in his mind of this as he had specifically triple-checked this detail.

"Didn't you just hear him, Robert? It was in June. He said June! Why didn't you fix this before the meeting?"

The CFO, a little shocked at Ron's reaction interjected, "I mean it really doesn't matter. Our movements in the Gulf of Mexico have nothing to do with an onshore seismic deal anyway. We just thought it was a very good slide and wanted to verify the data before showing it to our CEO. It's a great graphic – maybe something we could use going forward."

"Thanks David. I know, and thank you. It's just the principle of the matter. I expect my team to be on top of this sort thing, and I'm very disappointed when that doesn't happen. Robert, you're going to re-do this entire slide, triple-checking every piece of data, and we'll send it over by tomorrow afternoon." Ron's request suggested about forty hours of work to be delivered in the timeframe of approximately twenty-seven hours, assuming no sleep from here on. Furthermore, a promise made directly to a client was the worst assignment of all as failure or even the slightest imperfection was not an option.

"It's really quite alright, Ron. I think that your analyst might be right about those rig moves in May now that I think about it," noted the Chief Operating Officer.

"That's alright, guys. We will check it anyway and will get back to you."

Robert said nothing in response to Ron or the client. He looked down at his phone and back at Ron. In that moment, he realized that he was no longer afraid of this dickwad. After having pitchbooks thrown at him, after working the endless nights, and after taking abuse after abuse, Ron could no longer control his life. His destiny was finally his own again, or would be within a few minutes. Robert paused for a moment to collect his thoughts and to savor this moment for perpetuity. Collins Petroleum was now up 15.2%. Back of the envelope, they were likely just over $135,000 in the green.

"No, Ron…you're going to triple check it," said Robert as he stood up. "Consider this my resignation." He picked up his copy of the Ocean Management pitchbook and threw it across the table where it flopped, slid, and landed ultimately on Ron's lap.

The room went silent. Ron's whole face turned red as he stuttered, "What are you talking about? You can't quit. Nobody quits."

"As they say, looks like I just did," replied Robert with a smirk on his face.

"You little punk! You're going to regret this! You'll never work in investment banking again!" screamed Ron as the Ocean Management executive team stared on in complete disbelief

"Oh yeah, have a nice life asshole!" said Robert, making his way toward the door.

The younger Treasurer and Head of Corp Dev were snickering and desperately trying to hold off an outright burst of laughter. Ron grew redder, approaching the hue of a tomato; he appeared to be on the verge of passing out. While this startled him, the following series of events even Robert had not foreseen in his wildest dreams.

Mark opened his E-trade app to see the monumental gain in bold green numbers. He entered a sell order, and as soon as the confirmation arrived on his screen, he stood up as well. "Ron, I also quit. Thanks for nothing."

Ronald Lufkin could no longer tell if this was reality or some sort of sick nightmare. Nothing even remotely close to this event had ever happened to him before. Throughout his career, Ron had abused and pushed countless analysts over the edge but not once had they ever retaliated with such defiance, even in a private forum, let alone in front of a client. This was a revolt against everything Ron stood for. The Treasurer couldn't hold it in any longer – he burst into laughter and slapped the conference table. This set off a chain of events as the Head of Corp Dev followed suit unleashing a repressed cackle. There was a good chance that they had once been analysts themselves who took an exit-op to Ocean Management.

Next and least expected of all, Lenny Lee stood up. "Sir, it has been a pleasure working with you and thank you for giving me the opportunity to work at Latham Schroeder & Holt." Lenny stretched out his hand to Ron, who simply stared at it. Lenny awkwardly took his hand back and picked up his belongings from the conference table. Robert held the door to the conference room as Mark and Lenny joined him on the way out.

They took one last look at the plane wreck of a meeting behind them: Ron red-faced, the CFO and COO utterly confused, and the Treasurer and Corp Dev guy trying to regain their professional composure. As they exited the room, Robert felt as if he had been trapped underground for years only to finally feel the breeze and sunlight on his face again. This was freedom, and a client meeting that would go down in investment banking legend. The three smiled nervously at each other as they descended in the elevator.

Mark broke the silence, "Before we left, I sold half the options and kept the other half going. We've booked a profit of little more than $70,000 in cash."

"What the fuck! We did it guys! We fucking did it!" An outburst of joy exploded among the group with high fives all around and the stress of their confrontation easing. As the elevator doors opened, a very confused New Orleanean in full suit stood at the entrance. "What up PLAYA!" shouted Mark, laughing as the group jetted out of the elevator like a group of juvenile delinquents.

"Guys, we forgot that we brought Ron to meeting. He doesn't have a ride back," pointed out Lenny.

"Fuck him," said Robert. "That's his problem. And forget about the car altogether. I've got other plans. Lenny, cancel our reservations at the Best Western and see if the Royal Senesta in the Quarter has rooms. It's time to celebrate!"

"Fuck yeah!" exclaimed Mark as he jumped to slap the top of the glass door entrance before exiting the building onto the street, "Let's go!" They headed east toward the French Quarter, the heart of darkness less than a dozen blocks away. It was still daylight, but they eagerly awaited the New Orleans night and everything that it had to offer three newly minted young masters of the universe.

CHAPTER 14

LAISSEZ LES BON TEMPS ROULE

From his days of growing up in Mississippi, Robert was no stranger to New Orleans. Laurel was only a short two-hour ride away, and he had made trips to the city for years, both with his parents and slightly wilder excursions with his good friends. Mark was a rookie given his California roots and Lenny, though an occasional visitor, had never truly explored the city. "How about this for an itinerary? The sun is still out, and it's hotter than hell. What if we start by grabbing an early dinner somewhere nice like Brennan's and then we just figure it out from there?"

"Sounds like a plan. I'm starving," said Lenny. As the group marched through the CBD and crossed Canal Street, which marked the boundary of the French Quarter, the peculiar smell of Bourbon Street wafted through the air, a mix of damp humidity, old wood, spilled fruity drinks, smoke, and bodily fluids. One street over was Royal, a welcome escape from the more putrid smells of the city. There, they looked through the windows of the high-end French antique shops lining the street and occasionally paused to stare at the works of art in the galleries. While Robert had been down Royal Street many times, now he walked it with a new step and vision. The antiques were no longer inaccessible museum-like objects to be admired from afar. These were items that could actually be attained for his apartment should the desire strike him. The analysts walked past the Hotel Monteleone where Ron would be staying for the weekend. Its palatial entrance reaffirmed their decision to leave Latham, Schroeder & Holt. It wasn't simply that Ron had expensed the hotel for himself while making his analysts drive to New Orleans. It was that Ron did not feel bad about it for a single second. Through his eyes, he had earned this, and his analysts were lucky to be invited on the trip. As far as he was concerned, it was an honor and a pleasure to work for him every minute of their eighty-hour week.

Further down the street was Brennan's, a venerable New Orleans institution just opposite the courthouse. The restaurant is world-renowned, beloved equally by tourists and the elite of the city. The analysts were decades younger than anyone in the place other than a handful of Tulane or Loyola college kids dining with their out of town parents. Their investment banking attire set them above the rest of guests and reminded the staff of a time before Hurricane Katrina when Brennan's was a coat and tie establishment and casually dressed tourists were kicked to the curb regardless of their ability to pay. Given the realities of the post-Hurricane Katrina market, the dress code was relaxed to business casual and, to the chagrin of wealthy New Orleans natives, had never returned to its former formality.

"Let's go all out, guys. We got the money," said Mark. "Tonight's our night."

An immaculately dressed waiter approached the table with a wine list and menus. A second waiter precisely placed the silverware on the table.

"Hello gentleman, my name is Dustin. Can I start you off with something to drink?"

Mark commanded the wine list, an impressive eighty-two-page affair. "Let's see, Dustin, how about a bottle of Chateau du Seuil, Graves 2010 and then a lighter pinot to start the night, perhaps a bottle of the Domaine Perrot-Minot."

"Excellent choices, sir."

"And let's also begin with a few appetizers: two dozen Oysters Rockefeller and a dozen Oysters J'aime."

"They've got a 1988 Rothschild on the wine list," said Mark. "Maybe, we'll do it next time. $3,200 a bottle is still a bit much, even all things considered." The wine came out shortly and was poured by two separate waiters, their movements almost in lock step. Mark raised his glass. "I can't believe we did it. Let me offer a toast. To Collins Petroleum!"

"And to Wall Street!" said Lenny. "God, I love this business." The glasses were clinked, and each took generous gulps of wine. It wasn't long before the waiters were pouring another glass for the entire table. The oysters arrived shortly after, and the trio gored themselves in the appetizers. The wine was disappearing more quickly still.

Robert ordered another bottle and the next course. "Duck and andouille gumbo for everyone and let's do the blue crab ravigote for the table."

The vivacious spirit of the trio had caught attention of the entire Brennan's waitstaff, who exhibited that rare form of Louisiana fine dining which echoed hospitality with extreme professionalism while also retaining an element of spontaneity, fun, and personality. The captain introduced himself and stood always within a moment's call to fulfill whatever desire came to them. The sommelier sat down with the group and brought samples of several wine recommendations. For the main course, Robert had the black drum while Mark and Lenny ordered the redfish. After the main course, they were stuffed and skipped dessert. The decision was then made to switch from wine to a round of Vieux Carrés, a classic New Orleans mixture of cognac, rye whiskey, and vermouth served in chilled martini glasses. They toasted again.

"Don't even look at the bill. Let me pay it," said Mark, viewing the extensive tab. "Holy shit! Well…let's make it a little bigger why don't we?" exclaimed Mark, filling out an extravagant tip for the waitstaff.

The chuckling group made its merry way for the exit, escorted by a similarly joyous group of servers wishing them a pleasant and enjoyable rest of the evening. The wine and drinks were working their magic as the rhythm of the city pulsated through them. The humidity was no longer something to be struggled against; It was a warm embrace pulling them closer to the night, to that spirit of life in New Orleans which had called young men to the French Quarter for centuries. There was a sense in the air that anything could happen tonight, and they could be anyone tomorrow morning. The world was theirs for the taking.

From the restaurant on Royal Street, they sought something other than the serene and manicured galleries and antique stores. With a quick turn around the corner, they again approached Bourbon Street. With their extended dinner and drinks having lasted almost two hours, the worst of the heat was starting to give way. As they edged closer to the infamous street, the neon lights of the nearest bars became visible and the sound of music blasting from numerous doors and openings became more pronounced. Their first stop was the Tropical Isle for a hand grenade at Robert's suggestion. While a touristy location, it was a rite of passage on Bourbon Street that he wanted Mark and Lenny to experience. A hand grenade consists of likely cleverly disguised everclear, among other ingredients, served in long neon green plastic tubes with a frosty hand grenade-shaped smiley face at the bottom. The three looked strange making their way down

Bourbon in their banking attire and holding large glowing green drinks in their hands. Their $300-dollar shoes were quickly going to ruin in the street's terrible muck. Their ties loosened, and their jackets were soon removed as the group made its way farther down the street. On one side of Bourbon, a seven-member brass band belted out music to a gathering crowd. The sounds and the drinks began to take control of the young men's movements, all three were now walking and bouncing their heads with the groove, even Lenny. As they continued onward to their next watering hole, Robert noted, "You know that we got really lucky this time. I have no idea how one of our pitchbooks got to Bloomberg news, but it did."

"Don't worry about it, bro…sure, we got lucky, but I think that it would have worked anyway. Maybe our score wouldn't have been as big, but it still would have worked. Let's worry about it later, dude. That's a conversation for another night. Ease up. Take another sip of that hand grenade and forget about it," suggested Mark.

"You're right, man. Let's keep it moving, bro, and find a bar to lay our anchor for a little while."

The guys saw a group of five girls in front of them walking into the Cat's Meow, four of them blonds. "I think we found our bar," said Mark.

"Umm, yeah, agreed," added Lenny.

As they walked in, Robert immediately regretted his decision. The Cat's Meow was a karaoke bar filled to the brim by youngish tourists with plenty of drink and very little singing talent. A preppy southern kid with a torn white Ole Miss baseball cap was on stage giving his best version of "Pour Some Sugar on Me." Mark walked over to the bar and ordered three Abita Ambers. He passed two to Robert and Lenny and gave the bartender a $100 bill. "Give those girls over there whatever they want."

"Alright dude, hold my beer and watch this," said Mark, handing Robert his beer and walking over to the blondes.

"Awesome, free beer," said Robert as he turned the bottle skyward and chugged about half of it.

"Hey Robert. We're signing up Mark for karaoke. What do you say, *Jitterbug* by George Michael or *Material Girl* by Madonna?" asked Lenny, smiling.

"Oh man. That's a tough choice…I'm gonna say *Jitterbug*."

"Alright! This is going to be awesome." Lenny was almost done signing up Mark when they saw him motioning them over to the group of girls. From the look of things, Mark was doing well so far. The girls seemed to be having a good time.

"Hey guys this is Sarah, Stephanie, Susan, Kate, and Liz. Can you believe that they're from Texas also, Dallas to be exact?"

"Dallas, I never would have guessed," said Robert sarcastically. "Do you go to TCU?"

"No, we're at SMU. Are you from Dallas?"

"No, we're from Houston, but we're up there all the time for business. Robert and Lenny are also in investment banking with me." The conversation moved to SMU and their respective little towns of origin in East Texas, before it was cut off by the girls drunkenly beginning to sing along with the Brittany Spears song currently in rotation. The girls were all pretty hot but making it through the conversation for the rest of the night was going to be the hard part.

They hadn't quite yet moved to the endless debate between Dallas versus Houston, which was surely the next conversation topic, when the DJ announced, "Mark Edwards, you are up next with *Jitterbug* by George Michael!"

"What the fuck, guys, you signed me up for *Jitterbug*?"

Sarah egged him on. "Oh come on."

"I don't care – I'm not doing it."

"Yeah, we wanna see you sing!" said Katie, giggling. Lenny had already foreseen the girls egging him on, and Mark knew that his friends had caught him in the perfect trap. He couldn't back down without seeming uptight. His whole fun-loving laid-back persona would fall apart. However, Lenny hadn't predicted his next move. "I'm not doing it without you guys. Come on, Lenny and Robert – you're coming with me – fair is fair!"

"No way, I'm not doing it," said Lenny sternly.

Robert knew that there was no way out of it and that Mark had just ensnared them in the same predicament if they wanted any chance with these girls. Hesitation would make things only worse. Only bravery and over-confidence could save them now. Robert chugged three quarters of a full beer and slammed it on the table. "Fuck it, we're doing it! Lenny, you're in."

"Damn it," said Lenny grabbing his jacket and putting it on as he reluctantly climbed the stage. "Mark Edwards, don't back down now. Where are you at!" shouted the DJ again.

"I'm right here," said Mark as he climbed up the stairs to the stage.

"And I see that you've brought friends. Guys, give us your best George Michael!" exclaimed the DJ. The music sounded with the rhythmic snapping of fingertips. The three snapped their fingers in unison. Mark stepped forward, taking the lead center stage, his inhibitions down the bottle already. Robert and Lenny acted as his backup singers and dancers, belting out the tune to the best of their ability. Right off the bat, Lenny lost track of the lyrics, which he didn't know in the first place. Nonetheless, he still sung them at full volume about two words later than what was streaming on the screen. At first, it was sort of working, but about halfway through, their improvised dance repertoire began to fall apart. Mark's dance moves were getting increasingly creepy and Robert zoned out, attempting to delete this shameful incident from his memory before it could fully crystallize in his brain for posterity. They went through the "BOOM BOOM" in the chorus one more time knowing that the self-inflicted torture was almost over. Still, when the music stopped, the three walked off stage upbeat; even though they'd butchered the song, they fully expected the girls would find their antics hilarious. However, the audience's scattered applause after their performance gave them a hint of the cold reception waiting upon their return. The small talk continued for a little while longer and then the girl's group made a sorry excuse for having to call it an early night. It was only 9 p.m., which is practically broad daylight in New Orleans time. The young bankers politely parted ways, knowing for certain that George Michael had doomed their chances for the night.

"Oh well," said Mark. "Let's finish up these beers and march on. We cannot be stopped, gentlemen!"

They continued down Bourbon Street, ignoring the calls from the various doormen until Mark stopped in the middle of the street. "Guys, I think that it's that time of the night. We've had a very classy dinner at Brennan's, we've had some drinks, and now it's time for us to attend the ballet."

"What's he talking about?" asked Lenny.

Robert cleared his throat. "Um…the ballet, Lenny," he said, and pointed behind him at the lights of Scores. A large bouncer stood outside with a girl on his arm in clear plastic heals wearing a bright orange dress cut a solid foot and half above her knee.

"But we're not going to the first one on the block. Oh no. These are our options: Big Daddy's, Scores right in front of us, Rick's Cabaret, and Barely Legal," listed Mark.

"I'm cool with Scores," said Lenny. "Looks pretty good to me."

"No, no, no," answered Robert. "We have to do Rick's Cabaret.'

"Why Rick's?" replied Mark with genuine curiosity in his voice.

"Do I need to spell it out for your guys? RCI Hospitality Holdings Inc.…stock ticker RICK, it's the only publicly traded strip club in the world! I mean, we gotta go there!"

"Are you fucking kidding me? Dude, that's awesome! How great would it be to bank that company? Imagine the due diligence process! Ha!" added Mark as he pointed in the direction of Rick's. "Thataway!"

The young men paid their cover charge and entered the club. The lights were extremely dim on the inside and most of the furnishings were black or dark red. They grabbed three seats right next to the stage. One of the dancers was in the middle of sliding upside down from the pole with her dirty blonde hair leading the way. The crowd whooped and hollered and waved one-dollar bills in front of her. The dancer made a semi-circle on the stage collecting the bills, including those already held out by Mark and Lenny.

"Hey, I'll go grab us some beers." Robert walked over to the bar and got an ice bucket of Bud Lights. By the time he turned around, Lenny already had a cute younger stripper sitting on his lap and another one in her early thirties rubbing his shoulders. A petite platinum blonde was running her fingers through Mark's wavy hair.

"Man, that didn't take long, guys," said Robert as he sat next to them and watched the next girl step on the stage. Mark and Lenny were completely enraptured. So much for this being a group activity. A curvaceous brunette approached Robert and began with small talk which then turned to her rubbing his inner thigh. Robert bought a round of drinks and kept the conversation going. He appreciated her company given that his friends had bailed on him for the moment. He handed her half of his stack of ones. "Take these…and can you get the bartender to grab us another bucket of beers?"

"No problem, sugar."

Robert walked over to juke box, which was limited to songs of a certain length. Needless to say, *Stairway to Heaven* was not an option. It felt like a complete stereotype, but he knew that he had to do it. His selection began with *Girls Girls Girls* by Mötley Crüe followed by *Wild Side* by the same artist. He returned to his seat and finished his Bud Light while throwing ones at the stage like a broken ATM. By now, Lenny was busy getting a not-so-private lap dance in front of the stage, and Mark had disappeared to a back room. They had been drinking so heavily for the past few hours that the beer almost seemed to be sobering up Robert. It was that time of the night when the liver had regained some ground from the initial charge of the enemy, but while it fought back bravely, Robert knew that it would not win the day, or the night in this case. His eyes followed every curve on stage and lustfully gazed at the curves sitting next to him as another gulp went down his throat.

After what seemed like close to an hour Mark finally escaped the grasp of his succubus which had dragged him to her lair. His hair was uncharacteristically disheveled and half the buttons on his shirt were undone with this chest showing. He sat down next to the Robert and Lenny. "Hey, you guys wanna check into the hotel really quick before shit gets too crazy? We can come back later."

Robert said, "Let's do it, I'm ready to move on."

Another stripper sat on Lenny's lap. "You know, maybe I'll join you in like fifteen minutes."

"Right," said Mark. "Let's go. If we don't hear from you in thirty, we're coming back to get you." Since returning from the back room, Mark's tone was different, short and dry but determined. He had transformed from a sloppy Bourbon Street drunk to a man on a mission. Robert wasn't even going to ask what happened back there, but he could think of a few scenarios during the walk to the Royal Sonesta hotel just a few blocks down the street.

“You think Lenny will be alright?” asked Robert with genuine concern. He had never seen Lenny remotely close to this drunk, and they had just willingly left their cash-heavy and very drunk friend in the arms of a stripper. It is an unspoken cardinal rule of the French Quarter to leave no man behind, and they had just broken it, even if for the short duration of fifteen to thirty minutes.

“He’ll do alright, don’t worry. We’ll see him in a few minutes. No doubt about it. No doubt at all,” reassured Mark.

Robert and Mark clamored into the exquisite hotel lobby which seemed like a step back in time to a bygone era of luxury in the French Quarter, far from the neon lights, the drunks, and the whores waiting just outside. They stood in line behind a family which had driven in from somewhere in the Midwest. What were they thinking getting a room on Bourbon with their kids? Without noticing it, Robert was beginning to totter back and forth. At sudden intervals, he would take notice of his inebriated movements and regain his composure only to lose it again. Mark was in even worse shape, eyes agape and bloodshot staring around the lobby like a wild animal in the early stages of rabies. The two finally reached the front desk. Mark began to speak, but Robert cut him off before the words could exit his mouth. Information was exchanged, credit card numbers and IDs, as well as the room keys.

Mark texted the room number to Lenny and soon received a response.

Cool B there soon :-P

“Well, he’s alive after all,” said Mark holding up the text message. They entered the room and came to the realization that there was nothing to unpack as their car was still in a parking garage in the CBD. The events of earlier today at Ocean Management’s offices seemed light years away. “Man, I still can’t get over Ron’s face, fucking hilarious.”

“I know man – wasn’t it amazing!”

Robert turned on the TV and began rustling through the tiny bottles in the mini-fridge. “Where do you think we go next?”

“Maybe down to Frenchmen Street and check out some jazz. I think we have to as part of a proper New Orleans bucket list.”

Mark sat down at a black table next to the hotel window and cracked the curtains slightly to get a view of the passing parade of life in the street below. A knock came on the door, and Robert opened it without thinking. Thankfully, it wasn’t a mugger on the other side, but Lenny, who stumbled in and fell face first on the bed. “Man, nice room. Is mine this nice too?”

“Dude, you weren’t kidding on those fifteen minutes. You’re even punctual when leaving strip clubs!” said Robert, crouching down and continuing to investigate the contents of the mini-fridge.

“Hey, they got any mini-bottles of Jack in there?” asked Lenny.

“Yes, they do,” said Robert grabbing a bottle and tossing it to Lenny, who miraculously caught it from his position lying face first on the bed. Robert himself grabbed a Skyy vodka mini-bottle and cracked it open.

The minis didn’t seem to interest Mark who was digging deeply in his pockets for something. He finally found it. As Robert was about to turn the mini-bottle upward, Mark’s discovery caught him unawares. “What the fuck is that!” blurted out Robert. There, in front of Mark, was a tightly rolled up plastic baggie of a pearly white substance.

“Well, Robert, to me, it looks like a bag of cocaine,” said Mark as he gingerly unwound the bag and pulled the driver’s license from this wallet. “You guys never done blow before?”

“Nah, not really,” said Robert.

“Me either,” added Lenny. “Where did you get that anyway?”

“From Amberly,” answered Mark in a matter-of-fact tone as his driver’s license cut three small, thin lines.

“Amberly?”

"Yeah, Amberly from the strip club. You guys forgot her already? Don't worry, Lenny. She already forgot you," said Mark, chuckling as he finished rolling a hundred-dollar bill and then rapidly suctioning the first tiny mound. "Wooooooooooo!!!! Come on, your turn."

"I don't know man. I've never even smoked weed before," mumbled Lenny, trying to grasp what was going on.

"It's cool man," urged Mark, "This is what Wall Street guys are supposed to do, right? Big piles of blow and stuff like that. We're living the dream, Lenny."

Lenny pounded his Jack Daniels bottle. He sighed. "Fuck it, I'm in."

He was so drunk that he hardly had a clue as to what was going on, but that wasn't about to stop him. Lenny leaned over with the rolled up bill, precariously hovered over the table, and erased a line up his nostril. Lenny passed the bill to Robert. He hesitated for a moment, but then thought, "This is fucking Wall Street, why the hell not?" He bent over, took down his line, and began gagging as the powder hit the back of his dry nasal passage.

"There you go, man. Surf's up!" said Mark as he began chopping up more lines. "Glad you guys decided not to be a bunch of pussies." His next line was a behemoth, wide and nearly three inches in length. Nonetheless, Mark took it down in one fell swoop and then came up for air, snorting deeply, "Shit guys, I don't know how much coke is actually in here."

"Well, you did buy it from a stripper in New Orleans, bro," said Robert. They cracked up and began washing down the powder with a few more minis, which tasted like nothing across their cocaine-numbed mouths. They were jolted with chemical energy demanding to be exhausted. While Robert and Lenny were ready to hit the streets, Mark wanted to do some more coke, insisting on one last enormous line drawn in the shape of Texas. There was still more night to go. As the quality bottles were exhausted, Bourbon Street again called them forth.

The next few hours were a litany of generic bars playing millennial anthems and top forty hits. As the night wore on, Lenny had increasing trouble keeping up. The alcohol and cocaine had crippled his mental capacities to their most basic functions. He pulled himself down the street like a wounded animal – his jacket was already lost two or three hours ago. His heart thumped strongly as it struggled for oxygen in the humidity and struggled for a respite from the drugs. "Guys, guys I think I might be dying."

"You're not dying, Lenny."

Robert played the part of nurse for most the night trying to save both of his compatriots from the worst versions of themselves clearly on display. Mark was off his rocker, dancing to every song, ordering every drink, and talking with every girl drunk enough to put up with him. His luck was finally coming through as he found himself making out with a slim college girl in the corner of the Razzoo. Unfortunately for him, her friends came to her rescue and pulled her away. That didn't stop Mark. Before long, he found himself all over another girl, a little more heavyset. In this case, Robert did the saving and pulled Mark away, but not before snapping a few pictures on his phone for posterity.

The night was starting to wind down, with fewer and fewer patrons in the bars, but the gang insisted on keeping it alive by moving to yet another establishment with a greater quantity of desperate partygoers clinging to the night. Mark ordered a round of kamikaze shots, which finally broke all attempts to hold it together any longer. A luxury Uber took them back to the Royal Senesta, which was really not very far at all. They piled into the brand new Escalade and felt slightly embarrassed to be riding in such an expensive car in their condition. However, a glance at the driver's face told them he had clearly picked up a dozen different occupants in a similar state tonight. The seats had a slight odor of vomit to them, emanating from an unknown location in the car. A bunch of green Christmas trees hung from the rearview mirror in a sad, futile attempt to hide the smell.

Upon entering his room, Lenny fell face first into one of the double beds and passed out. Mark and Robert made some small talk as they washed up in the bathroom, getting the oily grime of Bourbon Street off their faces. Mark went to lie down, and Robert retreated to his room. He couldn't sleep and rolled in bed for a while with his clothes still on. Out of both boredom and restlessness, he exited the hotel and went for a stroll in the French Quarter. The hotel concierge looked at him suspiciously. The sun was slowly coming up, and the bar staff were power hosing the filth on the Bourbon Street sidewalks which was impossible to remove despite the daily washes. The morning felt cold despite it being spring ..it was likely that this was due to the drugs throttling through his system. He grabbed a twelve-ounce daiquiri from one of the 24-hour shops and aimlessly walked the side streets of the French Quarter. The older tourists with their maps and fanny packs were out and gave cautious looks in his direction. His body began to shake, and he held his arms close to his body. He felt deeply out of place. He couldn't tell himself what he was doing wandering the streets, sleepless, at this time of the morning when decent folk had begun to rise. His sense of direction was completely lost until chance or some miraculous force led him back to the Royal Sonesta. It was 9:30 a.m. Robert lay back down in the bed with his eyes wide open and stared at the ceiling. He prayed for sleep and wondered how he got here. Why he got here? This was their big day, yet all Robert McClure felt was shame and loneliness as he tried to close his eyes. After the lights and excitement of last night were over, there was nothing here but the same void that he felt on any given night in the last few weeks leading up to their big win. Finally, he slipped into sleep.

CHAPTER 15

ANOTHER ROLL OF THE DICE

It had been almost a week since New Orleans and the group had taken some well-deserved time off. However, it was now time to get back to work. Mark had let the rest of the position run for a little while longer and finally locked it in for a total profit of $160,000 on the trade. No doubt the Collins deal had been a success, but they were hardly set for life. They had tested the concept and it had worked for them – now came the task of turning it into real money. The group had unanimously decided that Robert's apartment would have to serve as the headquarters of their pitchbook forging enterprise. Robert spent the first hour and a half of the morning cooking breakfast and finishing the Netflix movie from the previous night. The last thirty minutes before Lenny and Mark's arrival would be spent on "cleaning". The place wasn't too bad by bachelor standards, with a couple of empty pizza boxes laying around, a short stack of dishes in the sink, laundry scattered all over the place and a few empty craft beer bottles here and there. Despite the downtime, Robert had somehow not found even a moment to clean. His goal this morning was to make the place tolerable, no one needed to see their reflection in the kitchen counter. He had just finished tossing the last of the laundry into the basket when there was a knock at the door.

"Welcome, gentleman, right on time." It was 9 a.m. The team had decided to maintain the same professionalism expected of any banker. Their pitchbooks needed to be exact replicas of those created by junior bankers working a hundred hours per week. Given they could be more targeted in their approach, maybe they didn't need to push those hours anymore, but they also couldn't get sloppy either. Perfect pitchbooks were not going to be created with a beer in hand and a movie in the background. Their work had to be as good as any investment bank on the Street. They had, however, relaxed their attire. Mark wore khaki shorts, Birkenstocks, and a polo. Lenny chose the banker casual Friday uniform: khaki pants, a button up Brooks Brothers gingham shirt, and expensive brown leather loafers.

"Hey, help us with these boxes man," urged Lenny, pointing to the stack in the corridor behind him.

"Sure, no problem. What is all of this stuff?"

"Just the basics," explained Lenny as he ripped through the cardboard, discarding the bubble wrap and plastic packaging on the floor. "I ordered a binding machine for the pitchbooks, a high resolution printer, a scanner, tons of glossy paper and some random office supplies."

"Oh man, this thing is sweet," said Mark with excitement while unwrapping the binding machine, a much newer model than the ancient contraption back at Latham, Schroeder & Holt.

"We're officially the only people on Earth to get excited about the latest model of binding machine," commented Robert.

"You better be excited…that thing is going to save hours of our life. Also, the last thing we want is to be printing fake pitchbooks down at the local FedEx."

"Who are you kidding, Lenny? I'm not binding anything. I just promoted myself to Managing Director," proclaimed Mark with a chuckle before sinking into the couch.

"So, the big item for today is figuring out our next acquisition target," announced Robert.

"What about RSP Permian?" chimed in Mark. "They're sizeable enough to have an options market, and it would make sense for Diamondback to buy them."

"Nah man. Can't do it. Remember that they're backed by NGP, a private equity. I think the fund is only halfway through its life cycle. NGP wouldn't exit for another five years or so. It would be a strange move for them. Someone might call a contact at NGP to ask about it. Our game plan has to stay simple and obvious where no one is going to second guess the acquisition, and no one is going to dig deeper into the details."

"Oh, come on, dude," retorted Mark. "Do you really think someone is going to second guess a professional pitchbook from a major investment bank? Why would a hedge fund manager care about how much sense the deal makes? We've seen dozens of downright stupid deals while working at Latham Schroeder. If you find a Goldman Sachs pitchbook for an asset sale, you don't ask yourself whether it's a good idea or not – that's the CEO's problem. You just take the information and trade on it."

"While I agree up to a point, the pitchbook still has to be in the realm of reality. It's not just the private equity ownership that's an issue here," responded Robert. "RSP bought thirty thousand net acres in Howard County a month ago and rolled out a twenty-slide presentation on their strategy for the next three years. Do you really think no one is going to question whether management is actually selling the company within two weeks of that presentation?"

"He's got a point," said Lenny. "We can't do RSP. It just doesn't make sense. It's a possible acquisition but not right now."

"Whatever, I'm just saying that I don't think it matters. Inside information is pretty simple, guys. We don't need to overthink this," said Mark, a little annoyed. "Well, do you have any other suggestions?"

"What about Pioneer Natural Resources?" said Lenny. "Everyone has been waiting for them to sell out to someone big like Exxon or BP. The acquisition would be a good way for the majors to get a bigger chunk of the shale action. They're still too focused on old-school international and offshore projects. They need a deal like that to diversify and move forward with their shale development."

"You're right, Lenny. That story fits our criteria perfectly. Just one problem…"

"…they're too big," said Mark, finishing Robert's sentence.

"Exactly. Even if a few hedge funds found our pitchbook, it wouldn't be enough to nudge the stock price of a $24 billion market cap company. The story fits, but it would be too hard to manipulate the market. So, that brings us back to the drawing board. Maybe we can look through a list of publicly traded tickers and brainstorm some ideas."

"That sounds like a good approach," said Lenny. "But before we do that, we have a few more items on our shopping list to take care of, if you guys are down for a run to the store. Ditching Latham Schroder is the best thing that ever happened to us but not so much in the resources department for the next pitchbook. We don't have Bloomberg any more, and we still need some more equipment and need to plan things out for the long term. For one, we gotta get some new laptops. Basically, I'm thinking that we just use burners, the less of a trace the better. After each pitchbook, we toss them out and replace them. It seems kind of wasteful, but if we're making tens of thousands of dollars per pitchbook, what's another thousand or two for new laptops every time? Consider it a transaction fee. I don't think we should buy them online either – too much of a paper trail. So, I was thinking of going to the store and paying in cash. As far as the Bloomberg, we'll just have to pull data directly from SEC filings and public releases – it'll be time consuming but it can be done."

"Good thinking. I like it Lenny, staying one step ahead of everything," said Robert.

After a quick stop at the bank to withdraw the necessary stack of cash, the group ventured to the local Best Buy. They weren't too picky with their laptop choices – PowerPoint presentations don't necessitate supercomputers. They paid for them with $2,400 in one-hundred-dollar bills, which unfortunately caused quite a scene. The shift manager was called to verify the bills and then the head manager inspected the cash again. This backed up a giant line behind them, and Lenny began to get nervous. He then remembered that there was no reason to be nervous because purchasing computers with legal tender was not a crime. Nonetheless, the experience still put him on edge. They bolted out of store with the laptops and a shopping basket full of assorted office necessities.

"Wanna grab lunch?" asked Mark as they pulled out of the parking lot.

"Sure, how do you guys feel about Smashburger?"

"Works for me."

They zipped over a couple of streets to Smashburger. The three slid into a booth and began chomping away at their burgers as soon as they arrived at the table. "OK, give me your list from best to worst burger," said Mark. "Hubcap, Christian's Tailgate, Five Guys, Smashburger, or Hopdaddy."

"Easy man: Hopdaddy, Hubcap, Tailgate, Smashburger, Five Guys," answered Robert without hesitating to think about it.

"If that's your list, what are we doing here then?" asked Lenny. "Here's mine: Tailgate, Hubcap, Hopdaddy, and I haven't been to Five Guys; so I can't say anything about that one."

Mark took a huge bite of his burger, "Are you serious? Tailgate over Hubcap?"

"Yeah, Tailgate has a better beer selection."

"We're talking about the burgers, not the beer. It's irrelevant."

"The hell it isn't – it's almost as relevant as the fries."

"Fries are another list altogether. What are you gonna throw in next, the milkshakes? We're talkin' burgers, man."

"Luther Williams!" said Robert out of nowhere

"I don't know man. I haven't had their burgers," said Mark.

"It's not a damn burger place, Mark," said Lenny. "It's an oil company. Luther Williams Energy to be exact. Sometimes, just for a second, I forget that you're from California and then without fail, you say something stupid."

Mark teasingly tossed a few shoestring fries at Lenny, "Haha, fuck you."

Lenny dodged to the left, avoiding the fries except for one that hit his shoulder. "Jeez!" he yelled noticing a grease stain on this Brooks Brothers shirt.

"Guys, hold on for a second, chill out for real," said Robert. "It's a classic story: a family-run business that's nearly run itself into the ground. Everybody around them is drilling wells in sixteen or seventeen days. The second worst company is doing it in twenty-five days. It takes Luther Williams almost sixty days to drill a single well, and when the wells finally come online, their production is about half as much as everyone around them even though the geology is the same. Their acreage is a gold mine, but it's operated by complete morons. The whole family-run thing is basically like hiring your cousin to drill wells for you instead of a professional oilfield services company. What could go wrong, right? As you can imagine, the stock price has been completely destroyed. However, the real problem is not the drilling but old man Luther, who is certifiably insane. It's not about the money for him. He loves the oil business – he's been doing it for fifty years or something like that. People have been waiting for him to sell for ages, but he just won't do it. What if we finally make this day happen? A pitchbook for the sale of Luther Williams Energy. The Street has been waiting ages for this one. We can't put a personal backstory behind the sale into a pitchbook, but I'm sure that everyone could fill in the blanks. Maybe old man Luther got cancer – he's only been smoking for sixty years. Or maybe the family trust is finally taking away the car keys. It's not a stretch by any means," said Robert.

"The market cap is right," said Lenny. "About a billion and a half dollars. That's enough for a hedge fund to push around."

"That's right, but there's even more to it than that. Over half the shares are owned by old man Luther and the family, which means less than half of the $1.5 billion is in the float. The trading volume is almost nothing," added Robert.

"Ah man, that could be killer," said Mark.

Lenny had already brought up additional metrics on his smart phone. "Check this out. Luther Williams has a 35% short interest!" Lenny lifted his phone, showing them the percentage. "Short interest that high on a company with a low float and low trading volume would rip the face off a couple of hedge funds. They've gotta be real cocky making a short bet like that. Whoever is in that short position has their balls out on the table."

Short interest is the percentage of the outstanding shares that have a bet on them that the stock price is going down. Typically, a hedge fund makes a short bet by borrowing shares from another investor and then selling the shares. So, for example, a hedge fund borrows a share of Luther Williams Energy, which is currently worth $50 per share. After borrowing it, the fund sells the shares and earns $50. However, they can't take that money to the bank yet. They still owe the shares to someone else who is also charging them a small rate of interest for borrowing them. To repay their position, the hedge fund eventually has to buy a share in the open market and return it to the original lender. When the price of the shares goes down, the hedge fund earns money by being able to buy back shares at a lower price and return them to the lender. If by this time Luther Williams has fallen to $30 per share, the hedge fund buys the shares for $30 and then returns them to the lender, which means that they get to keep difference – in this case, $20 cash per share. Shorting is how Wall Street bets against stocks.

The situation Lenny had laid out was something known as a short squeeze. If a hedge fund has a huge short position and something sends the stock price shooting upward, such as a very good earnings release, closing the position can be extremely painful. To exit their holdings and stop the pain from their position, the hedge funds must buy the stock in the open market, which sends the price even higher. Furthermore, positive news will draw additional buyers of the stock simply due to the good news. With the market filled with many buyers and few sellers, the stock price can skyrocket in a single day. And the more short-sellers in a stock, the tighter the short squeeze as multiple hedge funds desperately try to exit their short positions at the same time which only exacerbates their problems by pushing the stock price higher still. The short squeeze becomes a self-fulfilling prophecy, a kind of upward avalanche as good news sends the stock higher which makes the shorts close their positions sending prices even higher which forces even more shorts to run for the exit. A 35% short interest on Luther Williams Energy meant that over one in three shares in the float were borrowed by a hedge fund to bet against the company. That would mean an enormous amount of short-sellers would have to sprint for the door at the announcement of a positive and unexpected event…for example, an acquisition. Money was the biggest gratification of the Luther Williams scheme, but the other was kicking the smartest hedge funds on the Street in the balls at the same time.

The low float on Luther Williams Energy shares would make the short squeeze even tighter. As more than half the shares were owned by the family, it would be difficult to find a large amount of floating shares to purchase on any regular day. In a short squeeze, this low volume would force the price even higher as desperate hedge funds sought scarce shares to close their positions. Luther Williams shares were practically a dream come true as a fake pitchbook target.

"That is genius, Lenny. Nice job catching that short interest," said Robert. "Let's make it happen. You guys ready to royally fuck over some hedge funds?"

"Sounds good to me," said Mark. After a community fist-bump, they scooped up their trash and headed for the door of the Smashburger – they couldn't wait to get back to Robert's place to start on the pitchbook.

CHAPTER 16

MARK, THE MASTERMIND

With a tight deadline to finish their latest set of pitchbooks, it almost fell like their early days at Latham, Schroeder & Holt. The New York City International Petroleum Convention Conference, also known as the "IP double C" was just around the corner. Not only was it the biggest IPCC conference of the year, it was one of the biggest oil and gas conferences for the whole industry. The location, a thousand miles from Houston, was no accident. Beyond being a pleasure junket for executives and their wives, there was a strategic rationale for choosing New York. The goal of the event was to put Wall Street's top energy analysts in the same room as the industry's top oil and gas executives. Everyone attended, from household names in oil and gas to small cap players. Similarly, on the buy side, hedge funds managing $200 million or less rubbed shoulders with those managing tens of billions.

The conference wasn't cheap, with each registrant paying almost $2K per person, but it was well worth it. Executives often use the event as the sounding board for significant inter-quarter news such as acquisitions or new well results, but the real value of the conference comes from the private meetings and the breakout sessions that follow the public announcements and presentations. This is where the price of admission pays for itself. Within five minutes of the publicly broadcast speeches, the presenters leave the stage and rush for what is known as a "breakout room". Hedge fund analysts interested in that particular company follow suit. In the breakout room, management conducts a Q&A session – no mics and no recording equipment. Only the attendants inside get to hear the responses.

While this sounds very suspect in terms of SEC rules, most executives know how not to cross the line of inside information. Nonetheless, the grey area contained in those breakout rooms could be immensely valuable. A hedge fund analyst in the room still has an advantage, however marginal, over someone just reading the official press release on the company website. If for instance the company had publicly announced an increase from four drilling rigs to six that morning, an analyst in the room could inquire whether a further increase to seven drilling rigs would require hiring additional staff. Although the public press release does not mention the potential for a seventh rig, management teams will typically answer these types of questions. The answer is not so material that it will make or break an investment decision, but regardless, the attendees in the breakout session can now better assess future general and administrative expenses under a seven-rig scenario. Sometimes the advantage might be as slight as reading into a CEO's tone of voice. Did he sound confident when talking about the capital expenditure budget announced in the morning press release? Or did he hesitate?

Then there were the private dinners between investors and company executives. Investment banks host these dinners, with places reserved for the best hedge fund clients or those willing to pay several thousand dollars in trading commissions for an invitation. While the exact price of attendance is never specified, the expected payment is an understood gentleman's agreement. At times, these dinners occur prior to a big press release the following day; some hedge funds base entire strategies on non-verbal cues at these dinners and attend only to gauge management's mood. If management is energetic and jubilant, it could mean an important press release will precede their conference presentation within a day or two. If on the other hand they are tired, guarded, and sticking to the company line, one shouldn't expect much. Huge positions have been placed in the market based on the smallest of hunches over dinner.

With its grey areas and murky boundaries, and the participants' hunger for the slightest hint of a competitive edge, the IPCC was the perfect place for Robert, Mark, Lenny and their next stack of freshly printed pitchbooks. The conference was a shark tank, albeit one with very polite, hospitable, and sophisticated sharks. If anything, the former analysts from Latham, Schroeder & Holt were just another breed of shark, one that fed on its own kind, and their pitchbooks were the chum in the water. With Collins Petroleum, luck had clearly been on their side with the pitchbook falling into the hands of Bloomberg news. They couldn't rely on that kind of luck again. The conference could serve as a way of removing the element of chance from the equation as it almost guaranteed that a pitchbook would fall into the hands of a hedge fund.

Of course, there were also risks. While the oil and gas industry might seem large and impersonal to the uninitiated outsider, in reality it is a very small and insular community. Everyone at the conference knows each other to some degree. Someone might even recognize them from their Latham, Schroeder & Holt days. The team had attended dozens of management meetings with the companies presenting at this very event. Sure, Robert, Mark, and Lenny never said much at those meetings other than occasional coveted opportunity to explain the data behind a chart, but their faces would seem familiar. And since most executives are fairly sharp, they might even remember exactly who they are. Worse yet, there was the possibility that Ron himself could be lurking around any corner.

The second problem was their peers. Plenty of Lenny's classmates from Rice University were in the industry, and they too would be crawling all over the place, mostly working in servitude to one investment bank or another. Robert and Mark also had friends, contacts, and acquaintances in the business as a natural result of living in Houston. While these were risks, their novice status in the industry was also an asset. While there were plenty of people that could recognize them, there were far more who had never seen their face. As brand new analysts, outside of their friends, their colleagues at Latham, Schroeder & Holt, and a couple of management teams, they were safe from recognition.

Another issue was coming up with a backstory, especially one that made sense to someone who might know them. That's where Mark's idea came in – first, they needed a new employer. Obviously, they couldn't pretend to be still working at Latham, Schroeder & Holt. Posing simply as interested investors wasn't going to cut it either – registrants had to be oil companies, investment banks, or investment funds. At the moment, they were none of the three. However, the last option was the easiest to fake. After all, New York is packed to the brim with investment funds with billions under management, yet the average Joe has never heard of them. Funds like Citadel, Millennium, and Och Ziff manage tens of billions and are virtually unknown outside the finance industry and wealthy investor circles. As a result, no one would blink an eye at an unknown fund name claiming to manage a small billion or two. With this in mind, Mark filled out their conference registration forms and listed their employer as Gemini Capital Management. The fund name was Mark's tongue-in-cheek tribute to their penchant for pitchbook forgery. More importantly, it sounded equal parts mysterious, powerful, and ridiculous – the quintessential ingredients of any real hedge fund name.

Mark also began another special side project and kept his intentions secret until his big reveal. It had again involved copying a few items and making careful edits, but this time not with pitchbooks.

"Hey guys. I got something special for you today. Check these out." Mark threw a small stack of business cards in front of them. Robert picked up a few curiously, with Lenny leaning in to take a look as well.

The cards read, "Robert McClure, *Vice President, Mergers and Acquisition*, Energy Banking, JP Morgan."

Lenny stared at the cards in confusion. "Um, OK, what are we going to do with these? Is this why you asked for all our old business cards a few days ago?"

"Yup, I picked the simplest format from our card collections as an example, but we can really do this for just about any bank"

"They look awesome," said Robert, "but I'm in the same boat with Lenny. What's the plan here? What are we supposed to do with fake business cards?"

"Glad you asked. I thought of an idea for a side hustle. Something that we can do alongside the pitchbooks to double our chances of getting this right. What if we go beyond faking the pitchbooks…what if we entirely fake our identities? Instead of just impersonating pitchbooks, we impersonate bankers. You know, maybe we go out for drinks with the conference hedge fund crowd, we pretend to get hammered, and then, we start talking about acquisitions that won't actually ever happen?"

"That's the dumbest thing I've ever heard," said Lenny, unconvinced. "I mean seriously dude."

"No man, hear me out. Here's how I came up with the idea. Have I ever told you the story of my ex-girlfriend's sister Leslie?"

"Um no, what about her?"

"She is a complete sociopath. I don't mean that just as a word people use for an asshole at the office. I'm talking about a serious pathological liar. She would lie and manipulate everything and everyone around her, often for no reason at all other than her own pleasure. I'm talking about a clinical diagnosis here. No one figured it out for years because all of her lies were so normal. They were never outright fiction, instead they just bended the truth right to its limits. For example, when I first met her, she told me that she was getting a Master's degree in Music. Her family thought the same thing. In reality, she had flunked her senior year of college twice and was on her sixth year of undergrad. It's a long story on how everyone eventually found out the truth, but it took much longer than you would imagine. Since she was a musician, at least at the undergraduate level, it was pretty easy to get away with that lie.

"Think about it. If you met a girl at a bar tonight who said she was getting a Masters in History, would you doubt her for any reason? The lie is so realistic and plain that it's impossible to see through it. Furthermore, if she actually does know quite a bit of history, it's nearly impossible to detect the truth. Amateur pyschos get too elaborate with their lies. They make up stories about finding Tutankhamen's tomb on their Spring Break trip to Egypt in order to make themselves seem important. They never make up simple, believable and unelaborate lies such as getting a Masters in History when they've actually flunked out. But the simplest lies are actually the strongest ones."

"Dude, she sounds pretty fucked up," commented Robert.

"Yeah, tell me about it, but the lesson here is that we can do the exact same thing. If you meet someone at an exclusive conference like IPCC, you don't assume that they would lie to you. If a random guy in a nice suit at IPCC says that he works at JP Morgan, you take it at face value that he actually does. Why wouldn't you? Even if you have doubts for some reason, what would you think after he then gives you a professional business card with his credentials right there in all the correct JP Morgan logos and font? And if that person can talk shop about M&A and the industry, well, that seals the deal. You believe them without a single doubt in your mind. And even if you know someone who works at JP Morgan, the bank is so big that it's easy to escape an awkward conversation. 'Why, no, your friend Don doesn't work in my office. I'm with the San Francisco M&A team. We also do cleantech there, but I do see his e-mail address on group messages all the time.'"

"That's true. You'd have to be psychic to spot the liar," said Lenny, deep in thought as he analyzed all the different angles on the strategy.

"You got it. And just like Leslie, we keep our lies simple. We don't try to blow them out of proportion by mentioning billion dollar deals and our lunch with Rex Tillerson from Exxon. We just talk about football, Texas A&M versus UT, hunting, favorite neighborhoods in Houston, whatever the fuck. And then at some point in the night, you 'accidentally' let something slip about a small deal. They take that information and trade on it just like the pitchbooks. These business cards are only an example, but we don't have pretend to be a Vice President. Just say you're an analyst, an associate, or whoever. The game plan is the same. Hell, I might believe a new analyst yapping about deals more than a VP."

"It's pretty incredible, Mark," said Robert. "I'm really impressed, man."

"Yeah, I know, and the best part is that the more I drink, the more believable I become. I'm happy to volunteer as our bait."

"Hmm, I'm not a 100% convinced, but if you wanna give it a shot, then let's do it," replied Lenny. "However, let's test this out scientifically. We gotta choose a different company for your plan. That way, we can see whether it works or not independent of the pitchbook. Also, it gives us the opportunity to diversify across two stocks and spread the risk."

"Great idea, Lenny – saves us from doing another whole pitchbook," added Robert.

"Yeah, and given that we're not even finished with the Luther Williams pitchbooks, we better get to it," remarked Lenny. "Mark, can you take care of the final trip logistics while we wrap them up?"

"Sure thing, boss."

The Luther Williams Energy pitchbook was considerably more complex than the Collins Petroleum book. It had to be realistic and that meant detailing the operations with an in-depth analysis of potential value drivers. The pitchbook showed Luther Williams' under-stimulated frac jobs with only seven hundred pounds of sand per foot in their wells while the industry was now pumping fifteen hundred pounds or more. The well spacing was also obsolete, meaning a more-skilled operator could fit a greater number of wells on each six hundred and forty-acre section, in turn increasing the value. Furthermore, the company had not yet tested deeper intervals in the Wolfcamp zone, which offset producers were already exploring with success. Each topic required one or more slides and the detailed technical research behind each slide took hours and hours. On top of that, the basics were equally burdensome such as an acreage map calling out successful nearby wells, laboriously created from the Texas Railroad Commission website. In addition, they had decided to change the formatting from a Barclays pitchbook to Wells Fargo Bank. Since Barclays was not a lender to Luther Williams, this choice was more plausible. Wells Fargo did not have the top slot as a lender on the credit facility, but they still clearly had a relationship with Luther Williams. Also, the choice of Wells Fargo was believable as a top player in the energy space. At the same time, it was not as bold as forging a JP Morgan or Goldman Sachs pitchbook. The final product was much more than a simple forgery of a minor acreage sale. It was a sales pitch for the acquisition of Luther Williams Energy – it was good, persuasive, and most importantly, realistic.

In the meantime, Mark made the final arrangements for the trip. The conference was located at the Sheraton on 53rd and 7th Avenue, far too close to the zoo known as Times Square. Thankfully, Mark knew one of the key rules of any seasoned banker: never stay at the conference hotel. There were a number of reasons to choose a hotel several blocks away. First, you sometimes just need to grab a breath of fresh air away from the conference. After smiling and shaking hands all day, it's good to have a place for a mental escape. Second, and more importantly, there is the conference, and then, there is the after-conference scene. After a night of drinks, a professional can find himself in some awkward situations. You hardly want your clients to see you stumbling back into your room after a big night on the town. It can be equally embarrassing to see your clients dragging themselves back to their rooms, often raucous and sometimes with two hookers in tow. This all makes for strange conversations in the morning when what you really need to be focusing on is pitching an acreage deal to the same persons. The trained banker, the experienced banker who plans on entertaining, always gets a hotel room elsewhere. So for this reason, Mark booked three rooms at the Knickerbocker Hotel, a full ten blocks away.

"Guys, airplane tickets and rooms are booked," Mark announced to Robert and Lenny, who were still sunk deep into the couch with their eyes peeled to their laptops. "That was the easy part, but we have more important details to take care of before the trip. We gotta get some new suits."

"I'm all set, man. I got mine like a year ago. It's brand new," said Robert.

"Yeah, I can tell that it's brand new…brand new straight from the Jos A. Bank catalog, bro. If our business cards say Vice President, we need to actually look like Vice Presidents. We can't look like three junior banking analysts. It's not a discussion guys. I've set up an appointment at Sid Mashburn in River Oak in two hours."

Unlike Robert, Lenny, who was not shy about wearing $700 designer geek glasses and sleek European ties, filed no complaints and immediately began browsing the Sid Mashburn website. "Oh, sweet, man. Great idea! These are nice."

"Oh, yeah tell me about it. And a deal at only $1,300 bucks for the cheapest ones," pointed out Robert.

"You can take the boy out of Mississippi, but you can't take the Mississippi out of the boy," said Mark mockingly.

"Asshole," replied Robert with a chuckle. He peered over Lenny's shoulder to see the website. "Gotta say though that the custom-tailored shirts look pretty awesome."

"I know. They're sick. And I totally get it, Robert. They're pricey, and maybe we shouldn't be blowing this much money yet, but think of it as a transaction fee. It's a necessity to getting this done," said Mark. "I'm gonna do either a dark grey or navy suit with a pastel Vineyard Vines tie, you know the standard issue Houston banker look. If guys are going for our buy-side persona, then you'll need something professional but also laid back enough to fit in with the hedge fund crowd. I'm thinking confident and classy but not overdone."

"You should write suit commercials, man. I'm not even kidding. That's really good. Are you sure you don't want to measure me for the suit yourself?" teased Lenny.

“Ha…very funny.”

CHAPTER 17

THE CRIME OF THE CENTURY

Robert was again sleepless, a more frequent occurrence in recent weeks. The restlessness was no longer due to the stress of long hours – it was from the uncertainty that now defined his life. The human brain is hard-wired to play it safe and avoid high-risk situations, yet Robert's life had become a repeated gamble. Although the odds were in his favor, he still couldn't shake the gut-wrenching feeling of risking so much, even with a payoff beyond his wildest dreams. If their scheme continued to work, they could soon be sitting on a faraway beach and sipping drinks out of a coconut. On the other hand, they could wind up in jail or potentially somewhere in-between the two extremes, in former banker purgatory, unemployed with no money and a less-than-stellar recommendation from their previous employer. Their plan seemed airtight, but that wasn't much comfort. Every white-collar criminal in history had likely believed the same thing. By their very nature, white-collar crimes are premeditated and planned by smart and patient people. No matter where he redirected his mind, Robert couldn't escape the thought of being caught.

Just yesterday, Mark placed their order for $150,000 in call options of Luther Williams Energy, ticker LWE, and $50,000 on calls for Newstar Exploration, ticker NST, to test his business card strategy. Since IPCC was the biggest conference of year, they had decided to put their entire profits from the Collins trade and then some on the line. While they were tempted to save more of the funds for a rainy day, there wouldn't be another conference of a similar size for months. Furthermore, while the IPCC conference was open to any investment fund, most other major conferences were organized by investment banks and were reserved for paying clients – 'Gemini Capital' would have a tough time getting its foot in the door at these events. Perhaps, as Gemini grew, they could start sending some commission dollars to the banks in exchange for invitations, but at the moment their fund was a very small fish swimming in an ocean of capital.

Out of their two positions, the Luther Williams call options worried Robert the most. It was a thinly traded company and the option contracts were even more thinly traded than the common stock. The bid ask spread was sizeable given the lack of a liquid market. Thankfully, if the strategy worked, a couple of percentage points lost on the spread would be meaningless. They weren't looking for a 5% gain on the stock, but instead a double or nothing bet or even better. Liquidity wasn't the problem in the traditional sense – the main issue was that their position stood out. The open interest on option contracts is publicly available to anyone who knows where to click on *Yahoo! Finance*. Their position wasn't enormous, but it could catch someone's attention as very few bets had been placed on Luther Williams call options. What they had done was equivalent to placing a $500 chip on black at the casino roulette table when everyone else was betting just ten or twenty dollars. No doubt the bet catches every eye at the table, but at the same time, it is hardly the craziest thing to ever happen at a casino or in this case Wall Street. In any case, their chips were now on the table and hopefully some pit boss – or in this case some distant regulator – wouldn't think twice about them. Or so Robert hoped.

As soon as his mind relaxed for a second, it would quickly return to evaluating worst-case scenarios. He stared at the ceiling wide-eyed, not a moment closer to sleep. Their early morning flight was taking off in just a few hours. He considered abandoning all hope of sleep and checking the news on Bloomberg instead. Everything had been packed hours ago including his new neatly pressed suit from Sid Mashburn. There was no backing out.

****

Continuing to roll back and forth in bed, Robert remembered his last run-in with the law. It was almost seven years ago, in high school. The previous year's graduating class had taken the time-honored senior prank to the next level. In the final weeks of class, the seniors procured an enormous pig from one of the local farms. They had greased the pig and fed it until the thing was ready to burst. Then, late on Sunday night, they broke into the school and unleashed the beast into halls. Needless to say, the administration was less than thrilled to find the pig defecating throughout the building and causing a ruckus the following morning. The administration had only one choice: classes were cancelled and the school coaches chased the greased pig throughout the halls. While there were plenty of threats of expulsion within days of graduation, it came to nothing. As a small private school, the administration had little to gain by expelling anyone. In the end, the punishment was nothing more than damages paid and community service performed by the guys of senior class, which amounted to yard work on campus.

Unfortunately for the administration, this experience only emboldened Robert's class to top the prank next year. After all, the only thing better than the biggest prank in thirty years would be the biggest prank in thirty-one. Their small town class was comprised of only twenty-five guys, and everyone participated except for a few oddballs. While the greased pig was genius, it was fairly easy to clean up, and the story would continue to live on in myth only. The class of 2010 wanted to make a more permanent statement. Robert recalled the prank like it was yesterday. The night was crisp and overcast following an all-day rain. He had leaned the ladder against the wall of the school building and could feel it slide and shift on the wet roof. He and Matt, his best friend in high school, adjusted the ladder until it stood firm. The first of the guys climbed upward onto the roof. They looked like a motley band of vandals, most dressed in pastel-colored polo shirts with some taking things more seriously and wearing their hunting camou.

Robert climbed the ladder and did his best to avoid the giant puddles on the flat roof. Marcus passed a second ladder up to them, which was then lowered into the central courtyard of the school. Back at the parking lot, the others began to unload the necessary supplies from their trucks: picks, shovels, and cement mix. More seniors climbed the walls and distributed themselves evenly in a chain across the roof. From the base of the first ladder, they passed the picks and shovels upward, then across the roof, and finally down to the courtyard. The courtyard crew got to quick work excavating a pit in the center. As the crew dug, bags of cement arrived on the scene, and a small group was figuring out how to mix it. From a dark blue pick-up truck, they unloaded the centerpiece of their project. It had been finished only a few hours prior, an empty keg haphazardly spray-painted "Seniors 2010". As the chain passed the empty keg along, the young men snickered in anticipation of everyone's reaction on Monday. Almost every classroom's windows faced the inner courtyard – the whole school would see it. The keg made its way up the ladder and onto the roof. Robert grasped it momentarily, smiled, and passed it to the next man. The keg then traveled down the second ladder and was centered in the freshly dug pit. A group of camouflaged teens quickly began pouring the cement around it.

With the keg secured, the key operatives in the courtyard exchanged high fives, only to find their excitement short-lived. Without warning, red and blue lights illuminated the school halls, and sirens wailed from the parking lot. Some of the guys by the first ladder managed to run for it. The team in the courtyard reversed their ladder to the other side of the wall, climbed it, jumped down from the roof and ran across the football field to a tree line. Up high on the roof, Robert was trapped. He put his hands up in the air like a surrendering bank robber and his friends followed suit. Matt looked like he was scared shitless.

"Come on down, boys," he recalled Officer Larry Walters saying. While the police were hand-cuffing them in the front, little known to the officers, the cement was drying and hardening in the central courtyard – they had pulled off the greatest prank in their high school's history. The tale lives on in infamy to this day in Laurel, Mississippi and has practically buried into obscurity the previous year's greased pig incident.

Despite their confidence in avoiding repercussions prior to the prank, once faced with the actual possibility of punishment, they feared the worst, from expulsion to losing their college scholarships or even jail time. The uncertainty scared them most of all. Robert couldn't remember why they were so afraid. It's not like they were caught bagging heroin or robbing a liquor store. The small town arresting officer had probably done the same sort of stuff at their age, probably at the same high school. However, the police were the last of Robert's worries. His father came to pick him up from the downtown holding cell. Not a word passed his father's lips on the ride home in the early a.m. His father was a respected man in town, and his son had let him down. Robert offered a heartfelt apology, but it failed to break the silence. His father refused to even look in his direction. It was as if Robert did not even exist to him. He vividly recalled every painful, slow minute of that ride. When they reached home, he walked to his room. His father went to get a cold glass of water from the fridge. He slowly traversed to Robert's room and without warning slapped Robert so hard that he nearly lost his balance.

As bad as that was, it was not the worst part. Given that Laurel was a small town, he knew that his grandpa would find out eventually. The thought of explaining himself to his grandfather filled him with dread. While his father remained irate and cold for the next week or so, he eventually got over it, and things in the household returned to normal. However, when the time came to talk with his grandfather, the experience tore him to shreds. His grandfather didn't slap Robert like his father. He didn't yell at him. He didn't even have any words of wisdom, but the pain in his eyes could write chapters of his disappointment and embarrassment. That look haunted Robert over five years later as he lay sleeplessly in bed. There was no way to undo his grandfather's disappointment, and his passing several years ago made the memory hurt even more. In light of that, there remained little fondness for the senior prank in his reminiscences.

Robert returned to thinking about everything that that needed to be done tomorrow, and everything that needed to go right in New York, but the thought that wouldn't leave him was that of his grandfather's eyes staring back at him.

CHAPTER 18

COCKTAILS & TALL TALES

The gentlemen from Texas checked into the Knickerbocker and experienced the short-lived euphoria of every visitor in New York City – the grandeur of the hotel lobby overwhelmed them until the size of their actual rooms brought them back down to reality. They had decided to arrive before the official start of the conference to catch the social cocktail hours held the night prior to the main event. IPCC would certainly host one, and AllTrust Bank usually had a side reception as well. For his plan, Mark settled on assuming the identity of a young Vice President at BNP Paribas, an international French bank with a decent U.S. energy presence. He considered emulating a more respected bank in the energy space such as JP Morgan, but their size and influence would have made them a dangerous choice. JP Morgan bankers would be around every corner at the conference, and their team was well known in the business. While BNP Paribas was a respected international brand, it was not a powerhouse in the U.S or in energy for that matter. There would likely be only a few BNP Paribas bankers wandering the conference, if any at all. At the same time, BNP Paribas was still large and well known enough to get a sell side mandate for a company like Newstar Exploration. Maybe, they weren't the first choice for a mergers and acquisitions advisor, but it was still realistic enough. Lastly and perhaps most importantly, the bank's global presence offered an easy out if someone began asking too many questions. You could always claim to work on European transactions in the Paris office or even more obscure Middle East and North Africa deals.

Lenny and Robert decided to skip the cocktail hour as the less they were seen, the better. Their first task was setting up a makeshift office at the hotel room. Earlier in the day, they had purchased a small printer for the room, which they set up alongside the portable scanner Lenny had packed for the trip. Not only had Mark created fake BNP Paribas business cards, but he had designed Gemini Capital Management cards for the three of them as well. The cards were made of heavyweight board with a slick logo, the outlines of two maroon Greek-style faces staring in separate directions. To add the final flourish to their headquarters, laptops were placed on the hotel work desks and tuned to market news.

Robert reviewed the latest updates on Luther Williams and Newstar Exploration to make sure no unexpected press releases had hit the newswire, as can happen just before a major conference. In the back of his mind, he hoped for a scenario where the analysts could legitimately strike it rich by accident. With Luther Williams and Newstar both attending the conference, there was a decent chance that an important press release could be made right before their presentations. If the press releases were good news, the stocks would shoot upward. In this dream scenario, they could cash in their call options, pack their bags, and head home without breaking a single securities law. That would be nice, but Robert wasn't counting on it. Luck had gotten him nowhere in his brief Wall Street career, while forgery appeared to be his forte.

The next step of the plan was securing their nametags without arousing suspicion. Mark stepped out of the Knickerbocker and headed for the Sheraton. He walked with confidence in his new gray suit and $500 Italian leather shoes – also a necessary expense for the conference. Even he felt like a Vice President entering the conference hotel; it was amazing what a paycheck's worth of clothes could do for one's sense of self-worth. Mark approached the registration desk, which was covered with hundreds of nametags. He let the line ahead of him clear up a bit before asking for his tag. "Mark Edwards, Gemini Capital Management."

The IPCC employee flipped through the nametags, finally finding Mark's and handing it to him with a gift bag received by all attendants. In big letters, the nametag read, "MARK," followed by "Edwards" in smaller font and "Gemini Capital Management" in mid-sized font below that. Mark stuffed the nametag into his bag rather than put it on right away and quickly retreated back to their hotel. Upon his return, Robert and Lenny followed the same process and picked up their nametags.

When the three reconvened in their room at the Knickerbocker, Lenny got to quick work scanning Mark's nametag. IPCC was not just any conference. Security was a real concern. The nametags, typically worn on a lanyard around the neck, were the only way to access the conference. A couple of years ago, several enviro-nutcases broke into one of the meetings. A few of the protestors held up signs urging "climate science now!" Several others streaked naked through the halls to make their scientific point, while another group of would-be streakers were wrestled down by conference attendants. Since then, the security had been stricter. Lenny edited the scanned nametags on his computer, replacing "Edwards" with "Hollis" and "Gemini Capital Management" with "BNP Paribas". Despite security's attempts to keep the protesters out, this was almost too easy. Lenny's perfect replica was placed back inside Mark's plastic nametag holder.

Mark put the lanyard around his neck and examined himself in the mirror. "Nice job, Lenny. I'm gonna get to it. I'll text you guys a little later tonight with updates." Mark exited the room ready to start his mission while Robert and Lenny decided to kill some time at the hotel bar. They desperately needed to take the edge off and calm their nerves.

Mark Edwards, now "Mark Hollis", arrived back at the Sheraton just in time for cocktail hour and made a beeline for one of the bartenders. The spread wasn't top shelf but not half bad either. There were a few people in the line ahead of him and Mark took the opportunity to scope the room. While many people dread these sorts of social events, Mark thrived in them. Whether it was his old surfing crowd or his theater and film friends in college, he always enjoyed being the life of the party. Although that skill had no use in his college examinations, in the real world, its applications were limitless, especially in finance. What Mark lacked in Microsoft Excel skills, he made up in his ability to make anyone smile. As a natural-born extrovert, he truly enjoyed the company of others regardless of their rank or occupation and lived for war stories from banking industry old-timers. Mark was the rare creature who actually relished in small talk. Plus, he had a solid networking strategy: it was a numbers game. Get to know as many people as possible, even if they're not remotely in your same area of interest. If you're always thinking about how a conversation can benefit your career or goals, you inevitably seem inauthentic and flat. But genuine goodwill and talking with anyone and everyone naturally leads to other introductions, which then segue into yet more conversations. Sure, sometimes the conversations can turn into a dead end. However, the key is simply to keep enjoying yourself regardless. With that mentality, you can never go wrong at a networking event. And whether his plan worked or not, the drinks were free.

The guy ahead of him in the drink line didn't look like the hedge fund type; dark hair, in his forties, and by Mark's estimation clearly an oil company executive. "Jeez, I guess that I'm drinking Sam Adams tonight," said Mark.

"Yeah tell me about it. It's either that or Bud Light, or maybe a Jack on the rocks," said the man.

"I don't know why they can't get better drinks at this thing. I mean every year it's the same stuff. You'd think for a room full of executives and bankers that they could do a little better. If they're gonna serve this stuff, they might as well give us a couple buckets of Lone Star on ice to make us feel at home."

"Now you're talking my language," said the man

Mark stretched out his hand, "By the way, I'm Mark Hollis, BNP Paribas."

"Pleased to meet you. Alex Hanson, Chief Accounting Officer at Choctaw Energy."

Mark had been prepping with the team for this exact moment. He had tried to memorize a background summary of every major company in attendance. While Robert and Lenny were working on the final version of the pitchbook, Mark did his homework on the energy sector like never before. He studied website after website of company presentations. He printed the summary pages containing the acreage positions and the key facts for each firm and used them as flash cards. Lenny had even gone to the extent of quizzing him. Knowing the industry better would make for easier conversation starters, but there was only so much that he could learn in the last few days leading up the conference. Of the three analysts, his industry knowledge was the worst by a significant margin, yet he had to be as fluent as a Vice President of mergers and acquisitions in order to sound like the real deal.

"Oh yeah. I've heard of you guys. You have some acreage in the Anadarko Basin in Oklahoma and some up in the Marcellus in Pennsylvania, right?"

"Yeah, you got it almost right. It's about thirty thousand net acres in Canadian County up in Oklahoma, in the SCOOP/STACK play of the Anadarko Basin, and then we've got some acreage in the Uinta up in Utah."

Mark had already tripped on his first encounter and was hating himself for his stupid answer, but he did his best to roll with the punches. "Oh, that's right. Uinta and Utica is also next to Marcellus. I guess that I got that mixed up in my head. Man, is that SCOOP and STACK play heating or what? Are you guys next to Cimarex Energy?"

"Yeah, we've got some overlapping acreage with them, and we participated in a couple of non-op wells together."

A woman in her early forties, wearing a light grey pantsuit and a bright blue blouse walked over to the two of them. Alongside her was another gentleman in similar generic business attire. "Hey Alex, how's it going? Did you just get here?"

"Yeah, just got my drink. When did you all fly in?"

"Just now. We caught the last straight shot from Oklahoma City and checked into the hotel forty-five minutes ago," said the woman. "I saw half the town on the flight. Continental's management team was there, so was Devon's whole business development team, and about half of Chesapeake."

"Yup, that's basically half the town," said Mark. "By the way, Mark Hollis from BNP Paribas."

"Hi. Lindsay Harrison, CFO of Choctaw Energy, and this is Brent Stephens, Head of Investor Relations." Mark exchanged business cards with them. Thankfully, after some pleasantries, the conversation switched to the Oklahoma City Thunder. While the Anadarko Basin conversation wasn't a complete disaster, Mark didn't have much more to say beyond his initial commentary. Talking the Thunder versus the Houston Rockets was more familiar territory. He even held his own when the conversation shifted to local football rivalries between Oklahoma State and Oklahoma University. Lindsay, Brent, and Alex interrogated him about his favorite teams in California. Despite the state being thousands of miles from Oklahoma, they knew the rosters inside out. "How much football do these guys watch?" thought Mark to himself. Even Lindsay's knowledge of sports was nearly encyclopedic, but perhaps such knowledge was the price of being the rare female executive in oil and gas. Mark was genuinely having a good time with the Choctaw Energy team. Like many executives in the oil and gas industry, they were downright regular folks from Texas and Oklahoma. These weren't snobby East Coast Ivy League blue bloods or liberal West Coast intellectuals. These were regular people who liked nothing more than a college football game, a little deer hunting, and talking about the hydraulic fracturing of a ten thousand-foot horizontal well.

Mark was enjoying himself so much he had lost himself in the conversation. His pump and dump scheme for Newstar Exploration was not even on his mind as he went to grab another round of beers for everyone. When he returned with the drinks, he was met by two newcomers to the group in their late twenties or early thirties. Their dress code immediately hinted that these could be his targets. Each wore colorful gingham shirts with fleece sweater vests differing only in their shades of grey. Their hair was mopped with gel and styled somewhere between a 1950s greaser look and a modern hipster while also neat enough to pass the test in this business crowd.

"Thanks for grabbing these Mark." Lindsay smiled and turned toward the two younger men. "So yeah, we're exploring an IPO perhaps later this year if oil prices hold up. Like you said, we already have some public bonds outstanding; so we're prepared from a compliance standpoint. Brent here is our Head of Investor Relations, and he works with the credit investors for now, but he'll cover the equity side after the initial offering. So, we've already got a team in place to go public."

"That's really interesting, especially with so many other great public companies in your zip code. Speaking of...what do you guys think of Cimarex's completion design since they're in your neighborhood?" asked one of the young men. "They seem to be doing bigger fracs upfront like EOG. Do you think that will translate into a lower estimated ultimate recovery in the future?"

"Remember, I'm not an operations guy. But, speaking as the CFO, it really comes down to the internal rate of return so it's hard for me to say outright which completion method is better. If you're bringing enough value forward, it could make up for the drop off in production later on – a dollar today is worth more than a dollar tomorrow as we all know. But our completion design is more standard; so we're not trying to follow Cimarex."

"Do you know if you're using a hundred and fifty-foot spacing and thirty feet between clusters, or is it two hundred-foot spacing? It's a plug n' perf design, right?" prodded the younger of the two guys.

"Yeah, it's plug n' perf, but like I said, I'm not an engineer. I can't tell you much more than that."

Mark saw an opportunity to save Lindsay and Brent from this conversation going down a too technical route. "So, Lindsay, are you talking with our equity capital markets guys on the IPO? I'm mostly on the M&A side of things, but I'd love to get you in touch with our ECM team."

"No, I can't say that I have met with them, but you know shoot me an e-mail. We're still in the early stages of planning this out."

"Sounds good, we really like the SCOOP and STACK and would love to help you out. We've also got a sell side mandate for some acreage over there. It's not a huge position, but it might be something worth looking at."

"Really," said one of the slick, young and inquisitive men, "Where's the acreage?"

"Well, you know I can't say with confidentially agreements and all."

"Right, of course. We really like the SCOOP and STACK too. We're Continental shareholders and are always interested in what everyone else is doing in the basin."

"Oh yeah, the Continental team is great. I know Harold and all the guys there. And what group are you with?" Mark was already breaking his own cardinal rules for the cocktail hour. He was supposed to keep a low profile and not pretend to know everyone in the industry, but what can you do when you need to keep the conversation flowing. Hopefully, no one would call him out on his friendship with Harold Hamm, one of the richest people in Oklahoma.

"Sorry forgot to introduce myself. Bill Trevors from Quantico Capital," said the first of the two young men.

The other added, "Collin Shepherd with Eagle Sky Investments."

The sweater vests and the conversation so far had already given them away, but this was clear confirmation of their profession. They were too sharp for their age and a little too aggressive in their tone and line of questioning – all telltale signs of a hedge fund analyst.

"You guys from up here?"

"I've been in New York for a while, but I'm originally from Houston. I worked at Tudor Pickering and then got a buy side job here five years ago. So I'm not completely a New Yorker, but I'm starting to finally feel like one,"

"Nice, dude! Tudor Pickering is a great shop. Love those guys. Collin, what about you?"

"I'm from Connecticut so I've been around New York all my life. I got into the M&A analyst program at Bank of America and started in the energy group. Before signing on with B of A, I couldn't tell you the difference between a vertical and a horizontal well. Anyways, after my three years there, I got an offer from Eagle Sky," answered Collin. "We manage about $5 billion in assets under management with a focus on energy, debt, and distressed arbs."

"Dude, I hear you on the vertical wells. I'm a VP now, and I still can't understand half the stuff the engineers are talking about," said Mark. "So, I gotta ask Bill, as a fellow Houstonian, who's your team now? Don't tell me that you've sold your soul to the Giants or God forbid the Patriots."

"Man, I didn't watch the NFL back in Houston, and I have even less of a reason to now. Can't stand those overpaid assholes. That, and the Texans suck. I don't even watch the Super Bowl – I'm serious. I'm a SEC guy for life and went to Vandy for undergrad."

"New England Patriots for life," added Collin.

"Oh jeez, a Patriot's fan…we better run for it," said Brent from the Choctaw Energy team. "We can't be associating with these types of people."

"Well at least he's got someone to watch the games with. Bill's gotta be the loneliest guy in New York on SEC game days," said Robert, downing the last of his Sam Adams.

"Not at all. There's a hard-core group of fans up here. Almost every team's got a different bar for the games. Hell, I walked into a bar full of Aggies the other day. They were screaming 'Gig em!' at the top of their lungs."

"I've seen some strange stuff in New York, but that about tops my list," said Mark, laughing. "Hey, what are you guys drinking? I'm about to catch that bartender. It's not all about networking you know. You need to get your priorities straight at these events and grab a refill."

"Sure, I'll go stand in the line with you and get something," said Bill.

The conversation descended deeper into the SEC and college football. Mark was again glad to get away from technical talk, but at the same time, he was beginning to drown in this conversation as well. As a West Coast guy, he had at best a first year freshman's understanding of SEC football – Bill practically had a PhD in the matter. In fact, Mark was astounded that somehow Bill Trevors had ever left the South. They must have made him one hell of an offer to come up here. Hedge funds with a need for energy sector coverage were always pulling talent from Houston and Dallas. While it is possible to create a homegrown energy analyst in New York City, there is nothing like recruiting straight from those energy capitals. In Houston and Dallas, half your friends work in the business, half your girlfriend's friends work in energy, and that's not even counting contacts and acquaintances. You're talking about energy at work and then again at happy hour. That's the sort of all-immersive experience that even a New York energy sweatshop can't replicate.

By the time Mark and Bill returned from the bar with Jack and Cokes in hand, the Choctaw Energy group had dispersed. They surveyed the room, looking for the next group to join across a room full of grey, dark blue, and black suits. Waiters toured the room with hors d'oeuvres of bacon wrapped quail and miniature crab cakes indulging the various groups. As the two stood sipping their drinks and making further small talk, Mark glanced at the nametag of a passing executive from PDC Energy.

"Hey Bill, I don't know if PDC is in Quantico's portfolio, but I just saw their CEO walk by. You wanna go talk to him?" asked Mark.

"We don't own them, but let's do it."

They approached a large group encircling PDC Energy's management team. This team was even more laid back than the Oklahoma City group. PDC was one of the key representatives of the Denver tribe of oil and gas. All the tribes were here: Houston, Dallas, Midland, OK City, Tulsa, Denver, and even Calgary, a strange tribe of its own. The PDC team wasn't laid back because of their city of origin but rather due to their confidence as a leader in the Denver-Julesburg Basin and the hundreds of wells under their belt. They were swarmed by buy-side and sell-side analysts which gave Mark and Bill space for only a few questions. This was fine by Mark who used the opportunity to meet a couple more analysts: two sell-siders from Morgan Stanley and GMP Securities and then three buy-siders from Algernon, Robeco, and Blue Crest Capital, and some juniors from Alliance-Bernstein. The sharks swarmed PDC Energy with detailed questions, and Mark circled the sharks, cordially introducing himself and slow playing his hand.

CHAPTER 19

NEW BEST FRIENDS

As the pack of fund analysts surrounding PDC Energy swelled, sub-groups began to splinter and form. The waiters pushed more plates overflowing with hors d'oeuvres on the growing crowd. Mark gladly partook from a tray and traveled from one sub-group to next in order to maximize his networking efforts. He continued to play the part of the good time banker motioning the bartenders to bring more drinks and tipping them heavily to keep the cups full for his new best friends. The cocktail party had turned into a parade of introductions and business card exchanges, and his success was measured by the weight of those cards in his jacket pocket. Only an hour and half into the night and he must have secured a stack of sixteen or seventeen cards, and he had likely handed out the same quantity. Thankfully, no "fellow" BNP Paribas bankers were spotted, although he did run into a Lazard oilfield services banker and a JP Morgan guy, which made him glad to have chosen the BNP Paribas persona instead of those banks. While he had carefully thought through the reasons for avoiding a JP

Morgan persona, Lazard, as a boutique, had been on his shortlist of potential banks to imitate. Fortunately, the other bankers had no interest in conversing with the competition and evaded any meaningful interaction with him. Furthermore, they had no interest in his hedge fund acquaintances who don't engage in mergers or capital raises. As a result, they didn't steal valuable face time with his targets. This nonchalant attitude from the other bankers played well for Mark; in comparison to them, Mark seemed even more like a swell guy to the hedge fund crowd. He was the banker who enjoyed talking with anyone, not just potential clients and sources of fees. As a tray of red wine glasses passed his current group, Mark grabbed two glasses and then two more, passing them around to the buy-side analysts near him. They toasted each other and took generous gulps.

After mingling around the party by himself, Bill Trevor eventually found his way back to Mark's latest audience of analysts and executives. "Hey Mark, are you going to the AllTrust after party? A bunch of us are about to head down there."

"Oh yeah, for sure, where's it at again?"

"McHale's on 51st and 8th"

"Alright cool, sounds good. I'll see you there." Mark finished his conversations politely and promised the executive team to be at their presentation tomorrow. He sent a text message to Robert and Lenny: *AllTrust after party, 51st and 8th, wanna come? :-P*. He discarded his empty wine glass on a white-clothed table already riddled with empty bottles and glassware and journeyed out onto the street. The night was alive and called him forth. The energy of this city radiated something altogether different than a night out in Houston. The whole place vibrated with a sense of ambition. Bankers and lawyers paced the street hectically even at this time of night, but it wasn't all business. Avant-garde fashionistas, dread-locked Jamaicans, and every other variety of human being in between shared the streets with the business crowd. Mark traveled briskly to McHale's. A text message came back from Lenny and Robert wishing him good luck. So far so good, but he was getting nervous. The alcohol in his veins was working its dark magic. While not quite drunk, the details of his cram sessions with Lenny were becoming blurry, and it was getting harder to talk about reserve-backed revolving credit facilities and acreage prices in the Midland Basin.

After traversing block after block, the entrance of the bar mysteriously appeared before him. As he hesitated on the street, his mind went over his approach to the conversations ahead, but what he really wanted to do was get out of this place. While he enjoyed the drinks and the sophisticated company, Mark would trade it all in a second for a beach, the sun, and his old surfboard. Instead, he was stuck in this ghastly and dark city. Mark swatted away those childish thoughts and got back to doing what needed to be done in this moment. The whole night he had taken a slow approach by building trust with his new acquaintances. Now was the time to finally spring his trap. A deep breath filled his lungs with city air, and he stepped through the bar entrance smiling and exuding banker confidence.

AllTrust Bank had booked half the bar and had set up four poker tables in the back. It was the equity research group's annual poker event. The tables were packed with players and another three dozen or so hedge fund analysts and company representatives were socializing around them. The attendants were definitely a younger crowd, most of them in their mid-thirties. The ties were gone, and some attendants had quickly changed in their hotel rooms to a preppy chic or hedge fund casual look. Everyone cradled drinks in hand, and some held a shot glass as well as mildly attractive hostesses in black dresses passed them out. Those who tried to turn them away were egged on by the hostesses' warm smiles. Mark grabbed a mysterious shot from the tray and ordered another drink from the bar. He spotted Bill Trevors and Collin Shepherd talking with a group of other buy-side analysts.

"Hey, what's up Bill?" said Mark, "Collin, good to see you gentlemen again."

His new best friends introduced him to the three other hedge fund analysts in the circle. The names of their funds were blurring together, especially in his current condition, and the loud music in the bar didn't make it any easier to hear them – as best as Mark could understand, they were from "Oak Something", "Zenitar Something or Another", and "Something Something Strategies".

As the last of the shots were distributed by the hostesses, a red-haired man in his late forties with a receding hairline stood up from the poker table and raised his shot glass. Mark Edwards had never had the pleasure of meeting Ned Donaldson of AllTrust Bank in person but his reputation preceded him, and his characteristic receding red hairline fit the description of the many stories. This could only be *the* Donaldson of AllTrust Bank. Ned was a legend in his own time, one of the most quick-witted and hard-drinking equity research analysts on the Street. Ned wasn't the best analyst or even in the top ten in his sector. In fact, from a purely technical perspective, he might have been among the worst analysts. His research reports, which arrived daily in the inboxes of various hedge funds, were poorly written pieces of electronic trash, but Ned could not care less. Complex Excel models and insightful research pieces were not his strong points. His gift was the profound ability to drink anyone under the table and to entertain until four in the morning. Ned couldn't tell you half of what any management team was doing with their acreage, but he could tell you exactly how confident the Director of Corporate Development was about his latest acquisition at 2:30 a.m. after a dozen drinks. Furthermore, he knew everyone on a social level. Even if he wasn't privy to deep insider secrets,

Ned could tell you personal details about every management team in the industry. Were they driven? Cautious or ambitious? How many hunting trips had they gone on this year? Were they hands on with their team or hands off? Had they just bought a new house? Were they going through a divorce and whose fault was it? If you wanted to understand the personalities behind the management team running an oil company, Ned Donaldson was your go-to guy. This was invaluable information to a hedge fund, much more so than a model assembled by a pimple-faced MIT math whiz. Sometimes betting on the jockey is more important than betting on the horse.

Mark stared in awe at Ned Donaldson as his voice silenced the room. With a shot glass in his hand, Ned held court over his adoring Wall Street audience as his voice boomed, "Everyone! Thank you for coming to the 7th Annual AllTrust Bank Poker Night. Drink up and here's to $90 dollars per barrel again!" Ned raised his glass. "Hey Bob, you don't have a shot! Waitress, please give Bob a shot – it's been a great year in the Permian Basin – he deserves it!" One of the hostesses rushed to get a shot to Bob, whoever he was. "Alright gentlemen, raise them up." Following Ned's lead, everyone did so, pouring the shots down their throats. "Have fun and try not to completely rob me at the table tonight!" Ned sat back down and resumed the game, quickly pushing a stack of chips into the center.

"Man, Ned is hilarious," commented Mark. "I can't believe that you can get paid for drinking and having a good time. He's kind of my hero."

"I know. We're in the wrong line of work," said Collin.

"Livin' the dream man…livin' the dream," added Mark.

From the casual start, the conversation turned to horizontal well bore lengths and the quality of acreage in various basins, with Bill leading the discussion. Mark had done a tour of the room, and noticed that Bill had stayed close by his side, which was sort of strange. His constant presence was almost too friendly. Sure, this was an oil and gas conference, but Bill had lived in New York City for a while. "Maybe he's gay or something," thought Mark to himself. "You know not that anything is wrong with that," he reminded himself. Whether accepting of his sexual preferences or not, Mark was beginning to feel a little uncomfortable. Perhaps Bill was just clinging to the only familiar face in the room, he reassured himself. That's not uncommon in these sorts of social situations. However, this didn't seem to be the case. Bill appeared to be socially adept and certainly didn't need a crutch in a crowded room.

The poker party was dying down and thinning as the night turned into the a.m. A last poker table battled for the title of champion, and the remaining attendants were well into a long and growing bar tab for AllTrust Bank. Bill called to the bartender, "Six more shots over here…Fireballs." The waitress brought the shots to Bill, Mark, and the other hedge fund analysts. Another beer also arrived in Mark's hands. Two slightly older analysts in their late thirties turned down the shots and began to say their goodbyes.

"Oh, come on guys," said Bill. They again refused the offering. The rest of the group pulled back the glasses and splashed their tonsils with a round of cinnamon fury. "OK, Mark. Since they turned them down, we gotta do their shots," yelled Bill, handing him another as the aftertaste of the previous round was just beginning to settle on his palette.

Mark was now certain that Bill was gay and was trying to get him drunk. Self-consciously, he began to consider why Bill was trying to make a move on him. Had he been a little too friendly all night? Despite his suspicions, they slammed the shots together.

"We're gonna take off, guys," responded the older analysts, not amused by these boyish antics. Everyone exchanged business cards, and they left for the door. Mark was quickly losing his audience. At some point, he needed to bring up the Newstar deal while anyone was still there. Secondly, they needed the capacity to remember him saying something about the deal.

"Let's grab one of these tables," said Bill to the remainder of the group. "So, Mark, you said that you cover the SCOOP and STACK. What do you think that I should do with my Continental position? Should I hold onto it?" asked Bill.

Mark was trying his best to come up with an answer. He loosened his tie and sunk into his chair. His cognitive abilities were beyond impaired at this point and those shots had been the final nail in the coffin. If he didn't start dropping hints about Newstar now, he might not be capable of doing it at all. This whole night could turn into a waste. Mark rambled about the SCOOP and STACK and was screwing up badly. He mixed up the Meramec landing zone with the Osage and might have even mentioned the Wolfcamp drilling interval, which was actually in Texas, not Oklahoma.

"Those are great points, Mark. I mean you are so right about the Osage. What do we really know about it? It's a complete mystery like you said. Right on," commented Bill.

Were his answers actually making sense or was Bill just being nice? Mark tried to organize his next point on the SCOOP and STACK.

"Collin, what do you think?" asked Bill. "What the hell should I do with my Continental position? Is it overvalued now?"

"We don't own anything in the STACK, but I've looked at it pretty closely," responded Collin. He then went into the technical details of the basin's production decline curves and the economics throughout the intervals and whether a 5% or 6% terminal decline was appropriate for financial modeling purposes. Collin then touched on well spacing in the Meramec and whether ten or sixteen wells per six hundred and forty acres was the way to go when calculating the net asset value of the play.

Mark, sipping a new drink, kept nodding and occasionally saying, “Yeah, yeah.” However, he was barely holding on.

Bill also nodded in approval, listening attentively to Collin’s commentary. “So Mark, what about that deal that you mentioned in the SCOOP and STACK, what kind of valuation per acre do you think that you’ll get there in comparison to Continental’s recent purchase?”

This was very awkward. Everyone at the table was half drunk or worse. Why were they talking shop instead of college football, or the waitresses, who had mysteriously become more attractive in the past hour and a half. Then, it finally clicked! Mark couldn’t believe it. How could he have been so stupid? Bill wasn’t gay at all. He was pushing those shots for this exact moment. While Mark was trying to play him, Bill was trying to get him drunk and talking about the SCOOP and STACK deal he had mentioned earlier in the night. They were two black widows in a match to the death. Mark knew exactly how to play this. Bill Trevors had unwittingly walked into a much thicker and more intricate web.

“Well, it’s not exactly the same acreage as Continental. So, it’s not an apples to apples comparison. The package is in upper Kingfisher County with a little pouring over into Garfield County.”

“Um…er hhhem...” Bill cleared his throat. “You mean Newstar,”

“No!” answered Mark, feigning surprise. There were only two companies with significant acreage in upper Kingfisher County and some in Garfield County. Newstar was hardly a guess. “I mean, I can’t say…it’s just a public company with acreage in northern Kingfisher County.”

“Newstar is the only public company that fits that description,” said Collin, absorbing the significance of Mark’s statement.

“Look guys, I’m not saying it’s Newstar. Just don’t mention it to anyone, OK,” pleaded Mark. “I’m not saying it’s Newstar.”

"Well, who else could it be?" remarked Bill rhetorically with a twinkle in his eye and a smirk.

"Dude, just don't say anything alright?" mumbled Mark.

"No problem, man, it's cool," said Bill.

"Yeah it's cool. I get it. Don't worry," added Collin.

Houston black widow wins.

After this exchange, Bill and Collin suddenly grew very tired and had to call it a night for some reason. Under normal circumstances, such an abrupt end to a previously engaging conversation would have left Mark feeling awkward, but tonight he was happy to cut it short. He was done with these two targets. He took a deep breath and looked around the room. Less than a dozen stragglers remained at the event, most of whom had had too much to drink. Perhaps this was his cue to make his return to the hotel as well. Mark checked his watch. It was late, and there was plenty more work to do tomorrow. He grabbed his jacket and made his way toward the exit. On his way, boisterous shouts from the poker table in the back turned his head. One of the last players at the table had just taken in a big pot of chips, and Ned Donaldson was cheering him on. Suddenly, an idea struck Mark. No, he couldn't do it… oh, but he could. What better target than the legend himself, Ned Donaldson? Mark commanded his body away from the exit and back toward the poker table using all of his willpower to drag himself there. Ned was closely watching the cards on the table and the last three competitors. "Hi, Ned, I wanted to introduce myself. My name is Mark Hollis from BNP Paribas. I've heard a lot about you, but I don't think that we've ever met. Thanks for putting this whole event together."

"Hey, no problem. Pleased to meet you, Mark. I'm glad that you're having a good time. Who do you think is gonna win between these three? The investor relations director from WildHorse or the two guys from Collins Petroleum?"

"I got my money on Collins Petroleum."

"Are you only saying that because you bank them or is that what you really think?" asked Ned jokingly.

"Heh, no we don't bank them at BNP. I just like the company. Would love to bank them."

"I hear ya," responded Ned. "So what do you do over at BNP?"

"M&A or A&D…however you want to say it."

"Working on anything interesting at the moment?"

"Oh you know this and that. I've got a mandate for something in the SCOOP and STACK at the moment," said Mark while purposefully swaying back and forth "Oh shit, look! The corp dev guy from Collins has two kings in the hole!"

"Nice job, Tim!" said Ned with a laugh. "Very nice job! Waitress, get this man a shot of Glenfiddich 15 year. I've got to reward Tim here and give WildHorse a better chance of getting ahead." Ned returned to the conversation, "Oh really? Are we talking Canadian or Kingfisher County?"

"Kingfisher with some overlap in Garfield," responded Mark as if he was saying nothing important. The same line had worked just minutes ago, why not give it another try.

"What like the Newstar acreage?" asked Ned confused.

"Something in that general area," mumbled Mark.

"You know…I know those guys pretty well, and I just don't think Herb Walters would sell, at least not for a few more years. That's what he told me about three weeks ago when I was on the road with him and the rest of the management team."

"Well shit, you know how it is with CEOs. They tell you one thing and before you know it, they're doing something completely different," responded Mark.

Ned gave a smile and pushed a hand through his thinning red hair. "You know Mark. Just a side thought here. I mean completely out of the blue and don't take this as an offense, but something about you doesn't strike me as a banker. Did you do something else before entering the business? Were you an engineer or a geologist or something like that from the technical side? I just don't know…something about you just doesn't tell me, 'banker'. And again, don't take it the wrong way. I don't mean that in a bad way."

Mark forced himself to take another sip of his drink. A million lies could get him out of this situation, but nonetheless, the question, straight out of nowhere, stunned him for a moment. Of all the things he was expecting to be asked, an attack on his credibility was not one of them. He needed to quickly make up some bullshit on the spot.

"No, I'm a banker...a banker at BNP Paribas." Jeez, could he have said anything dumber than that? During the night, he had fumbled various geologic terms and mixed up basins and intervals, but this feeble response topped them all. The room began to spin from the abundant alcohol in his blood stream as he contemplated this mistake. There was no longer a need to pretend severe inebriation, it was there – he was fully in character as an inebriated banker foolishly spewing trade secrets to whomever would listen.

Ned looked at him strangely, trying to make sense of the mixed signals and the weird expression on Mark's face. Ned Donaldson was a true professional, and Mark knew that he was out of his league here. While many fools considered Ned a terrible analyst and a cheap hustler, when it came to reading people, he was a social genius on par with an Einstein or a DaVinci. No longer on top of the food chain at this gathering, Mark was the one now in the leopard's cage. The leopard saw meat in front of him but questioned its scent. So, the leopard prodded some more before taking a bite. Ned switched the conversation to transaction comparables and acreage prices. Somewhere from the cerebral parts of his brain ingrained through rounds and rounds of Lenny's flashcards, Mark reflexively summoned a few numbers from memory. They seemed right. Ned prodded again, asking more specifics about the geology of northern Kingfisher County. Mark mumbled, guessed and tried his best to conjure a halfway intelligent response. Ned nodded but before he could speak the corporate development guy from Collins pulled in a massive pot of multi-colored chips. That was it! He was the champion of the 7th Annual AllTrust poker game. The celebration pulled Ned's attention back toward the table. Before returning to his hosting duties, he turned back to Mark, shaking his hand. "Mark, it was great meeting you. Thanks for filling me in on the STACK. It's always good to get a little color from the bankers behind the scenes. Give me a call sometime when you're back in Houston, and we'll catch up over a drink, OK?"

"Sounds good, Ned," replied Mark. "Thanks for the drinks and the great night, dude."

Mark said his farewells to a few of the remaining new acquaintances and staggered out of the bar. At least, he wasn't waking up early for the conference tomorrow. That was Lenny and Robert's job. As "Mark Hollis" departed the bar, Ned gazed in his direction and pondered this peculiar encounter. "Something was off about that guy," thought Ned to himself. "But then are a lot of strange guys on the Street. That aside, the tidbit on Newstar was magnificent." As soon as Ned awoke the next morning, he planned to dial a short list of his best hedge fund clients in exchange for what he knew would be hefty trading commissions. As usual, the event had been a success, with his clients happy and entertained, but it was the BNP Paribas banker's tip that would pay for the event tenfold. Business as usual – it was a successful game of poker.

CHAPTER 20

URBAN COWBOYS

Mark was passed out like a rock the following morning. Robert and Lenny assumed all went well, but were both sound asleep by the time their third compatriot had stumbled into the adjacent room. Robert examined himself in the mirror. His jacket was immaculately wrinkle-free, and his tie was properly aligned. Everything about his outfit was straight, neat, and obnoxiously perfect. Lenny was doing the same last minute check in the bathroom. Other than the deer-in-headlights expression on his face, everything was fine. They packed two handbags with pitchbooks, but did not overload them so as to avoid looking awkward or drawing attention.

The first stop on their mission was a presentation at the conference. They didn't even check the schedule to see who was speaking at that particular time, but instead judged the conference rooms by the number of attendants. After finding a rather crowded presentation hall, they entered and searched for open chairs. The room was filled with eager hedge fund analysts taking down notes on paper, laptops, and tablets. In addition, representatives of other companies in the oil and gas industry spied on their competition. Nearly every chair was taken, with only standing room in the back for overflow. Lenny found one open chair embarrassingly close to the speaker's podium at the front. Robert scanned the room for an opening and pounced on a seat vacated by a very large and fat hedge fund analyst well past his prime.

His knee bounced incessantly with stress throughout the presentation, his hands constantly playing with the free hotel pen and notepad on the table. After the presentation, he didn't even remember who had spoken and on what subject. As soon as the speaker rose from the podium, throngs of hedge fund analysts bolted to the breakout session room for the Q&A session. About half left their seats, which were shortly occupied by another round of analysts ready for the following company's presentation. Robert got up as well, leaving a pitchbook on the table intermixed with the various brochures provided by the conference. The next person to sit there would potentially take a peek. Lenny had done the same thing at his table near the front before the two reconvened together in the hallway.

"Hey, Lenny rather than go to the next presentation, I got another idea. What about giving them a little bathroom reading material? Someone might not touch a pitchbook in public, but the john is perfect. With no one to see you and nothing else to do, it's gotta be read."

"You are a genius, sir."

The two refilled their coffees at the drink stations near registration and scanned the lobby. They were primarily keeping an eye out for familiar faces as well as Wells Fargo bankers since their pitchbook was a forgery of the Wells format. In addition, they watched out for the rare possibility of someone from Luther Williams Energy. Before dropping each copy, they always made sure to check any potential danger around them. If a pitchbook fell into the hands of a Wells Fargo employee, things could hit the fan quick.

After dropping off a few more copies, they followed separate paths around the building on a routine search, mingling in the hallways outside presentations and closely examining nametags for "Wells Fargo" or "Luther Williams". After making their rounds, Robert and Lenny reconvened at the coffee station and exchanged notes. In total, the count was five Wells Fargo bankers so far. That was a lot for a short spin around the room. After pointing them out to each other, it would be easy enough to avoid them. However, it was impossible to know whether a dropped pitchbook would fall into the wrong hands.

That said, this was not the time to think about the worst-case scenario. It was time to get to work. First, they covered all the stalls in the bathrooms. Next, there were a couple of easy drop spots such as couches throughout the conference halls, the hotel bar, and a nearby Starbucks. Halfway through the day, the two returned to the Knickerbocker to reload on copies. Since the Sheraton itself was pretty well covered and there was a chance of overdoing it at the conference, they peppered a few nearby hotel lobbies on their way back.

Before depositing any further pitchbooks, they reviewed their previous drop spots at the Sheraton. Some of the books were still in their places while others had disappeared – hopefully into the hands of hedge fund analysts rather than housekeeping. In the spots with missing pitchbooks, Lenny and Robert refilled their traps. At this point, potential locations were running low, which led them to some sloppier deposit choices. A few were randomly discarded in the halls and a couple were placed at elevator landings and foyers. The Sheraton could not be any more canvassed, and it was time for a break. They had successfully transformed the hotel into a roach motel for hedge fund managers.

In the lobby, the two killed time checking their e-mails and stock prices. Oil was down 2%, ticker NST for Newstar was down 4%, and ticker

LWE for Luther Williams was down 5%. This price action was no surprise given that smaller leveraged companies typically moved twice what oil does in any direction. However, understanding the market movements didn't change the fact that their losses were piling up. Robert was not yet worried, but this was definitely not good. Even if their plan worked, the losses were still a problem. There was no point in Luther Williams spiking upward by 10% if the stock had slid by 12% in the days before that.

Suddenly, Robert felt a hand firmly grab his shoulder. He froze as the unfriendly grasp tightened. This was is it. How could they have been so stupid? They had put out too many copies; they should have been less sloppy with the hallways and couches. Too many people could have spotted them. So far, Lenny and Robert had counted seven or eight Wells Fargo bankers and junior analysts. That was way too many In light of those numbers, the right call would have been to scrap the whole operation. Absolute terror pulsated through his body and would not let him move. The expression on Lenny Lee's face only confirmed his worst fears. This was the end.

The unknown assailant pulled him closer and whispered harshly in his ear, "You fucking piece of shit. Didn't I tell you to never show your fucking face in this business again?" Robert was still scared shitless, but felt a moment of relief as the voice was familiar. He turned to see the glowing red face of Ronald Lufkin.

"Um Ron…sorry, I didn't know you were here."

"Now you fucking know," said Ron. He pulled on Robert's lanyard to read the nametag. "Who the fuck is Gemini Capital Management? Oh, don't worry. You don't have to tell me. I'll find out, and then I'm going to call your fucking boss and we're going to have a little chat about your employment history at Latham Schroeder Holt. What do you think of that you stupid little piece of shit!" His snarl then turned to Lenny and his nametag. "So, you work there too! Great, that will save me an extra phone call. I'm giving institutional sales a call tomorrow, and they're going to put me in touch with whoever is running Gemini. I'm about to ruin your fucking pathetic little lives."

"Um, sir," Lenny managed to get out. He was still fearful of Ron's wrath despite being away from Latham, Schroeder & Holt for months. It was a fear that would likely stay with Lenny into his old age given the abuse at the hands of Ron Lufkin. "We don't have a boss. Robert and I started our own fund. That's what Gemini Capital is."

"You gotta be fucking kidding me! You losers have your own fund? You couldn't even properly balance a model at Latham Schroeder. What are you investing, your mom's life savings, $50,000?" Sadly, Ron was not far from the truth.

"No, Ron, we've raised $25 million, and we're here to raise more funds."

"Bullshit," replied Ron. By now, Robert had escaped his grasp. "I'm gonna make sure that no one at this conference invests in your fund, not one cent. And, I'm going to talk to the IPCC about blacklisting you two losers. At only $25 million under management, which, by the way, is a totally made up fucking number, you guys aren't even supposed to here. You know what, I bet your whole fund is just made up. I bet what you're really doing up here is networking and passing out resumes. Mark my words – I am about to fuck your world in every orifice." Ron marched with determination toward the registration desk.

Robert and Lenny exchanged glances of sheer terror. Lenny sent an emergency text to Mark. *Ron is here! WTF!! He is trying to kick us out!!!!*

Oh shit! FML!!!! replied Mark. *Meet me at that Italian restaurant across the street.*

Robert and Lenny rapidly made their way to the exit before the registration desk could figure out what to do with them. They entered the restaurant to see Mark standing next to the bar, which was occupied by only a handful of businessmen.

"What the fuck, guys!" exclaimed Mark. "I was just on my way to the conference after waking up when I got your text. How did he see you?"

"I don't know, man," answered Robert. "He came out of nowhere!"

"Well, what do we do now?" asked Mark.

"Let's have a drink and lay low, then we'll go back in later," said Robert. "Ron will probably attend one presentation, network for a bit, and then call it a day. We know that lazy dipshit. We were the ones doing all of his work."

"But I think that you're safe to go back in. Ron didn't ask about you. So you should be cool, man," said Lenny. "Just be careful and keep an eye out."

"Fuck. I'll lay low with you guys for a bit. Let me order a coffee real quick. I still feel like crap after last night." Mark motioned to the waiter for his order.

"How did it go, anyway?" asked Lenny.

"Ah man, it was fucking awesome. Only problem is that I waited too long to start talking about Newstar so I didn't get that many confirmed hits. I'm going to circle up with a few contacts from last night. I gotta figure out where the party is tonight."

"Stay on top of it man, this isn't a vacation," said Lenny, louder than necessary as he was beginning to lose his cool with the stress of the situation.

"Whoa, chill man, I know. Don't worry about it, bro. You know, fuck this coffee. I better get back to it and grab a table at the conference lunch. Can't let a good networking opportunity pass me by. Good luck to you lads.

Text me if you can't make it back in." Mark slapped Lenny's back and put a five-dollar bill down on the bar top to pay for his coffee which hadn't yet arrived.

After Mark left, Robert had a scotch, and Lenny joined him. It seemed like he always had a drink in his hands these days to help calm the nerves for one reason or another. The scotch was the first drink of several, desperately needed to summon enough liquid courage to return to the conference. Robert would have much preferred to stay put for the rest of the day, but there was work to be done. After drink number three and multiple reassurances to Lenny, they stood up from their bar stools, which had grown increasingly comfortable. Before again entering through the revolving doors of the Sheraton, they laser-focused on the faces in the lobby to make sure the coast was clear.

"Sirs, excuse me," said a big, broad-shouldered security guard as he stepped in front of the young gentlemen entering the lobby. "Mr. McClure and Mr. Lee, you are being asked to leave the conference."

"We registered like anyone else. We have every right to be here," said Lenny defensively.

"Gentlemen, your registration fee has been reimbursed, but you are being kindly asked to leave the property immediately. We want to resolve this as discreetly as possible." The guard was about to place his hands on Robert, but the two decided to leave without further protest. As they retreated back to the Knickerbocker, Robert texted Mark. "You're on your own now. We got kicked out. Good luck man and be careful!"

"What the fuck? I can't believe this shit. Just when you think that you've gotten away from Ron," muttered Lenny as he paced back to their headquarters.

"I know, man. I know"

Back at the Knickerbocker, Lenny fired up their laptops and watched the market closely. This felt like banker detention. The trip was over for them. There were a few coffee shops left for pitchbooks drops, but honestly, the area was already more than well canvassed. They might as well start packing for Houston. The stock market was about to close for the day. "Hey Lenny, check this out: oil is still down 2%; Newstar is down 4%; and Luther Williams is down only 1%."

"Something has got to be pushing it up," said Lenny. "But it's too early to tell. After all, we only just handed out those pitchbooks this morning. Keep your fingers crossed."

The rest of the afternoon was spent moping around and occasionally raiding the minibar for peanuts and liquor bottles. By the evening, tiny Skyy Vodka bottles littered every corner of the hotel room, where they were tossed haphazardly in despair following each serving. This was the greatest city in America, yet all they could bring themselves to do was watch Bloomberg and crack open another mini bottle. With the taste of defeat and vodka still fresh on their tongues, nothing about New York City seemed exciting tonight.

Thankfully, Mark Hollis, Vice President at BNP Paribas, was doing better back at the IPCC. His newfound friends from the previous night all wanted him at tonight's events. He had nailed down the locations of several management dinners and after parties. His game plan was to touch base with as many acquaintances from the previous night as possible. While he didn't drop enough hints about Newstar then, the previous evening had still been time well spent, as his targets now trusted him even more. With today being the last major day of the conference, it was now or never. This would be his last shot to pull off the new strategy and prove himself to the team. As a result, Mark got drunker quicker and became much more blatant about the Newstar deal starting with the seven o'clock post-conference mixer. Mark felt no shame in playing the fool blurting out all sorts of details about the transaction. The hedge fund analysts were lapping it up. From the conference mixer at the Sheraton, the location quickly changed to yet another event held by BMO Capital Markets at a bar a few blocks over. Everyone was looser and livelier now that the main part of the conference was done, and the drinks were going down more rapidly and in larger quantities. Rather than a few stragglers left at the bar like the night before, the after party was still packed approaching midnight. This was almost too easy and almost too much fun.

In a few cases, he perhaps pushed his boundaries too far. At around 11:30 p.m., Mark took a few steps back from his conversation circle with a bunch of hedge fund guys to make a call. "Hey Leonard! Great, you're still at the office. Look, I'm going to need you to finish the model for project Xavier tonight. Run different scenarios at forty, fifty, and sixty dollars per barrel," yelled a clearly inebriated Mark above the boisterous bar crowd of analysts in the background. "Oh yeah and one more thing. See if Vinson and Elkins are done reviewing the purchase and sale agreement for the Newstar deal. It's supposed to be signed by next Friday so we can't wait on them any longer. We need that PSA finalized now!" He feigned a pause as he pretended to listen to answers from Lenny. "Alright, great Leonard, thank you! I don't want you guys to stay up all night working on this, but I do want it on my desk first thing tomorrow morning."

Mark turned back to the group of hedge fund analysts. "Damn first year analysts, you know how they are. You gotta stay right on top of them, or they're going to run out of the office the first minute you slip off to a conference," he said. The buy-siders chuckled and mentioned nothing about Newstar although everyone had heard Mark loud and clear. With his body barely responding to the wishes of this brain, Mark dragged himself over to the jukebox and loaded it full of 80s classics: Bon Jovi, Poison, and Bruce

Springsteen. He ordered a round of kamikazes for the group. The night was slowly but surely getting out of control. This was their second bar of the evening and given the group's energy level, it would not be the last. Mark loved this – it sure beat the hell out of being analyst at Latham, Schroder & Holt. It was even better than being the managing director. This was the life for him…

CHAPTER 21

AFTERMATH

Robert and Lenny awoke just before the market open, eagerly anticipating the day's first price action. Robert brushed his teeth in the bathroom while Lenny scrolled through his newsfeed. "Hey Robert, come check this out!"

Robert spit out the last of the toothpaste and rushed over to the computer. Ticker NST was up 3%, and LWE was up 2%. The price of crude oil was flat. Most other exploration and production stocks were flattish or half a percentage point in the red. A couple of other tickers were up in the 1% to 2% range, but not many. This wasn't a smoking gun, but it was a good sign. They packed the last of their luggage and checked the progress of the tickers practically every five minutes. The conference would still continue for another two days, however, the final days focused on private companies or bottom bucket publicly traded companies. Anyone who was anyone considered yesterday the "last day," which meant that it was time for them to head back to Houston.

"We better call the front desk to extend the checkout time. I don't think Mark is waking up anytime soon."

With the market turning in their favor, Mr. McClure and Mr. Lee decided to treat themselves and went to the Waldorf for breakfast, a century-old Street tradition. To start, it was the classic eggs benedict, always a wise decision. Newstar was up 3.5% and Luther Williams Energy reached toward 3%. In light of this progress, an order of mimosas arrived at their table. They sent a text message to Mark giving him the good news. There was no response.

To kill some time, they strolled through midtown Manhattan and walked past the monolithic lobbies of various corporate offices: Barclays, UBS, and Nomura. The grandeur of their tall windows, slick designs, and colorful abstract artwork on the walls surpassed anything in Houston. It was crazy to recall that just a few years ago these buildings were among the central characters in the worst recession since the Great Depression. Robert had still been in high school at the time and never felt the full sting of the crash, but he imagined now what it must have felt like for a regular New Yorker to walk in the shadow of these decadent displays of extreme luxury back then. As the financial system teetered on the brink of collapse, and multitudes of people lost everything they owned, these buildings faced the street as opulent and pristine as ever. Even though years had passed since the crash, hatred for the financial sector was still fresh in the public's mind and continued to simmer. And perhaps there was good reason for the animosity. After all, just look at what he and Lenny were doing to game the system. The Barclays building in particular brought these thoughts home. The two stared in awe at the same blue corporate colors on the outside walls that they had laboriously used to forge the Collins Petroleum pitchbooks. In Robert's small apartment, the investment banks of New York seemed so far away, but seeing the physical edifice of the Barclays building made their high stakes game feel much more real.

Their financial tourism next took them to Nasdaq and Morgan Stanley. The bright-eyed young financiers stared in awe at the lights shifting across the screens. Although they had struck out on their own, deep down they still wanted the prestige of venerable institutions like Morgan Stanley; however, they knew that their role in the finance would forever be somewhere on the edges. But then again, was their newfound place in the world of finance truly on the periphery of the business? Was it really so different from the bankers and brokers working inside those walls? During the financial crisis, the major banks purposefully sold dodgy financial products to their investors. Even after the crisis, blatant conflicts of interest still exist between clients and the banks. For example, equity research analysts write reports on companies while the investment banking division earns fees from those same clients. By no accident, the overwhelming majority of Wall Street research analysts have "Buy" ratings for their banking clients. In fact, nearly every company is Buy-rated or at worst Hold-rated. Even if a company isn't a current client of the bank, they are still a potential client, so why rub them the wrong way? Sell ratings are practically unseen. When boiled down to its root, the relationship is no different than stuffing white envelopes with cash in exchange for favorable ratings and research reports. In the 2008 crash, this exact problem played out with bond ratings when credit ratings agencies traded consulting fees for favorable ratings. While this type of activity has since been curbed in the bond market, it is alive and well in equities. Institutional investors and regulators both understand how this works, but not everyone is in on it. When a small-town financial advisor recommends a Buy-rated stock to the local dentist, guess who ends up holding the bag when the shares of the company go south? The small town dentist loses, but the investment banker and the bank, who helped that same company raise capital or do an M&A deal, keeps their multi-million dollar fees regardless of where the stock price trades.

This is the prestigious world of legal and "legitimate" finance, and it is hardly the only such game being played on Wall Street. There are plenty of other "respectable" and legal frauds in finance. Think of the financial advisors who place their clients in high-fee funds to earn greater commissions or encourage trading in and out of positions to rack up transaction fees. Or consider the fact that financial advisors do not even have a fiduciary duty to their clients – they are not bound to act in their clients' best interests. When new laws threatened to mandate fiduciary responsibilities for financial advisors, the industry fought tooth and nail to stop them.

And what of the investment banks who hire a politician to give an "insightful" thirty-minute speech for $250,000? What special insight warrants such a fee? While this is pure and simple bribery of the most ordinary type, it is perfectly legal. To add to the hypocrisy, society jails politicians accepting cash bribes in envelopes and praises those giving useless speeches for personal checks. In this twisted paradigm, one can be utterly corrupt without ever breaking a single law. And so Robert and Lenny did not feel particularly unjustified in taking their slice of the pie from a couple of hedge funds, even if their means were less than legal. And at the very least they were scamming hedge funds and not the general public. In some sense, you could even argue that the members of Gemini Capital were nobler than those laboring in the hallowed halls of the bulge bracket investment banks.

On their return to the hotel, Robert compulsively checked his phone. Luther Williams was up by 6%, and Newstar stood at a solid 4.5%. Everything else in market was stagnant or showing a small gain, around 1%. "Lenny, this isn't a coincidence anymore. I think we did it!"

Lenny sped to open his phone. "I can't believe it Robert – we fucking did it again." Lenny actually hopped in his stride as he shouted with joy. His eyes beamed with excitement behind his stylish black hipster glasses as they eagerly returned to the hotel to wake up Mark.

As they entered the room, they yelled, "Mark, we fucking did it! We did it!"

Lenny climbed on top of the bed and began jumping up and down. Mark raised his head from the pillow. "Huh? Whaaa?" His blond hair was a mess, pointing in every direction from the unfortunate mixture of rolling in bed and his hair gel from the previous night. His button-up white shirt was still on, and he reeked of smoke. His face glistened with traces of glitter all over it.

Robert laughed. "Someone went to ballet again. Either that or you were mugged by a leprechaun last night."

"Man, look at you," said Lenny, grabbing his phone and snapping a picture. "I'm putting this one in the company history section of the Gemini Capital website."

"Dude, shut the fuck up. I feel like shit." Mark grabbed an empty bottle of water next to him and threw it on the ground. He tried to clear his nostrils and rubbed his eyes. "Guys, leave me alone."

"Did you not hear us, bro? We did it! NST is up 4.5% and Luther Williams is up six!"

"Dude, I seriously don't fucking care right now!" Mark groaned as he reached for his phone. On his screen, an alert flashed the NST and LWE stock prices. Seeing the numbers for himself snapped him out of his stupor. "Oh fuck! And oil is flat, man. This is one hundred percent us!"

"We know!" yelled Lenny. "That's what we've been trying to tell you?"

"AHHAHAHAHAHAHAHAH!" screamed Mark as he jumped out of the bed and pounced around the room in excitement, "Yes, yes, YES, YESS, YESSSSSS!"

They all shouted in unison and exchanged far too many high fives, followed by strong pats on the back and then outright hugs.

"Hey," said Lenny. "I hate to burst everyone's bubble, but we gotta check out in thirty minutes."

"Take it easy dude, who gives a shit? What are you they gonna do? Charge us an extra $300 when we just made $75,000 and that's our profit for this morning alone?"

"Come on, guys. We still got all this stuff to do, like throw away the printer," retorted Lenny.

Once Mark got moving, he hastily assembled his belongings as if he was escaping the scene of a crime…which he was. He scrambled for a six-minute shower and was out of the bathroom sans his usually well-manicured banker hair. Despite his long night, Mark was now exploding with energy. In the taxi, he kept giving occasional high-fives to the team for no reason at all and exclaiming, "Fuck yeah!" By the time their taxi arrived at LaGuardia, LWE was back down to 4%, and Newstar was up only 2%. That was OK. The market tends to overshoot reactions to anything, especially in low-volume stocks. Judging by the chart and the high volume, someone, or perhaps multiple players, were trying to build a position. Throughout the rest of the day, whenever the prices descended down to a 3% or 4% gain, someone would start purchasing LWE shares again sending them back over 5%. Then the trading volume would calm down and the price would again slide only to repeat the process. The gyrations were not a big concern. The most important part of the equation was that the plan was working. They weren't going to sell their position quickly like last time.

Patience was key. This was about winning the war and not the battle. Day one was a victory, and they hoped it would continue in the weeks to come.

When they arrived at their gate, Robert suggested, “You know, why don’t we treat ourselves one more time on this trip. Let’s upgrade to first class. We made enough money, right?”

“Killer idea, Robert!” said Mark.

At boarding call, the team went to the front of the line ahead of the plebeians and ordered wine before the flight had even finished boarding. A few familiar faces from the conference passed them, but thankfully it was no one with whom they had spoken directly. The three were tired of pretending to be someone else for the past few days and dreaded the thought of carrying on the façade with a seatmate for the duration of the flight to Houston. The wine tasted sweeter as they watched a group of red-eyed and exhausted investment banking analysts and associates pile into coach. The passing analysts were talking about the layout for an upcoming pitchbook due next Friday. Hearing someone else suffer this drudgery rather than themselves was music to their ears. They were no longer those slaves to the bank and office – they had escaped, and handsomely so.

“Did you hear those guys?” said Mark while clinking Robert’s glass. “Oh, I am so glad to not be them, oh so glad!” Most of the plane had boarded, and the team awaited liftoff. The stewardess was about to close the door when a final passenger came rushing down the gate and onto the plane. To their dismay, the face was very familiar, and his ticket was almost certainly for first class. Their jaws dropped, yet given his hurry, Ronald Lufkin didn’t seem to notice his former analysts sitting at the front of the plane. Ron was dead tired and retreated to a seat about three rows back. His former analysts stared at him as he placed his bag in the overhead compartment and handed his jacket to the stewardess – they jerked away as he turned to sit down.

The plane soon took off and reached a cruising altitude. The stewardesses came down the aisle, promptly attending to the needs of the first class passengers. Their row was among the first served. After receiving a round of champagne, Mark asked the stewardess, "Excuse me ma'am, could you send a double shot of your best scotch to the man in D5? He's an old friend of ours."

"No problem sir," she replied and continued serving drinks to the other flyers. The three of them watched eagerly as the stewardess approached Ron's seat. They could see her reach over to hand him a drink. Ron warmly smiled at her. She then pointed over at his former analysts in the rows ahead. Lufkin's smile instantaneously transformed into a frown and his face turned into its characteristic red – the same shade it had been during the Wellco Solutions meeting in New Orleans. The three burst into laughter. Mark was cackling and rolling around in his seat. His seatmate stared at him in fright and confusion. Surrounded by potential clients in first class, Ron could say nothing, but Robert could see him mouthing, "You motherfuckers!"

For the rest of the flight, their laughter was mostly controlled but at random intervals, bursts of giggles and demands for more champagne would explode from their seats without warning. As soon as the plane landed, they literally ran out of the cabin with their carry-on baggage and only rested after enough distance had been put between them and Ron. It was not that Ron could really do anything to them, but it still seemed like the right thing to do given the circumstances.

****

Over the next few weeks, Gemini Capital slowly began exiting its positions. The first to go was Newstar, as Mark had mentioned a definite timeline of "next Friday" for a possible purchase and sale agreement to several of his targets. Over this time period, NST had risen approximately 13% while the rest of the market had moved less than 2%. After closing the position, Gemini Capital was $115,000 in the green. Mark had nailed it with Newstar, and best of all, he had fun doing it. He was more than thrilled at the prospect of repeating it, and if there had been a conference next week, Mark Edwards would have happily attended with a new potential acquisition. However, the newfound strategy could only have a limited run. As the oil and gas industry is very tight-knit, the fake identity would only work for so long. "Mark Hollis" had introduced himself to at least a quarter of the attendants in his networking blitz. Some of those would recognize him the next time around. Maybe, if properly spaced between conferences, he could do it again. Or perhaps, the next time, he would attend a West coast conference with slightly fewer familiar faces from New York. However, even if he succeeded in the same scheme a second time, it would be even tougher to do it a third time and probably impossible and downright dangerous on the fourth try. But they didn't need to worry about that for a while. The Newstar Exploration trade was a huge success, and they had plenty of cash to keep themselves well fed.

Despite their finance background, which preached diversification, the team plowed its profits back into energy stocks. In the following weeks, they spent their hours not creating fraudulent pitchbooks, but actually researching public equities for once. Part of the plan was to make Gemini Capital seem more legitimate for legal and tax purposes, and so they invested both in equities and call and put options. Of course, these option contracts never risked as much as their big wins, but nonetheless, the trades seemed similar enough to the Luther Williams and Newstar positions to be an effective smokescreen. Gemini couldn't have three huge winners on call options while the rest of the portfolio simply followed an index – the high risk and high reward payoffs had to seem like the fund's normal strategy. Otherwise, the stocks in the portfolio would seem like an obvious cover up.

From the outside looking in, their strategy was not much different from any leveraged special situations hedge fund.

While the team chose their picks to the best of their ability, whether they gained or lost on the trades didn't matter. Even a loss had value as it provided legitimacy for their wins. For a few weeks, Robert's apartment became a real active hedge fund. The team would drink craft beers at night and get into raging arguments on what to put in the Gemini portfolio. They even bought Collins Petroleum again. Hey, it was a good stock!

The run on Luther Williams had been even more amazing than Newstar, and Gemini began slowly unloading its position after three weeks. By the fourth week since the IPCC conference, the stock had risen 32%. The rumors on Wall Street had spread like wildfire. During the rise, the team was tempted to sell several times, and it took every measure of their willpower to keep them from doing so. After two more weeks, the stock price rose even higher, and they took a little more of their position off the table. Then, the run up flat-lined, and the share price began to decline. Seeing the writing on the wall, Gemini unloaded the last of its position.

After their final shares were settled, the trade netted a profit of approximately $535,000 in cash. Combined with the NST payoff, the IPCC trip had yielded around $650,000. Even the legal side of the portfolio was beating the market; the energy sector index was up 3% while their bets averaged a 4% gain. This hedge fund business wasn't so hard after all. However, the harder part would be getting the money out. Mark had no issues cashing in since Gemini was basically his personal brokerage account. He had already placed a down payment on a Tesla, but for everyone else, access to the funds was becoming a serious issue. Thankfully, their lifestyle, still in one-bedroom apartments, didn't necessitate large cash transfers. Nonetheless, eventually distributing a greater portion of the funds to Robert and Lenny could be far more complicated than creating fake pitchbooks on glossy paper.

CHAPTER 22

GARY GREENE

Gary Greene was at the end of his rope. His fiftieth birthday was within three months, but today, he already felt sixty-seven, beaten down by three decades of working on the Street. His hair was thinning and receding, but his depreciating physical appearance was only a part of the story. On the inside, he was withering at an even quicker pace. It had been a tough year for his portfolio at Acreage Reserve Partners. They were down 25%. When oil prices had declined to the high $70s per barrel last November, his fund doubled down on oil and gas stocks, predicting that this was the bottom. Oil prices were now in the low $50s, and 2015 was already a losing year for the portfolio. Worse yet, his fund was underperforming all the major energy indices, which put Gary's career in a very precarious situation. Despite working at Acreage Reserve for seven years, his tenure had no meaning. Every quarter was judged based on what was hunted and killed in those three months. If it wasn't enough to feed the fund, he didn't eat either. And

Gary hadn't eaten in several quarters. If this went on any longer, he was done for. Gary could see the writing on the wall.

Despite the rough start to the year, his confidence had returned in the past month just like in the old days. He could see it all coming back again, the big bonuses and the admiration of his peers. It had started at the IPCC conference, where he stumbled across a Wells Fargo pitchbook detailing the sale of Luther Williams Energy. This was the answer to all of his problems – it would make his year. Best of all, he literally just found the thing laying abandoned on a coffee table in the lobby of the Sheraton. No one could prove that his inside tip came from a friend or an insider. It was as if God himself had smiled down upon Gary Greene, welcoming his prodigal son back into the fold of successful portfolio managers. The day after the conference, Acreage Reserve Partners rolled millions into LWE and watched it begin spiking upward. Luther Williams was so illiquid that his position had to be grown slowly over time. He phoned several brokers, searching for bigger block trades, but with little luck. Over the next few weeks, Acreage Reserve patiently and steadily piled more funds into the stock, a little at a time. LWE kept rising, but not simply because of his trades. It was clear that others were actively buying as well. The leak had to be bigger than just him. LWE continued to move skyward despite the lack of any official press releases or company-related news. This only reaffirmed Gary's conviction of an imminent deal.

Within five weeks, Acreage Reserve Partners had accumulated 2.9% of Luther Williams' total shares. A week later, LWE peaked and then slowly but surely began to slide downward. Gary thought of selling at this point, given the gain in his position, but with the expected deal still unannounced, the shares could spike even higher at any moment. Instead, he saw it as a buying opportunity. The share price had retreated, yet the sale was still imminent. "Oh the suckers," thought Gary as his fund added more shares to the portfolio. By the time Luther Williams had dropped 25% from its relative peak, Acreage Reserve Partners owned 4.2% of the company. While slightly worrisome, Acreage Reserve was still about even on the trade. As one of LWE's top stockholders, his office even received an inbound call from the Director of Investor Relations at Luther Williams who was interested in meeting their new mysterious shareholder. Rarely did someone take such a large position in a company without first meeting the management team. This call was the first troubling sign that something was amiss. Why would a company on the verge of selling itself care about meeting a new sizeable shareholder? According to the pitchbook, the final bids should have likely come in sometime around last week.

Anxious over this conundrum, he stopped purchasing additional shares, but still had enough faith not to exit his position. But to his dismay, the stock continued its downward spiral with another 25% decline over several weeks. The LWE chart looked absurd. Within the period of about two months, the stock had shot skyward on no news whatsoever and had then plummeted steadily again without a publicly disclosed catalyst. The reality of his dire situation was becoming more apparent. This could be the position that finally sinks him. Even if he wanted to get out now, escaping a 4.2% ownership position in an illiquid stock would send the share price even lower, worsening his losses as he tried to offload the stock.

He wasn't quite ready to sell yet and still held out hope for an acquisition. Gary waited for the next quarterly earnings report which was over a month away. It was his last shot, as the company could potentially announce a sale alongside their quarterly results. Finally, the month had elapsed with sideways price action, leaving his position in much the same spot. In the minutes leading up to the release of the quarterly report, his knuckles were white with tension and anticipation. When the earnings report was finally released, there was nothing in it to save him. No sale, nor any other good news. And even worse, Luther Williams had missed consensus analyst estimates yet again and was bleeding cash. The stock was down 10% on the press release and another 4% the day afterward. Watching the screen, he sunk his face into his hands in despair. Gary couldn't bring himself to sell the position, but now, he was forced to. Acreage Reserve Partners began liquidating its position as methodically as it had been built, which sent the shares down further.

The financial loss wasn't the only damage. Gary had been telling everyone at Acreage Reserve that this would be his pick of the decade. He had played it up to the limit. As far as he was concerned there was no way for him to lose, given the discovery of the pitchbook and his "inside knowledge". But, here he was now, likely within days of being fired. Maybe, he could hold on until the end of the fourth quarter. Despite being well-paid over the years as a portfolio manager, he had saved almost nothing. And tonight, on Tuesday August 10th, he sat alone in his living room on the forty-second floor of a Manhattan sky rise with a bottle of thirty-year-old scotch and a .38 caliber pistol. He knew that he wouldn't kill himself tonight but maybe soon. He could at least give himself a week, maybe two. Gary cried. He screamed. He dug his nails into this scalp and took another swig of the scotch. There was just one more thing that might rescue him from this predicament. He knew that the following phone call was long overdue and likely too late, but he had to make it anyway. Gary opened the pitchbook to the contacts page and searched for the name of Will Stephens, the Managing Director at Wells Fargo. He probably hadn't talked to Will in decades, but they used to be close. At least as close as two associates can be working ninety hours per week at Goldman Sachs almost twenty-five years ago. He dialed the number.

"Hi Will! This is Gary Greene calling you. How is it going?" There was clearly a slight shakiness in his voice that the scotch could not obfuscate.

"Heya Gary. Haven't heard from you in ages. Are you still over at Acreage Reserve?"

"Yup, sure am. You know, things are going great It's been a tough year for energy, but we're pulling through and are staying afloat."

"That's great. You know it has been too long. We really should get together for lunch and talk about our old Goldman days."

"Oh yeah, that would be great Will, but you know, I wanted to call you about something very specific. It's something sort of strange that I wanted to ask you about."

"Um OK. What's going on, Gary?"

"Well, I was at the IPCC a couple of months back. And I found this pitchbook."

"Oh yeah, I was there too. Can't believe that we didn't run into each other, but I guess the conference just keeps getting bigger every year."

"Yeah, you're right, but about this pitchbook. So, it's one of yours for the Luther Williams deal."

"What do you mean, Gary?"

"It's one of your pitchbooks, a Wells Fargo pitchbook for the sale of Luther Williams Energy. I just found it sitting around the conference. It's good that I picked it up rather than someone else."

"I'm confused, Gary. We're not doing anything with Luther Williams Energy."

"Oh, come on Will. Don't fuck with me! How long have we known each other? I'm holding the pitchbook right here in front of me, and your name is on the contacts page as the lead managing director on the deal."

"Look, Gary, I'm really not trying to be difficult here. I'm not on the deal. I don't know what the hell you're talking about. If I was, I would let you know, old pal."

"Bullshit, man. I'm looking at it right here. Do you swear on your mother's grave that this isn't yours?" said Gary, his voice getting more irate as he took another gulp of scotch.

"Gary, calm down. I promise you that we're not working on a deal with Luther Williams. They never do any M&A deals with us. I promise, OK? They always do their deals with JP Morgan. Look at their last few transactions. JPM is the banker every single time."

"I just don't get it then. This pitchbook has to be fake or something. Someone is trying to trick the market."

"I don't know what to tell you other than it isn't ours. I'm still wrapping up a few things at the office here for a meeting tomorrow, but let's get together in a couple of weeks, OK?"

"Alright, good deal."

"You take care of yourself, Gary."

What a scumbag, thought Will Stephens to himself. He hadn't spoken with Gary in years and when he finally calls, it's to try to scam him out of inside information. He doesn't have a fake pitchbook. He probably heard a rumor on the Street and was trying to verify it. What an asshole.

As he hung up, Gary finished the rest of his glass. He was red-faced with anger. He had known Will long enough to know that his former colleague was not lying. To confirm, Gary searched online for the transaction history of Luther Williams Energy. Will was exactly right. Every single acreage transaction and capital raise was led by JP Morgan. Wells Fargo seemed to hardly ever do business with the company and only played a minor part on the credit facility. If anyone would get the final deal for the sale of the whole company, it would be JP Morgan without a doubt, not Wells Fargo. Someone had screwed him and screwed him very badly. This would probably be the end of his career, but in the morning, there was one more thing that Gary needed to do – a final hail Mary. His will to live returned, if only to catch the bastards that did this to him.

****

The next morning, Gary put in a call to Alex Sinovic, an investigator at the Securities and Exchange Commission. Alex had worked as an intern for Gary at a previous employer almost fifteen years ago. Gary had taken a liking to the kid and kept in touch with lunch meet-ups about once a year when Alex made it to New York from D.C. Alex Sinovic was a brilliant kid and would have done great in the hedge fund world. However, after the internship, his girlfriend received a job offer in D.C. He followed her and got a role at the SEC, given the lack of buy-side opportunities in the Beltway. The original plan was to work a year or two in D.C. and then cajole his girlfriend into returning back to New York City, but as soon as he settled in, there was no leaving. Life in the government sector was amazing. While the Wall Street guys thought they had it made, Alex was working a relatively zero-stress job while earning a six-figure paycheck. Despite the stationary job and being close to his forties, Alex's relaxed schedule allowed him to maintain an immaculate physique. He was tall, wiry yet muscular and wore fashionable dark glasses with short-cropped dark hair. His position at the SEC afforded him all the time in the world to enjoy his favorite hobbies, including pickup games of soccer and lacrosse, Civil War re-enactments (Alex always chose the Union side), hiking, and constant vacations around the country with his generous off days. In D.C., government employees are no sacrificial public servants working on shoestring budgets. This was the good life. Maybe, the job wasn't as prestigious as being a hedge fund analyst, but what fool would trade this life for that?

On the professional side of things, life was good also. The longer your tenure at the SEC, the higher your pay grade went, more or less regardless of performance. And the work was easy. Every year, they busted a couple dozen small time financial advisors on some sort of obvious scam. Usually, it was a poorly constructed Ponzi scheme that collapsed before it even got started, and sometimes it was just blatant theft from client accounts. But only rarely did they get the chance to take a run at a professional hedge fund, which is where the work actually got exciting. Alex craved more of this type of action, just to add a bit of excitement to his life. That's why he was so intrigued when his old mentor Gary called regarding the fraudulent pitchbook.

While he was thrilled to start working on the case, the situation put him in a conflicted position. It was clear what was really going on here. Gary had acted on the information, and he had likely lost big, as evidenced by the recent stock chart for Luther Williams Energy. While his former mentor was clearly breaking the law, it would be no problem to get him immunity. Nonetheless, this was still an uncomfortable position, but Alex was senior enough now to pull some strings and make it work. Forging pitchbooks was a completely unheard of scam. He hoped that the pitchbook was as good and professional as Gary had described over the phone. Busting this racket could put him on the map at the SEC. This was both an opportunity for recognition in a faceless bureaucracy and an escape from the boredom of his daily routine. Finally, he had a test worth flexing his intellectual muscles, which had atrophied with years at the agency.

Alex flew into LaGuardia and grabbed a taxi headed to a discreet and quiet restaurant. As the car traveled down the streets of Manhattan, he stared up at the skyscrapers, and the skyscrapers stared back down at him with displeasure. The buildings seemed so large, so powerful, and so out of the reach of his influence at the SEC. Chasing down big hedge funds was his dream, but he knew that the glamour of that chase came with a price. It would mean saying goodbye to the amenities of his comfortable life and rolling up his sleeves. He could forget about the hiking, the soccer meets, and all of his extracurricular hobbies. While ready to work, he also secretly prayed that the case would not take up that much time. After all, Gary was practically handing the case to him. No resources or leg work were spent so far, just one flight to New York and one hotel room on the government's dime.

At the restaurant, the two men exchanged smiles and handshakes, but underneath Gary's smile, Alex could see that the years and the market had worn down his old mentor. The Street had pummeled his spirit into submission. He was against the ropes and almost ready to fold. Gary handed over the pitchbook. Alex took plastic gloves from out of his side bag, put them on, and turned the front cover. "Sorry, Gary, I don't mean to be overly formal, but we're going to have to fingerprint this, and I gotta follow procedure. Don't worry. You're at no risk. I'll take care of everything."

"Thank you, Alex. I really mean it. You were always such a good kid back at the fund."

Alex flipped the pages and marveled at what he saw. This looked exactly like a Wells Fargo pitchbook. Even the numbers throughout were consistent. The level of detail was tremendous. The biggest giveaways in any sort of forgery scheme are the careless mistakes made by the scammers in comparison to real corporations. Phishing e-mails, for example, can often be identified simply by the ridiculous misspellings and sentence structure of Russian or Chinese hackers. This presentation had no such imperfections. "Gary, this is really something. And you said that you talked with Will Stephens, the managing director at Wells Fargo about this, and there is no such deal going on."

"That's correct."

"Incredible." After flipping through it, Alex produced a five-gallon Ziploc bag, placed the pitchbook inside, and wrote the date on the front of the bag. The waiter looked at them oddly as he approached the table and related the lunch specials.

Gary Greene recounted his story of discovering the pitchbook at the IPCC conference. He didn't incriminate himself and both of them pretended as if Gary was no partner to a crime here. Next, they went over the short conversation with Will Stephens, word for word. Gary stared at his phone on the table. LWE was down another 5% today. The low liquidity was compounding his losses. He bit into one of the scallops he had ordered. It tasted of nothing. With so much distress on his mind, even the taste of the delicacy would not register with his brain.

"So Alex, have you heard of this happening anywhere else with other deals?"

"Can't say that I have, Gary. This is a first and that's what makes it a big deal. I'm going to make this a top priority. We're going to find out who did this."

"Thanks, Alex, I know you can do it. You're a smart kid. You always were…you'll catch these guys. Do it for me will ya?"

"You got it, Gary. Don't worry about it."

Gary knew very little about the scam that had sealed his fate. There wasn't that much more to say, and so the conversation turned to more casual topics. Alex was now married with two kids. Time had flown by so fast. Gary was divorced with three kids, two of whom were in college. He didn't talk to them much. The Wall Street life tore him away from his family and had a lot to do with tearing it apart as well. His children were nearly strangers to him after years of long nights at the office. They wrapped up lunch and parted ways. Alex stopped at the SEC office in New York to deal with some administrative duties and spent the night at the airport hotel. He was eager to return to his desk in D.C. as soon as possible to begin working on the case.

CHAPTER 23

UNION STATION

Like every weekday at 8 o'clock, Alex Sinovic was on the Orange line train at the Vienna station about a fifteen-minute drive from his house in Fairfax, Virginia. While the life of a government employee afforded him many luxuries, a good commute was not one of them. Following fifteen minutes of snail's pace traffic and five more minutes navigating the oversized parking garage, he could look forward to another thirty minutes on the train to Union Station followed by a four-minute walk to the SEC office. Thankfully, as the first stop on the Orange line, finding a seat on the way into the city was easy, but on the train back, the passengers were packed like sardines until almost the final stop. Nonetheless, this morning, the train car was already crowded. Within a handful of stops it would be filled to capacity.

Instead of his usual morning reads, the free *Washington Examiner*, a financial newspaper, or the latest corporate thriller, Alex examined the pitchbook for probably the thirtieth time. The craftsmanship of the forgery was stunning. Only someone from the industry could have done this. Sure, there was the remote possibility that a skilled forger had copied the layout and design of a pitchbook perfectly, but that seemed unlikely. Still more telling was what he found upon carefully researching the pages behind the industry overview section. While Alex wasn't an expert in oil and gas, his research verified that the overview was up to date with the latest news and occurrences. Furthermore, the oil and gas lingo of "completions", "horizontals", and "spuds" in the pitchbook certainly seemed to be written by someone who knew their stuff. If the creators came from energy banking, as he suspected, the first place to begin the investigation was with fingerprints. During the FINRA registration process and as part of the licensing exams, all investment bankers and equity research analysts are fingerprinted before even being allowed to talk with their first client. If the maker of this pitchbook had ever worked for an investment bank, his or her prints would be in the system. It was a starting point.

The train went underground on its approach to D.C. By now, the car was stuffy as the passengers squeezed in tighter. There wasn't enough space to review the pitchbook any longer, so he tucked it away for safe-keeping from the crowd. After enduring the cramped conditions for a few more stations, the train halted at McPherson Square where the majority of the sharper suits departed for K Street. Everyone else, including Alex, disembarked the train at the following stop, Metro Center, and switched trains to every which direction in D.C. Alex briskly raced through the crowd to grab the Redline toward Union Station. After a very short ride, he arrived at his final destination and pushed his way toward the escalators, and more importantly, fresh air and sunlight. He passed beneath the station's enormous archways and Doric columns holding up statues gazing outward to Congress only a few blocks away. While the station and its surroundings on Capitol Hill were majestic and several tourists were already fawning over the grandeur this early morning, Alex didn't even notice the architecture anymore. He walked over to the SEC, a building adjacent to Union Station, and entered his drab office, hidden deep inside the building and far from the impressive, striking, and misleading edifice that presented its face to the outside world.

His first task was handing off the pitchbook to his secretary and ordering the fingerprints. If a few strings were pulled, maybe the fingerprints could get done within a reasonable timeframe. He gave her the number of a friend in forensics who might be able to speed up the process and hoped for the best.

At his desk, Alex flipped through a collection of business cards from hedge fund analysts. Over the years, he had developed friendships with quite a few contacts in New York, including from his own time as a hedge fund analyst. In most instances, his contacts and connections weren't used for anything overly serious but rather to ask questions about the inner workings of the financial sector. You can't be an expert in every part of the market from interest rate derivatives to futures contracts on soy beans and pork bellies. As a result, it was always helpful to know a contact who could explain specific market dynamics when internal sources were unavailable. To this end, he made a call list of several analysts among the bigger funds, only those managing over twenty billion. Analysts at these firms were practically the nerve center of the Street. They were connected to everyone and everything as their commission dollars made them first in line for the latest rumors floating around the brokerage houses and investment banks.

Alex dialed the first number. "Infinity Investments, how may I help you?"

"Hi there, could you transfer me to Matt Turner, extension 7527? This is Alex Sinovic calling from the Securities and Exchange Commission."

"No problem sir. Just wait one moment."

"Thank you," said Alex, before waiting several minutes to be connected.

"Matt Turner, Infinity Investments Energy Group"

"Hi there Matt. It's Alex Sinovic. Been a while since we talked."

There was a slight nervous pause and then Matt responded in an overly jovial way, pretending it never occurred, "Alex, yes, of course! I didn't recognize your voice for a second. How can I help you?"

"Hey Matt. Yeah, I know that it's been a while. Sorry for not calling to catch up earlier. Hope you're doing OK with everything happening with oil prices."

"The phone is still working, which is more than I can say for a lot of funds out there. As you probably know, we're a traditional long only fund with $60 billion in assets. It takes a lot to turn the ship when the winds start changing. Even if we decided to get out of oil and gas tomorrow, it would probably take us a year or two to finally do it."

"Good to hear you're hanging in there. From what I've heard in the business, not everyone has been so lucky. Well, to cut to the chase, I'm hunting down some rumors in the energy space, and I was hoping you could do me a favor and share anything you might have heard on the Street."

"Uhh… umm… yeah… yeah… definitely… uh, sure," responded Matt.

"Specifically, I'm looking for M&A rumors in the energy space. Have you heard anything? We're investigating some peculiar price action on a few stocks. Remember that this is all confidential and off the record. I'm just asking as one colleague to another, not as an SEC agent."

"Do you mean that strange price action on Noble Energy or WPX a few weeks ago?"

"No, no that's not it."

"I mean I wish that I could tell you something, but I really haven't heard anything. I don't know what else would come to mind."

"What about Luther Williams Energy?"

"Oh yeah. They did have some interesting price action lately, but it's a small stock. You know, I did actually hear something there about a possible takeout for Luther Williams."

"But you just said that you hadn't heard any rumors?"

"Yeah, of course. I thought you meant credible rumors. If you want to talk about every time this year that I've heard non-credible rumors of a potential acquisition, we'll be talking until the market closes. So, yes, I heard from someone that Luther Williams might be selling. Did I act on it? Absolutely not. I can have compliance send over our trade records and research notes right away if you want them."

"No, that's not necessary. Like I said, I'm not after Infinity Investments. I'm sorry if you misunderstood my intentions. I'm after some rogue group that pumped the Luther Williams stock and could be doing the same to others in the energy space."

"OK, cool. I'm sorry too. The way that you mentioned the rumor put me on the defensive as I'm sure you understand. I don't want to get Infinity Investments in trouble. We're all good Alex."

"No, problem. And to be clear, so far I've just been speaking as a colleague and friend, but I do have to ask one question in my role as a SEC agent and I need one hundred per cent confidentiality on this. And I mean confidentiality far beyond a typical non-disclosure agreement. I'm only asking a few contacts about this specific situation. So, if it comes back to me – I'm coming back to you."

"Oh man, do I want to hear this?" said Matt Turner with a chuckle.

"Oh, I think you do. So, this rogue group has been faking pitchbooks that illustrate impending acquisitions of public companies. They're immaculate. Had to be done by someone in the business. Have you heard of anything like this in the past year or so?"

"What the fuck, Alex! What the fuck did you just say to me, man?" muttered Matt incredulously.

"OK, I regret mentioning it already. I know this is wild stuff, but not a word!"

"Nnnnoooo, I've never heard of anything like that. I can't believe something like that even exists. How many times has this happened?"

"Look, I'm sorry Matt, I've already said too much. Thank you for your time. Don't ask anyone about this as it could jeopardize the investigation, but if you happen to hear anything, let me know right away." Alex then promptly hung up without even saying goodbye to solicify the seriousness of the matter. He made several more calls to other trusted industry sources. None of them had heard a whisper about the existence of such a deceptive trading strategy. In fact, like Matt Turner, most were stunned to consider the depth of this scam. Hopefully his questions had not triggered his own rumor mill, but if so, it still might mean stopping these frauds the next time they hit the conference circuit.

Unfortunately, these endless phone calls were part of the necessary drudgery of the job. Next, Agent Sinovic dialed Gary Greene to dig further into the details. At their lunch, the two had covered the pitchbook's discovery, but after a few days to think about the forged pitchbook in detail, he had a few more questions.

"Hey Gary, how you doing buddy?"

"Oh, I'm OK Alex, how is the case going? Have you found out anything?"

"Yeah, that's what I'm calling about. Would you mind if I recorded this conversation for the official record? I'm trying to nail down the timeline."

"Sure, Alex. Whatever helps," said Gary who sounded drained.

"Great, this is Agent Alex Sinovic beginning the recording with Gary Greene of Acreage Reserve Partners in regards to case number 873352. Let me start with the first question. Mr. Greene, when and where did you find the forged pitchbooks?"

"It was the IPCC oil and gas convention in New York City on April 5th. I was taking a break after the Concho Resources presentation at the couches outside the main presentation hall. I glanced over at a small table next to me and saw the pitchbook. I examined it for a minute and decided to take it for safe keeping."

"Thank you. And what time exactly was that, Mr. Greene?"

"Oh, I don't know. A little after lunch."

"Could you be more specific?

"Umm, yes let me look in my e-mail for the conference schedule," said Gary. For a minute, only typing was heard on the line. "Umm, here we are. The Concho Resources presentation ended at 1:30 p.m. eastern. So, I must have sat down on that couch five minutes after that."

"And had you noticed this pitchbook at this location earlier in the day?"

"Honestly, I had not sat in that couch up until that point. So, I couldn't say for certain whether I had passed the pitchbook previously. It's certainly possible."

"And Mr. Greene, could you describe the exact location of these couches?"

"Yes, they were right outside the main hall. So, you walked past the registration desk in the main lobby and then took a right down the hallway. There is an alcove with several couches and a few sofas on the opposite end of the corridor. This was the couch in the alcove."

"Thank you sir." Alex stopped the recorder. "Thanks Gary, I stopped recording. Apologies for the boring questions, but we had to get these details down. I've been reaching out to contacts and have found nothing so far, but then I had an idea. What if the Sheraton has security tapes of the conference? We could end this all right here."

"That's a great idea Alex. You were always a smart kid. Thank you so much again for doing this. You have no idea how much it means to me."

"Don't worry, Gary. I love being able to help out an old friend, but honestly, I'd want to bust these guys regardless of who was involved. Thanks again and I'll give you a call when I have something more substantial."

"Sounds good. Thanks, Alex."

Shortly after hanging up, Alex rang the Sheraton in New York. The operator tossed him around to the front desk, then a random security guard, and then the head of security. Finally, he was connected to someone with access to the hotel's video surveillance. The surveillance system manager explained the hotel's standard procedure for retaining surveillance footage. Alex explained back the inadequacy of such a procedure. The manager clarified that this was the Sheraton Hotel, not an international spy agency. Bested in this exchange by a lowly security guard, Alex hung up and moved on. Having that footage would have been a little too darn lucky…

CHAPTER 24

LUNCH IS NOT FOR WIMPS

After the exhausting phone calls, Alex stepped out of the office for a sandwich and to collect his thoughts. He purposefully chose a lunch spot several blocks away rather than Union Station, which had an extensive underground food court. The longer walk provided him more time to think. Also, lunch underground was the last thing on his mind after being cooped up in trains and offices all day. Besides, the weather was refreshing in the late summer. The line at the deli was excruciatingly long and ended with an uninspiring sandwich. While the lunch was bland, Alex's mind raced with excitement as he thought of more angles on the case. He couldn't wait to see the suspects sitting across the table from him, but given the evidence so far, that goal was still far away. Throwing his sandwich wrapper into the trash, he eagerly exited the deli to enjoy the pleasant weather again, even if only for the short distance to the office.

On his walk back, Alex called Danny, his junior analyst, and instructed him to get in touch with a mergers and acquisitions analyst on the Wells

Fargo deal team. It was best for the juniors on both sides to have the first exchange. His hope was to find out from a low-level Wells Fargo employee whether Luther Williams was a client or not. His goal was to get the case moving as soon as possible without becoming entangled in the massive bureaucracy associated with this kind of casework. In financial crime cases, the paperwork was always a nightmare, but when it came to requesting information from a major bank, you were basically asking for a mountain of lawyers to get involved in the process. While a formal inquiry would be needed at a later date, for now, all he needed was a simple "yes or no" answer. If Danny could cajole a Wells Fargo analyst into giving away that much, it would be enough to double check Will Stephens' claim and confirm the pitchbook as a fake.

With a sigh, Alex sat back down at his desk and once again lifted up his phone to continue his lonely crusade, this time with a call to the International Petroleum Convention and Conference. Thankfully, after a short conversation, it took surprisingly little convincing to get a list of attendees and their registrations. Alex thanked them for their time and arranged for a short meeting at their D.C. offices later in the week as their lobbying arm was only a short skip from his office. The registration list would cut down the potential list of suspects by thousands. Alex's original idea was to narrow down FINRA license holders to a small group with an energy background and the psychological profile of the culprit. The problem was that even this smaller grouping would have been excessively large. The IPCC registration, however, only had a couple of hundred names – his suspect or suspects were on here somewhere. Whether the names were aliases or not was an altogether different question. Nonetheless, this was a solid starting point. To shorten the list further, he also requested the attendee lists for the past ten years. By comparing the latest attendees with previous years, perhaps an anomaly would make itself apparent. Likely, the management teams and reputable investment funds in attendance for a decade were not his suspects. The profile for his target was someone new, hungry and scrappy who had been to the conference perhaps only once or twice – someone who was trying to stay below the radar. With a small enough list, his junior SEC analysts could cross reference the trading records of the suspicious outliers. With some effort, the list of several hundred attendants could be trimmed down to a couple dozen potential suspects. That process would take forever, but it was something. Hopefully, a better clue would present itself before turning to these painstaking lengths.

Alex's junior analyst, Danny, knocked on his door.

"Come in."

"Hi Alex. I talked with an analyst at Wells Fargo," stated Danny with this eyes darting towards the floor. "And it didn't go so well."

"Oh, jeez. What happened?"

"Well, I called and tried to ease into the conversation just like you taught me, a little bit of small talk and industry conversation. And then, I told him that I was calling from the SEC investigation unit and inquired about Luther Williams. After that, the tone of the conversation completely changed. I got rerouted to the compliance department which then notified the legal department. And then I got a long speech about client confidentially and non-disclosure agreements."

"Oh, boy. That's OK Danny. It's not your fault. It's amazing the hoops we have to jump through for simple, 'yes' or 'no' answers. How long did they say it would take for us to talk with legal?"

"Well, we have to make a formal information request and from there it would be a few weeks."

"Damn it. Well, I guess there's nothing we can do for now. I'll catch up with you later. Just close the door on the way out."

"Thanks Alex. And I'm sorry again about this."

The door clicked shut. Alex knew that, sadly for the investigation, the Wells Fargo analyst had made the correct decision from the bank's point of view. When the SEC calls your bank, the right move is to escalate the request to compliance – it is not to wing it and tell them whatever they want to know, even if the requested information seems innocuous. A slow army of SEC lawyers would resolve this with time, but for now, Wells Fargo was another dead end. Alex turned his attention to knocking out some administrative work and filings. It had been a long day with few tangible results. At 4:30 p.m., he packed his bags, headed for the metro, and prepared himself for the overstuffed metro ride home. This investigation was not going quite as smoothly as he had first hoped…

****

Several days later, the fingerprints arrived to the office, which was almost record time. During the wait, Alex had distracted himself with a few other cases, mostly small town financial advisors. When the prints arrived, he immediately shut all other open files on his desktop and dropped everything to examine the results. Based on the analysis, Gary Greene's prints were all over the thing, but there were five other prints on the front cover. And those prints belonged to a Robert McClure of Houston, who until recently had been registered with FINRA as an Investment Banking Analyst at Latham, Schroeder & Holt. The FINRA profile for Robert McClure on the BrokerCheck website was incredibly short. With only a year at Latham, Schroeder & Holt and a business degree from the University of Texas, Mr. McClure had much less experience than Alex would have expected for someone who could pull off a crime like this. Was this actually his man? Or was McClure just some rookie analyst who had picked up the pitchbook at the conference and, unlike Gary Greene, had been smart enough to put it back where he found it? Whatever the explanation for the fingerprints, Robert McClure was the SEC's only lead at this point.

Alex immediately set Danny and the rest of the junior staff to reviewing Robert's trades as well as those of family and close associates. The team also cross-referenced the IPCC attendee list. Almost instantly, they discovered Robert McClure among the attendants registered under "Gemini Capital Management", a fund which did not exist according to the SEC's registration filings. More importantly than this curious fact, additional potential conspirators, Mark Edwards and Lenny Lee, had also registered under the same fund name. According to their FINRA registration timeline, Edwards and Lee had been on the same team at Latham, Schroeder & Holt as Robert McClure. Even more strangely, all three had resigned on the exact same date. Alex didn't know what to make of that, but it was odd to say the least, and it connected the three even prior to Gemini Capital. Perhaps there had been a disciplinary event at Latham, Schroeder & Holt, yet no such event was recorded on the BrokerCheck network, which is specifically designed to warehouse a history of these types of incidents. What only days earlier seemed like a case fated to rest in an unloved cabinet somewhere within the SEC's offices was now coming into shape.

After further investigation, it didn't take long to discover Mark Edwards' trades in LWE call options which stood out like a sore thumb. The size of the open interest had been considerable for the thinly traded position. Mr. Edwards' recent trades included short-term call options on LWE, NST, and CPO and only recent purchases which would appear to be a more rounded energy portfolio. Wells Fargo had not yet responded to his inquiry regarding Luther Williams, but this was enough to get the wheels rolling on the investigation, and Alex did not want to wait any longer. This information was practically a smoking gun. What else could he ask for? He finished filing the paperwork for the search warrants and sent it to the judge. He ordered Danny to schedule interviews with Robert McClure and his associates for later in the week and booked flights to Houston for himself and two other senior agents who would assist in the search and seizure of files and documents. He could hardly wait to get there.

****

On the morning of his flight to Houston, Alex arrived early to the airport and picked up a breakfast croissant from one of the vendors. The bread was stale and the strange pale yellow substance, claiming to be eggs, did not entice the appetite. After two bites, he decided to play it safe and wait for lunch in Houston. He opened the *Wall Street Journal* and scanned the cover stories. Nothing out of the ordinary. The market looked like it was in good shape. Occasionally, he had busted a few financial advisors with the story ending up on page ten of the *WSJ*. Maybe this case would be big enough to get his team closer to page one. It all depended on the true size of the Gemini Capital scam. The public jumps on the stories with the most zeroes on it. Unfortunately, that was the single thing missing here. McClure and his gang seemed to be only making miniscule trades in the big scheme of things. If billion-dollar hedge funds had been using their pitchbooks in this way, it would easily make the headlines. However, it would be harder to prove who those actors were. Alex imagined what Robert McClure, Mark Edwards, and Lenny Lee would look like... almost certainly a bunch of slick-haired and well-heeled hedge fund types. He wondered what they might be like beneath their outer shell. What was motivating them? What has to happen to a group of analysts to go rogue like this?

Agent Sinovic browsed his text messages and responded to a friend organizing a pickup game of lacrosse with some buddies. His wife had sent him a couple of messages and a few work e-mails kept him occupied to pass the time. He also phoned Gary Green briefly to let him know the chase was on. This trip would be a nice escape from the office. Houston wasn't an elegant destination, but it was still a chance to escape the staid predictability of DC. He searched the internet for some fun activities while in the city.

Perhaps, he could stop by the Menil Collection – could be interesting. Other than the tense interviews ahead, his goal was to make the trip as enjoyable as possible. Alex stared down at his phone. Only twenty more minutes to boarding time.

****

As Alex Sinovic boarded the plane at Reagan National Airport, Gary Greene's day in New York couldn't have been more different. He was in the middle of being fired. Today, Gary didn't review the *Wall Street Journal* or *Bloomberg News*. None of that mattered to him anymore. His termination came with a pitiful severance, enough to widen the eyes of most people on Main Street but nothing by Wall Street standards. Shortly after his departure from the office, his positions were being taken over by the junior analysts at Acreage Reserve Partners with orders to liquidate the last of the LWE holdings among other unfavorable tickers. After receiving his notice, Gary spent a few hours drinking overpriced beer with his head buried beneath the glass, not even looking up at the bartender to order another. He wandered the streets aimlessly looking for a sign, for something to guide his way forward in all of this. The thought of seeing his family came to mind but vanished upon realizing the impossibility of that. He briefly thought about Alex and his trip to Houston. According to his old friend, the SEC was close to catching these guys, but even that thought gave him no pleasure. It didn't fix his current predicament. It did not give him his life back, his entire career. Tired to the bone and to the heart of his existence, Gary eventually returned in misery to his condo. He did not shoot himself that night with his .38 revolver. He jumped from the window of his forty-second story apartment onto the pavement.

CHAPTER 25

TIME TO PAY THE PIPER

Mark was adjusting the new 75-inch TV screen on the wall of his apartment. The box had just arrived that day and the packaging lay strewn about the floor. It was one of the many newfound toys which now littered the small space, including two full-sized arcade games: Pac Man and Street Fighter II. His furnishings had also been upgraded to white leather couches and a $5,000 sleek modernist table as the centerpiece to the room. Although Mark had no problem spending his new wealth, it was becoming more difficult to withdraw money from his account and then anonymously re-deposit the cash into Robert's and Lenny's accounts without triggering anti-money laundering limits. While their expenses were minimal – rent, student loan payments, and a few new purchases to reward themselves – things still added up quickly. There had to be a better way of redistributing the cash.

Lenny got to work finding a solution, and soon enough, Gemini Capital Management was born as an actual entity, a legal hedge fund. They had spent the past few weeks meeting with lawyers and filling out paperwork.

As their filings had to be immaculate, no expense was spared on lawyers. To further legitimize the legal entity, the team searched for real, physical office space. On this, they budgeted carefully, given their still-modest means in the big picture of things. Thankfully, the Galleria had plenty of well-located office buildings from the 1980s. At one time, these monoliths were on the cutting edge of office design, but were now worn down and dated, bleeding clients both due to their age and the decline in oil prices. After an extensive search, Gemini Capital found its new home in a small office with a central reception area and three individual rooms on the fifth floor of one such unloved building. The office came equipped with furniture which had seen better days to say the least. Despite its poor condition, the used furniture gave them one less thing to worry about, and anyway, Gemini Capital wasn't exactly worried about impressing potential clients like most hedge funds – they had no real clients. The view, barely above the ground, stared squarely at the roof of a giant corporate apartment block across the street. While lacking the niceties of their former offices at Latham, Schroder & Holt, the lease was, most importantly, dirt-cheap.

Lenny and Robert worked out the logistics and lease contracts. The printers and scanners were transferred from Robert's apartment, and they continued to use their current laptops until the new ones arrived in the mail. Lenny encouraged them to visit as many sketchy websites as they wanted since these computers would soon be scrapped anyway.

Mark filled in the organizational gaps, which meant purchasing a ping-pong table for the reception area, a kegerator, a large fridge for other beer options, several futuristic lounge chairs, and a giant pillow for the newest addition to the team, Rusty, a golden retriever pup bought the previous week. The dog was the finishing touch – you weren't a successful hedge fund until you had a dog in the office. Lenny had wondered if Rusty's addition was too soon and a little presumptuous, but was soon won over, and the team welcomed the new rambunctious member of the Gemini pack. In addition, each office had TVs mounted to the walls with yet another 75-inch in the reception area. When not tuned to ESPN, each screened blared the latest *Bloomberg* news. Along with the aesthetics and the animal companion, the tech side of their operation also needed an upgrade. Lenny ordered four computer panel screens for each of their desks – two more than their setup at Latham, Schroeder & Holt – matching the same functionality of any major hedge fund or bank. With the overhead TVs and the new four-panel screens, their office soon resembled a miniature trading floor.

Robert was carrying the new screens across the floor of the office when his phone began to buzz wildly in his pocket. He placed the boxes on top of the desk and checked his phone to see a strange 202 area code. "Probably just an automated telemarketer," thought Robert as he let it ring out. To his surprise, the phone beeped, indicating a voicemail. Telemarketers don't usually leave voicemails.

Mark's phone then started to vibrate as well. "Hey Mark, it's your phone."

By the time Mark had walked over to it, the phone had stopped ringing. "Huh, strange. Washington D.C. number," said Mark.

A voicemail was again left behind. With only the slightest sense of disquiet, Robert lifted his phone to his ear and listened to his message. "Hello, this Alex Sinovic, agent with the Securities Exchange Commission Enforcement Division. I'm coming into Houston next Tuesday and wanted to talk with you about Gemini Capital Management. Please give me a call back at 202-555-3758 so that we can schedule a convenient time."

"Fuck," said Robert.

"What is it dude?" Mark asked anxiously.

Robert played the message again but on speaker this time for everyone to hear. Mark turned pale and checked his voicemail, hoping that it was different, but it was not. Lenny seemed to be on verge of crying. "Oh God, what are we going to do?" said Lenny. "We're in deep shit." As those words left his mouth, his phone also began to ring with the same D.C. number flashing on the screen.

He reached to answer it as Mark yelled, "Dude, don't fucking touch that thing."

"Chill out for a second, guys," said Robert, trying to calm the group. "What could they know? Maybe they just think there were irregularities in our trading? I mean our positions were pretty big. Let's not jump to conclusions yet. It's possible that they don't know anything about the pitchbooks."

"But why did we all get the phone call?" asked Lenny. "Mark was the only one trading from his account up until we formally registered Gemini. How are they tying us together?"

"We did all register as Gemini Capital at the IPCC," noted Robert. "But I don't see how that makes us guilty of anything. We gotta play this smart. We can't get too worked up. First thing we do is call our law firm. Let's get them to sit with us during the SEC interview."

"Well, what other choice do we have?" said Lenny.

In many ways, the timing of the SEC visit could not have been better, all things considered. By setting up the hedge fund entity, they were already clients of a securities law firm and had a mostly professional office. If this phone call had come a few weeks earlier, the three of them would have had to do the SEC interview in Robert's apartment unassisted by legal counsel. At least now their office was legitimate, with the right legal papers, a pay roll, and a law firm to back them up.

Lenny sat down heavily in one of the new lounge chairs and buried his face in his hands. "Who's going to call them?" said his muffled voice. Rusty jumped up beside him and began to lick Lenny's hands and Lenny flinched with surprise.

"I'll call," said Robert. "I just… need a little space."

He took his phone, went to the bathroom, and locked the door behind him. Robert leaned against the bathroom door for a moment before dialing their law firm, Watkins & Watkins.

"Robert," said Skip Mathewson, their attorney, when he finally got through. "What can I do for you?" Doing his best to sound casual, Robert outlined the voicemail from Agent Sinovic. On the other end of the line, Skip listened patiently before advising them not to worry too much about it. "Sure, it's a little strange," said Skip, absentmindedly tapping his pen against his desk. "But it's likely just something to do with the hedge fund registration process – purely routine."

Skip was confident in the accuracy of their filings; however, it was possible that the SEC found the transfer of assets from Mark's personal account to the new hedge fund entity troublesome. Robert hoped so. Even with attorney client privilege, he didn't feel comfortable telling Skip about the pitchbooks. Nor could they disclose the truth regarding the Collins Petroleum, Luther Williams Energy, and Newstar trades. Robert mentioned to Skip that the leveraged bets could seem irregular to the SEC. However, he emphasized that their trades were based on hundreds of hours of research and that Gemini Capital wasn't going to apologize for their hard work and success.

"Nor should you," said Skip. "All the same send over your trade records to us and we'll do our own due diligence. We'll play a little devil's advocate in case this comes up so we've got our bases covered. Take care now Robert, and don't get too concerned about this."

According to Watkins & Watkins' independent evaluation, there was absolutely nothing abnormal about the trades other than their size. The purchase and sale dates were never close to any significant press releases or events. This fact alone would make an insider trading case almost impossible. Even the Collins Petroleum purchase right before the Bloomberg announcement wasn't proof of anything. Sure, it was very lucky, but the announcement wasn't an official release. Ultimately, the Bloomberg release proved to be a false rumor, further invalidating any claim of insider trading. Unless some kind of collusion between Bloomberg and Gemini Capital could be proved, nothing could link their clients to wrongdoings. That said, similar cases had actually occurred in the past where brokers were caught trading ahead of news stories written by friends at major financial publications. While this sort of conspiracy potentially could explain the Collins trade, it did not fit the Luther Williams or Newstar trades.

Gemini Capital's buy and sell orders were spectacularly successful almost without rhyme or reason. By all accounts, their success could only be explained by amazing timing and nothing else. Skip had originally thought his clients were punk rich kids playing hedge fund, but after studying their trade records, he reached a newfound respect for them. And as his research dug deeper, Skip couldn't help but admire their skill. When this interview was over, he would ask Mark about investing in the fund. They were young but obviously very talented. He called Alex Sinovic to schedule a meeting for the following Tuesday at Gemini Capital Management's offices.

After speaking to Skip, Alex stood up from his desk and anxiously walked a circle around his drab office, his excitement about the case building. He had worked cases against Watkins & Watkins in the past. It was a fierce and venerable institution. On the downside, litigation against a sophisticated securities law firm could become a long, drawn-out process. Even when caught absolutely red-handed, it often took the SEC years from discovery to actually putting the crooks behind bars. That was going to be the tough part. However, on the upside, the presence of Watkins & Watkins potentially signified something else. The firm was far too high-powered for a simple hedge fund registration, especially for a new fund with almost no assets under management. Gemini Capital could have easily gone through the registration process with a much cheaper rate. Why Watkins & Watkins? Something was going on here for sure….

****

On the day of the SEC agents' arrival, nothing got done at the office. The appointment at 2 p.m. left the members of Gemini Capital Management worrying about the interview the entire morning. From his appearance, Lenny had only managed a few hours of sleep last night, if any. Robert and Mark didn't look much better. They said little to each other throughout the day, and all secretly hoped that this was truly an interview regarding the hedge fund's registration process.

Lenny had told himself that he would get work done in the morning despite the looming meeting ahead. The portfolio's positions still needed a review and the financial news did not stop for their interview. Despite his best laid plans, anxiety won the battle and not a single minute was spent on any productive task. Bloomberg news was open on his desktop and was turned on the TVs in the office, but Lenny read nothing and paid no attention. Instead, he flipped through Facebook and burned time aimlessly clicking through his friends' pictures, stopping most often on those friends from Rice University who were still in banking and doing quite well for themselves. Everyone puts their best life forward on social media instead of reality; still, surely none of his former classmates were harboring secrets like Gemini Capital. The morning passed minute by excruciating minute until lunchtime, which came and went with no fanfare.

Skip Mathewson showed up an hour and a half before the SEC to give them some preparatory remarks beyond what they had already discussed in the days leading up to the meeting. Skip reassured them that everything would be fine. His clients' serious and somber mood was a bit perplexing. Perhaps they were just inexperienced kids who simply didn't know any better and any interactions with the SEC, however harmless, scared the daylights out of them. To him, they seemed to be taking this much too seriously. Sure, no one likes being interviewed by the SEC, but there was nothing really to fear.

Alex Sinovic arrived in their office exactly on time with two agents accompanying him. His agents knocked on the door, which Skip volunteered to open as they clearly did not have a receptionist. The government employees were from a different world. Alex's suit was nothing impressive but adequate, likely a purchase from Macy's, and it had seen years of use. As a government employee, there wasn't anyone to impress, inside the office or out. A sharp suit was pointless, even though he could easily afford a better one. The two agents with Alex similarly wore plain black outfits of even shabbier quality. Mark, Lenny, and Robert were in their Sid Mashburn suits but with no ties. Mark wore large aviator sunglasses. Their goal was to avoid looking too formal or concerned, but the sunglasses were perhaps a bit much. Robert sent him a couple of distasteful glances toward Mark, but could not gauge his reaction behind the shades. The only one with a tie and the sharpest of the group was Skip who had shown up fully suited with a very stylish and professional briefcase. In his early fifties with a stocky frame and a slowly receding hairline, he looked the part of the elder statesman of financial law in this room. Mark welcomed Alex into the office with a calm and casual smile. "Hi, Mark Edwards, welcome. Would you like something to drink?"

"Sure, a water would be great?"

Mark crossed the room to grab a water from the fridge which had been installed only days before. As the fridge opened, Alex spotted row after gleaming row of beer bottles. At least the agents wouldn't see the freezer, which was packed with chilled bottles of Belvedere. Alex scanned the room along with the other agents who raised an eyebrow at the ping-pong table, the arcade machines relocated from Mark's apartment, and of course, the kegerator. Robert tried to play it down, noticing the attention garnered by their furnishings. "We don't really use those much you know. We're much too busy most of the time."

At that moment, Rusty, the golden retriever pup, came romping from his bed in Mark's office and ran circles around the team before retreating to Mark's side. "Heh, yeah, we have Rusty here as well You know that's pretty normal for a lot of hedge fund offices," said Robert. "He's kind of our mascot."

The two agents exchanged quizzical glances and fought the urge to roll their eyes. While there were plenty of comforts to working at the SEC, an in-office kegerator and dog were not on the list of agency benefits. The group sat at a small hand-me-down conference table crammed into the side of the reception area. Alex introduced himself around the table and last to Skip before asking, "Why the lawyer, guys? We haven't even started talking, and things are so formal already."

Robert was about to answer, but Skip cut him off. "My clients have hired Watkins & Watkins to help register and incorporate Gemini Capital Management. Watkins & Watkins provides turnkey services to our clients as part of the registration process which includes our participation in this interview. We hope that our assistance will help both our clients and your agency in resolving any registration issues in an efficient and expedient manner."

"Very well," said Alex. "So, let's start with some basics. When did Gemini Capital Management begin?"

Robert answered, "Well, we knew each other from Latham, Schroeder & Holt where we were all analysts on the mergers and acquisitions team, and…"

Skip cut him off again. "Gemini Capital Management filed its paperwork on August fourteenth, 2015. This is the first date of the inception, and my clients did not manage any client funds other than their own prior to August fourteenth."

Alex was starting to see that this was going to be difficult, but he wasn't concerned. This wasn't his first stare down with a skilled attorney. Furthermore, in his briefcase was the Luther Williams pitchbook, his big surprise for these kids. The current discussion was only the warm up round. "So gentlemen, the three of you worked at Latham Schroeder & Holt until March 2015, correct?"

"Yes, that's correct," answered Robert.

"And is this an error in the FINRA records or did you all resign at the same time from Latham Schroeder?"

"No, that is not an error."

"And, what is the reason for resigning on the same date?"

"Well, this project didn't come together at once. We had been researching investments for months leading up to our resignation. As I'm sure that you can tell from our trading records, we bought call options on Collins Petroleum while we were still analysts at Latham Schroeder. When we saw the initial success of our strategy, we decided that it was time to step away from the firm, but it was something which was a long time in the works."

"Hmmmm. And by 'we', you really mean, Mark Edwards here?" said Alex, pointing to the man with the shades.

"Yes, correct. Mark managed the portfolio from his account, but our investment decisions were made together."

Skip's eyes went wide, and he was ready to jump into the conversation, but Alex stopped him. "It's OK, Mr. Mathewson. Managing the assets of multiple individuals from a single retail account is technically a minor offense, as I'm sure you know, but that's not why I'm here today. Now, let me ask, how did your employer take all of this? Certainly, having three analysts suddenly leave put the firm in a tough position, am I right?"

"I agree with you Agent Sinovic that perhaps it is unusual to leave a job in this manner," responded Robert. "And perhaps it was not the best way to treat an employer or our own future career prospects. Nonetheless, the opportunity which we saw with our trading strategy was worth pursuing, even if it meant burning a few bridges. We couldn't continue to put in eighty hours a week at Latham Schroeder while also researching our own trades, and we were forced to make a very difficult decision."

"Interesting. Would you mind if I talked to your former supervisor, Ronald Lufkin?"

"No, not at all."

Lenny glanced over at Robert nervously.

"OK, thanks. Now on the subject of the timing of your trades, could you walk me through your last few transactions? I have the dates of each trade here in front of me."

"Sure, that's no problem," said Robert, growing more nervous as this was clearly moving in the direction of trades rather than the fund registration process.

"As you noted, Gemini Capital Management's first trade, or should I say Mark Edward's first trade, was just ten days prior to your resignation. Could you explain the timing of that transaction and why it was done with call options, and why the options were sold so quickly?"

"Oh, yeah dude," said Mark, feigning confidence.

Lenny looked at him, annoyed, and took over the conversation before Mark could continue. "Like Robert just said. We didn't have the capital or time to diversify. As a result, we placed our bets on our best idea after spending weeks analyzing Collins Petroleum," said Lenny nervously. "However, we sold out of the position given our good, uh, fortune with the *Bloomberg* news acquisition announcement. Were it not for the, uh, announcement, we would have held the position much longer as we felt, uh…the stock was considerably undervalued. But, with the run-up in the price after the *Bloomberg* news story, it made sense to exit the position after the spike in value."

"Coincidental timing wasn't it?"

Robert uttered sternly, "Yes, it was very fortunate timing for us, especially as a first trade, but we are not willing to apologize for our success. We thought the security was undervalued, and it made complete sense that someone would bid for the assets as *Bloomberg* news reported. Just like everyone else, we had no clue that the story was not credible. After all, *Bloomberg* is a highly reputable news source. Could you elucidate what you're getting at here?"

Alex Sinovic changed the subject. "And what about the other trades, Luther Williams Energy and Newstar Exploration? You entered into these a week before the IPCC conference. Can you explain the logic for those trades and the subsequent quick exits to both investments?"

"After leaving Latham Schroeder, we had more time to research our own investments, and we zeroed in on two companies. Per our energy and special situations strategy, we saw Luther Williams as an opportunity to buy an extremely distressed equity that had underlying strong assets despite a weak management team. Newstar similarly had key acreage in the emerging SCOOP and STACK play which had experienced considerable consolidation from major players such as Devon Energy and Newfield. We always look for undervalued assets which the market fails to appreciate," said Robert.

"That all makes sense as a strategy, but why sell out of the positions so quickly?" asked Alex.

"Why not?" replied Mark as he took a sip of water from the glass on the table. "Our position was in the money, and we decided to take a profit. It's basic trading. Buy low and sell high."

"But, why use leveraged call options yet again?"

"I admit that options are riskier than equity. However, we knew that if Gemini Capital was going to make a splash in the business and attract new investors, we had to show a few more big wins. As a young team, I'm sure that you can understand how it can be more difficult to attract investors to our fund. So, we wanted to let our results speak for themselves."

"Also, Agent Sinovic," added Lenny, "you'll notice that our portfolio today is much more diversified as our assets under management have grown. Since we've achieved a significant track record for the year, we don't need to use options as aggressively anymore, although they do continue to be a part of our long-term special situations strategy."

"Alright…well, what about those other Gemini investors? Who are they, and how is your marketing of the fund coming along?"

"The fund currently has no other investors, and no investors were solicited prior to the fund's official registration," answered Skip.

Skip's response gave the Gemini team a reprieve from the stress that was causing them to trip over their own words. Letting someone else talk even for a short while gave them a much-needed break in this interview, which had quickly transformed into an interrogation. They would happily pay any sort of legal fee if Skip could handle the rest of this thing himself, but this they knew was not possible. Agent Sinovic smiled slightly, giving nothing away, his next question already prepared.

"You were all in attendance at the IPCC conference about four months ago, correct?"

"Yes," Robert answered. "All three of us were there. It's the biggest energy conference of the year. We wouldn't miss it for the world."

"And as I understand, the three of you were no longer working at Latham Schroeder & Holt at this point, correct?"

"That's correct."

Alex wrote on a notepad as they answered the questions. "And under what name did you register at the conference?"

"Gemini Capital Management," said Lenny. Mark grew increasingly nervous, and despite saying little so far, he became visibly unsettled and fidgety in his seat.

"Right, that's what I thought, but let me get this straight. You registered at the conference as Gemini Capital Management three months before it was registered with FINRA and the SEC. So, you were basically lying to the IPCC about your identity."

Skip stepped in again. "Look, I don't know where this line of questioning is leading, Alex. While my clients may have registered for an industry conference under the Gemini name, doing so is not a financial crime nor a violation of securities law. If the IPCC has an issue with our registration or would like to file charges for this innocent and educational conference attendance, then we can have that conversation. These are three very talented young fund managers, and they have violated no SEC rules or regulations here."

"I disagree," said Alex, his demeanor turning suddenly cold. "Did you solicit clients as an unregistered investment advisor at the IPCC?"

Skip was taken aback. He knew that Alex could actually get them on this point, and worse yet, he still had no clue where this was all going.

"No sir," said Robert. "We were there to see company presentations and hear about the latest events in the industry, just like everyone else."

"I find that hard to believe. You guys have a brand new hedge fund which is very low on assets under management; you're at the biggest energy conference of the year; and you didn't solicit any investors at the conference? Do you expect us to believe that?"

Skip jumped in before his clients could reply and answered sternly. "Alex, as we just discussed. The fund has no investors other than the three gentlemen in front of you. My clients have said that they did not solicit any investors and over four months after the conference, they still have no investors in the fund. If they did solicit investors, they were certainly unsuccessful in doing so."

"Damn, Skip is good!" Robert thought to himself. "We picked the right guy."

"What do your clients have to say about this?" Alex reached into his bag and took out a large five-gallon evidence Ziploc bag containing the pitchbook. Skip stared at it in confusion. Everyone else felt not confusion but fear jolt through their bodies. Their hearts collectively pounded in their chests. Lenny's eyes were getting teary.

Robert tried his best to play stupid. "I don't know what that is."

Alex proceeded to take the pitchbook out of the Ziploc bag and flipped to a few key pages. "As you can see, this is a pitchbook found at the IPCC conference for the divestiture of Luther Williams Energy."

"I had no clue that they were selling the company. That's fascinating, but I don't understand what this has to do with us," stated Robert. "This is a Wells Fargo pitchbook. We used to work for Latham Schroeder & Holt.

If you have questions about Latham Schroeder, we could definitely help you out."

"Sure you can help, Mr. McClure. We found your fingerprints on this pitchbook. You do remember having your fingerprints taken for your FINRA registration and the Series 79 test, right?" Alex tossed a photocopy of the prints across the table.

Up until this point, everything had gone so well. For every push by Alex, their answers pushed back almost perfectly without incriminating themselves. All of a sudden, the tables had turned – they felt like trapped animals who only now realized the cage was already around them. Sheer panic went across their faces which no preparation for this interview could hide. The gears in Robert's brain began working on all cylinders to find a solution for their predicament. What could he say now? Even under the most stressful of times at Latham, Schroeder & Holt, his body had never felt sheer terror like this.

Yet, there was still hope. There was one more card to play here. As Robert gazed at the photocopies of the smudged fingerprints on the outside of the pitchbook, he spoke. "So, which one of these fingerprints are mine exactly?"

"We identified yours on the front cover of the pitchbook."

"So, that doesn't mean that I opened the pitchbook, right? I probably just found it on a seat and pushed it aside. It doesn't prove that I saw the contents of the pitchbook," replied Robert.

"It also doesn't mean that you didn't," Alex jabbed back. "And, since your fingerprints are the only ones on here and no one else's other than our informant, we're sitting here and talking today."

"This is all very coincidental," said Skip. "Did you fly all the way down here to harass my clients over circumstantial evidence?" Skip was frightened as this was heading in a very strange and unexpected direction, but he had a duty to protect his clients. His complete ignorance of the truth made his defense sound that much more authentic, and he was personally glad to not know the truth at this very moment.

"No, I did not, Skip," said Alex. "Were Gemini Capital's call options on Luther Williams coincidental as well?"

"Are you implying that we got inside information from this pitchbook?" said Robert. "If you look at our trading records, we entered into our LWE position a full week ahead of the conference. Also, we've been out of the position. If we had inside information about an asset sale, wouldn't we still be holding onto the call options. I'm sorry to disappoint you Alex, but this just isn't adding up."

"No, that's not it," replied Alex as he paused to assess the situation before making his next revelation. "I don't think Wells Fargo created this pitchbook. I think the three of you made a fake pitchbook in order to manipulate the market. Your fingerprints and those of our informant are the only ones on the pitchbook. You registered at the conference under an illegitimate fund name, and as you pointed out in detail, Gemini Capital was not there to solicit clients for your new fund. So, what were you doing there? Let's be honest now."

"A fake pitchbook? You gotta be kidding me? That's crazy," chuckled Mark.

Skip was in a state of shock. What had started as an administrative proceeding was spiraling deeper and deeper into something much more concerning and sinister. "Alex, I think that it's time for my clients to end this interview until they can receive further legal counsel. Thank you for your time."

"I'm afraid that it's not over, Skip," said Alex with a broadening smile. He was beginning to enjoy this. He reached into his side bag again and pulled out a stack of papers. "This is a search warrant for the premises as well as the personal residences of Mark Edwards, Lenny Lee, and Robert McClure."

Lenny buried his face in his hands. The two SEC agents, who up until this point had said nothing, began to stand and make their way to Robert's computer. "Thanks guys, yes, start with that one." The computers were brand new and had arrived yesterday morning. However, the burners were still in their apartments and were very hot with the files used to create the Luther Williams pitchbooks. While they would not be found right away, it was only a matter of hours until their discovery.

Skip frantically turned the pages of the search warrant, attempting to find the smallest inconsistency to invalidate it. This was hardly his specialty in law, but he knew enough to be dangerous. A voluminous amount of law literature and case precedents exist for just this sort of situation. A hundred technical reasons could throw out a poorly written search warrant. Unfortunately for Skip, page after page, there was nothing to help him strike the warrant. It appeared absolutely air tight. His quiet afternoon was rapidly turning into pure horror.

Lenny couldn't even process the situation before him. His mind was a million miles away thinking about what his strict, proud Asian parents would do to him after finding out about this. Their reaction was more frightening than jail time.

"We're going to need your cell phones as well," added Alex.

Mark looked around the room…at his ping-pong table, at the kegerator, and at Rusty's big puppy eyes staring back at him expecting a ball to be thrown across the room at any second. It would all be gone. Everything that they had built. He just wanted to soak it up one last time while it was all still theirs. It had been a good dream.

In his despair, Robert thought of the embarrassment of explaining this to his dad. The worst part is that it wasn't a simple confession such as telling your dad that you broke a window with a ball. His father didn't understand the first thing about banking or capital markets or hedge funds. To him, the SEC was an agency about as far away as the planet Mars. Robert would have to describe it all step by step which would make things only more painful. There was nothing else to do now.

He laid his phone down on the table. Lenny and Mark did the same. As one of the agents reached over to sweep them, Robert's ear faintly caught a familiar word from the TV screen in the reception area turned to Bloomberg news. "Wait! Hold on!" The confused agents stopped in their tracks. "Did they just mention Luther Williams on the news?" Robert paced toward the remote on another table and turned up the volume, but before the sound was even on, the banner at the bottom of the screen flashed: "LUTHER WILLIAMS ENERGY ANNOUNCES SALE OF COMPANY TO CONCHO RESOURCES".

Robert smiled. "Lenny, check your inbox. Is this real?"

The Bloomberg newscaster announced, "Just released on the wire Luther Williams Energy is to be sold to Concho Resources for $2.1 billion. This is another transaction on the tail of other red-hot deals in the Permian Basin of Texas. While oil prices in the sector remain subdued, this has not stopped consolidation of acreage in the area. Up next, we'll cover a preview of tomorrow's Fed minutes and what investors need to expect."

Lenny scrolled through his inbox and said with elation, "Found it! The official press release came out from Concho Resources almost thirty minutes ago. The deal is for $2.1 billion with $1.0 billion in stock and $1.1 billion in cash. The anticipated close date is October thirty-first."

Robert traversed across the room to see the release himself on Lenny's phone and then tossed it over to Alex Sinovic. "Here you go, Alex…read this." Alex perused the news and turned ghost white.

Robert proclaimed out loud, "Well, I guess that disproves your fake pitchbook theory, doesn't it?"

Mark exploded with laughter like a pressure gauge snapping off a pipe. Skip glanced at this unexpected reaction and tried to return the conversation to a professional level. He stood up and firmly strode over to the two agents, who had already packed one of the computers. "Please cease your activities. Your warrant is no longer valid. Under the law, your search warrant is based on false assumptions and stale information. If you would like to continue your search, please do so without legal consent, and we will strike this warrant down in a court of law along with all the gathered evidence." The two agents stopped in their tracks and waited for direction from Alex.

Agent Sinovic paused to think and motioned them to return to the table. "You aren't out of the woods yet. Let's check to see who was the financial advisor on the deal. If it isn't Wells Fargo, you are still in deep shit. I'm going to make a quick call to a Federal judge and our D.C. office and we'll get this resolved momentarily." Alex forcefully opened front the door and exited the office into the hall as his agents stayed behind staring down their suspects. So far, he had managed to hide the extent of his anger, but in the privacy of the hallway, his face twisted with frustration as he searched the press release on his phone. Sometimes, transaction advisors were disclosed toward the end of acquisition press releases. However, about half the time, they were not. This was ultimately a coin flip.

On the other side of the door, the three former analysts also searched their phones in desperation for the transaction advisors paragraph or the lack thereof. Robert silently prayed in his head as he read the release, pleading to a higher authority that the financial advisors were not disclosed. Maybe all those long mornings at church throughout his childhood would somehow payoff in this crucial moment. He wasn't exactly sure how praying could change a public press release, but he continued doing so nonetheless. With a head start, Robert reached the end of the press release first. Lenny and Mark didn't need to read any further given the look on his face…a big smile.

No financial advisors cited.

By now, Sinovic had realized the same, but remained in the hall. While the former analysts were quietly ecstatic, they were still unsure if this was enough to halt the investigation. The passing minutes felt like running out the clock in the final moments of a football game. Even the seconds seemed to last forever. Team Gemini was winning, but they were still within distance of a trick play which could turn it all around again for the SEC's side. Their knuckles were clenched white with anticipation as they awaited Agent Sinovic's return. Robert had ceased his prayers only to resume them again. Lenny seemed to be on the verge of a nervous breakdown, and Mark got up from his chair and began pacing around the room, followed by Rusty, who seemed perplexed by his master's peculiar behavior.

In the hallway, Alex was ready to punch a hole through the wall. He walked further down to avoid the others hearing his conversation, which might be held in an elevated tone. There was still a chance that the agents could go through with the warrant today. His first call was directed to the investor relations department of Luther Williams Energy to verify the financial advisor on the transaction. Such information was not material to the transaction, and as a result, investor relations could share it freely. After about twenty rings, Alex couldn't get through. This was not surprising in the slightest given the momentous corporate announcement. He left a message, but there was no telling when investor relations would get back to him.

His next call was to his offices at the SEC and the legal department to advise him on the matter. In perfect government fashion, no one wanted to take responsibility. Each lawyer that discussed the issue with him gave a similar response, "on the one hand this and on the other hand that". Even after reaching nearly the top of the legal department, he still couldn't get a concise answer or a green light to move forward. At this point, he had been out in the hall a full twenty-five minutes making calls back and forth with the legal team and had no progress to show for it.

Alex couldn't be certain that Wells Fargo wasn't the advisor on the deal. Furthermore, even if Wells Fargo was not on the deal, it was certainly possible that the bank was hired first but then another advisor was brought on later after a failed deal, sort of like switching real estate agents. This wasn't extremely likely, but it was possible. Nothing short of a call back from a managing director at Wells Fargo could give him complete certainty. Meanwhile, Skip was right about the new revelation. There was enough reasonable doubt to invalidate the search warrant. Going forward was too great a risk. The clear-cut case behind the warrant had fallen apart in minutes and proceeding any further could potentially jeopardize the case even more. This wasn't the end, but it was enough to stop Sinovic and his agents today. He firmly clenched his phone, ready to smash it into a thousand pieces on the floor and waited a moment for the oxygen to return to his head before walking back into Gemini's office.

As he entered through the door, the punk kids sweating profusely looked guilty as hell and Sinovic knew it. He was angry at them, but even more at himself for dropping the ball. He should have been more patient and just followed procedure, even though the case seemed open and shut. The only thing that the agents could do now was return to D.C. and take this through the proper channels, only now his targets would know he was coming for them. Alex didn't even look in the direction of the three analysts and Skip. He barked orders at his agents to collect the bar codes from the laptops to prove no obstruction of justice should the computers mysteriously disappear on their next trip. Skip objected, but despite his counsel, Gemini Capital happily provided the information. After all, it was the laptops at Robert's apartment that would disappear. As the agents collected the barcodes, Sinovic passed the time by examining his e-mail and occasionally sending glances of burning hatred toward the analysts, particularly Robert. The government agents then finally left the office with their tails tucked between their legs. Sinovic promised himself that this wouldn't be the final say on the matter, but for today, he had been defeated by a bunch of kids almost twenty years his junior. It stung.

As the final agent departed from the office, the analysts and Skip breathed a sigh of relief. Rusty romped and jumped on the legs of the group as he barked with excitement realizing the difference in the room's atmosphere.

"Dude, that was real, bro," said Mark, finally removing his sunglasses.

"Yeah man. That was real," replied Robert as he watched Lenny, still on the brink of tears, struggling to regain his composure

CHAPTER 26

TAKE THE MONEY AND RUN

As promised, Alex Sinovic didn't give up. The Director of Investor Relations from Luther Williams Energy eventually called back and confirmed that Wells Fargo was not their financial advisor on the transaction and never had been one. As Will Stephens, the managing director at Wells Fargo, had suggested to Gary Greene, the advisor was JP Morgan. Several days later, lawyers from Wells Fargo confirmed the same and informed him that the bank had made no mergers and acquisitions pitches to Luther Williams Energy.

The SEC investigation team made a flight to New York to specifically get Will Stephens' direct opinion on the forgery. Upon examining the pitchbook, Will couldn't believe what he was in front of his eyes. With the turn of each glossy page, he felt not only astonishment at the accuracy of the formatting but deep guilt for not believing his old colleague, Gary Greene, when they last spoke. The pitchbook could have fooled anyone. Will confirmed that this was not a Wells Fargo pitchbook, and yes, it was created by someone with investment banking experience and knowledge of the energy sector. These were no amateurs or scammers working out of India. Will agreed to testify to the same in a court of law.

With confirmation from the legal department and the personal attestation of a managing director at the firm, the SEC team had enough to go back to a Federal judge and secure a second search warrant – one that even divine intervention could not undo. As soon as the warrant was issued, the SEC was back in Houston searching Gemini's offices and the residences of Robert McClure, Mark Edwards, and Lenny Lee. However, this trip was entirely different. The three quivering former analysts were nowhere to be seen. Instead, Alex encountered three confident men completely unshaken by his visit as well as two more lawyers accompanying Skip Mathewson. Any additional questions at this point were promptly interrupted by the legal counsel and few meaningful words left the lips of Gemini Capital Management.

While a search by Federal agents is always embarrassing, there were no complaints from Gemini Capital or the firm of Watkins & Watkins. Their belongings were strewn across their apartments, and their brand new laptops were confiscated. Their computers would likely be several years out of date by the time of their eventual return. But the trio had made the most of their time since the last SEC visit, and the burner laptops had been destroyed shortly after the SEC's first visit. Their cell phones were confiscated as well. The SEC scoured through the data and tried their best to interpret the text messages from the IPCC conference with no tangible results. For a moment, the SEC thought that they were onto something when they found a message on Mark's phone: *AllTrust after party, 51st and 8th, wanna come? :-P*.

That message sent them a long way down a rabbit hole as they suspected the party could have been a drop off point for more of the pitchbooks. As a result, they contacted Ned Donaldson from AllTrust and interviewed anyone that could have been at the after party. Of course, no one in attendance had met anyone from Gemini Capital, seen any pitchbooks, or heard anything out of the ordinary regarding Luther Williams Energy. And, those that had heard about Newstar Exploration, like Bill Trevors from Quantico Capital and Collin Shepherd from Eagle Sky Investments, were in no mood to incriminate themselves. While this inquiry wasn't about Newstar, the investigation was too close to home, and both Bill and Collin remained tight-lipped about meeting a "Mark Hollis" from BNP Paribas at the after party. Naturally, Ned Donaldson was very careful with his recollection of that night as well. While cooperative, he certainly didn't say any more than what needed to be said. The lead went cold as quickly as it had seemed hot to the SEC.

Next, the SEC investigated the background behind the analysts' resignation at Latham Schroeder & Holt. While Mark, Lenny, and Robert had given perfectly satisfactory answers to those questions, Alex was convinced there had to be more to it. During his visit to Houston, Alex scheduled an interview with Ronald Lufkin about his former analysts, and Ron couldn't be any happier to oblige. Ron tried to inflict the most damage possible on his former analysts in the conversation. He pretended to barely care about his former analysts so that his scathing descriptions of them would seem unbiased. His true goal was to deliver the most misery and harm possible. Ron depicted his former employees as conniving and manipulative underlings with no sense of loyalty whatsoever. His version of the Wellco Solutions meeting in New Orleans was embellished and edited to the extreme. In his recollection of the story, Ron was an innocent victim who had placed his trust in a trio of monstrous sociopaths. He also happily volunteered information about his run-in with Gemini Capital at the IPCC. Ron described them as "sneaking around the conference" and surely searching for inside information, which, ironically, was true in a way. Before the SEC left his office, Lufkin made one last gracious offer to assist the investigation in any way possible.

This was getting somewhere. While not exactly solid evidence, Ronald Lufkin would be an excellent character witness, especially as a respected managing director and former supervisor. Based on Ron's testimony, the psychological profile of the culprits was coming together. Alex also talked with John Granton, who was more than thrilled to be interviewed by the SEC. It was a great story that he could tell his friends and acquaintances to make himself seem more important. Due to Ron's embarrassment over the New Orleans trip, John had never heard the full story behind the analysts' departure from the firm. Ron had made up a thinly detailed alternative version about firing Robert, after which Lenny and Mark had quit since they couldn't take the additional workload. John Granton had already been using them as a cautionary tale of poor work ethic to the new class of recruits working themselves to the bone. When John offered up this entirely different version of events surrounding the departure of the trio, Agent Sinovic was perplexed. In addition, Granton sketched an entirely different portrait of the analysts as lazy, dumb, unqualified slackers. In his opinion, they were the worst analyst class in the history of investment banking. When Alex inquired about the possibility of the group forging a pitchbook, John laughed and said that they were completely inept and too stupid to do something like that. In no way was John trying to save his former analysts, he was just offering up his honest opinion. In his own mind, John Granton was a financial genius while everyone else on this planet was an imbecile on the level of an insect.

With such a divergence from Lufkin's description of the "conniving" geniuses, Alex asked John to explain the contrast between his description and that of his managing director. John explained that Ron simply hadn't known the analysts well enough. If Ron interacted day-to-day with them, his opinion would match John's accurate description. In addition, all of their work was verified by him before reaching Lufkin. If everything seemed perfect, it was only because *he* made it so as the associate and gatekeeper to the managing director. The analysts were essentially taking credit for his work and effort – that's why Ron thought that they were so talented for a bunch of young analysts. Agent Sinovic had a couple of more administrative questions, but John couldn't answer them now. Ron was violently texting him with demands for a dozen new slides and the removal of another twenty from the latest pitchbook. After a rushed apology, John ran in desperation toward his desk, hoping to make the pitchbook changes quickly enough to avoid further wrath.

****

Despite the mess, the financial cost of the computers, and more significantly the cost of their legal fees, Robert and the guys felt lucky. At the end of the search, the SEC was in the same position as it had been two weeks prior. Furthermore, their only informant was deceased, and other than five fingerprints on a forged pitchbook, they had nothing. While there was plenty of circumstantial evidence like Gemini's recent ownership of LWE shares and the completely blank brand new computers, there was no hard evidence which could stand beyond the shadow of a doubt in a court of law. Alex Sinovic pressed the issue further for a while longer and searched avenue after avenue, but despite his best efforts, he soon eased back into his old comfortable routine of weekly soccer pickup games and lacrosse meets. It wasn't long before the whole ordeal was all but forgotten.

After the close encounter with the SEC, Robert, Mark, and Lenny decided to lay low for an extended period of time on new pitchbooks. They still came to the office every day, but only to perform legitimate research. Their stock portfolio was earning legal and, strangely enough, solid returns.

Mark purchased an even larger kegerator with multiple taps along with several pinball machines to complete his arcade for the office. With a legal payroll, the winnings so far were easily distributed to the rest of the team. Lenny bought his first BMW – his parents were very proud and impressed. Robert chose to save his funds for the moment.

Mark became the busiest member of Gemini and was growing into his new role. He even studied the energy market closer than ever, not to make smarter investments but rather to stay conversant in the industry over cocktails. Each morning, scores of research reports and commodity price outlooks were piled high on his desk. More importantly, his downtime was spent gathering investors for the fund, first beginning with his father and family friends. With a successful track record, Gemini Capital had no problem marketing itself. In addition, Mark began to dress and act the part of a successful young hedge fund manager. He leased a brand new Porsche, hoping in time to upgrade to a Lamborghini. His daily schedule was packed with lunches, drinks, and dinners with potential clients. His favorite lunch spots were anywhere that his potential clients could observe the valeting of his Porsche upon his arrival. Given his innate ability to attract people and this marketing blitz, Gemini's assets under management grew by the millions.

Lenny Lee dove head first into managing the portfolio. With the luxury to research and build his own Excel models rather than work on pitchbooks all day for some managing director, his stock picking abilities began to shine. However, their founder, Robert McClure, unexpected by the rest, grew more distant from the Gemini operations. He broke their strict early morning regimen and came and went from the office at his leisure. There was no reason for him to be perturbed or upset. The team had dodged the biggest bullet of their careers. This was the part of the story where the heroes enjoy their piña coladas under a palm tree, yet something didn't feel right. After the dust settled, morose and existential considerations began to plague him again. In the heat of the moment with a SEC agent sitting across the table, it was easy to dismiss these penetrating thoughts. But now that the immediate threat had passed, the thoughts crept in. The same unsettled feeling had kept him awake in New Orleans, and since then, it had grown stronger and could not be ignored anymore. The feeling seemed to have an intelligence and volition of its own, but it would not speak. It willed him to do something, but like a ghostly messenger, failed to communicate its demands.

After a particularly restless night, Robert drove an hour south to Galveston to walk alongside the surf and brown sand as the sun was rising. He strolled aimlessly, barefoot in khaki shorts and an expensive Vineyard Vines polo. The water today was partially translucent with two feet of visibility, which was pretty good for Galveston given its water quality ranged from chocolate milk to several feet of clarity under the most pristine conditions. The breeze gently whipped his skin with occasional powerful bursts blasting him with more intensity.

Earlier that week, he had read a disturbing story on *Bloomberg* about an energy portfolio manager who had taken his life by jumping from his high-end Manhattan condo. The story shook Robert. There was something wrong with this business. After so much money and so much success, the man's life ended alone and without meaning. His career would have been the envy of any young business student, yet that career ultimately provided him with no deeper sense of satisfaction. In fact, it may have been what drove him over the edge. Robert shared the news story with Mark and Lenny. They didn't seem to care much about it, and the tragedy didn't strike them deeply in the same way. According to Mark, this guy was just another faceless casualty of the market. It was simply something that occasionally happens. But for Robert, the story stayed with him the whole week and haunted him even this morning on his walk up the beach.

As he wandered Galveston's shores, he recalled a lecture from way back in his high school history class, long before he had even thought of becoming an investment banker. The class had been studying the Great Depression and among the many hardships of the era, the teacher related very similar tales of stockbrokers jumping to their deaths and the excesses on Wall Street which preceded the Crash. Was is it a mere coincidence that similar suicides still happen today in the financial sector and with more regularity than most would like to admit? Or, was there something intrinsic to this line of work that led its participants down a dark path?

And thinking of history, Robert realized that in his own small way, he, too, was a part of it. This energy slump was its own minor depression in Texas, and it had its own casualties. Instead of reading about the events in a book as a student, this recession was the story of his own life, and he had become a character in the book. Hard choices were no longer discussions of business school case studies; they were the very stuff of his life. Robert McClure, the struggling young student and young banking analyst, no longer existed. In his place was a successful portfolio manager, yet for some reason, he felt no more satisfied than at the beginning of his journey. Robert did not much like the person that Robert McClure had become. This portfolio manager felt so far away from the guy who grew up in Mississippi enjoying a much less complicated life.

He wondered if others felt the same in secret. Even people like Ronald Lufkin weren't particularly happy. Yes, they enjoyed their life, bought expensive cars, and seemed to have a good time, but there was something miserable at their core. If Ron's life was so great, why did discontent define his every action and anger flow from him so easily? While Ron was overjoyed with his big bonuses, the money could never fill a certain void within. Robert was no different; happy and comfortable on the outside, yet deeper down something tugged at his soul and left him feeling unsettled. Money did not seem to weaken the deep pull. In fact, it was even more noticeable now that both money and leisure were more available than ever.

On the other hand, plenty of people on Wall Street did seem to exist happily without ever thinking twice about the big picture. Any number of young business students would love to be in his shoes, but Robert felt far from victorious. Why did he want to be a banker in the first place? An easy answer was the money, but that old cliché didn't fit his motivations, or those of Mark or Lenny either. According to most folks on Main Street, investment bankers were the luckiest guys on the planet – supposedly the world is your oyster. In reality, when you became a banking analyst, you couldn't wait for a promotion to associate. And even after a promotion to associate, you were really nobody until you made it to vice president. But achieving that just made you more conscious that you weren't a MD. Of course, becoming a MD was supposed to be a transcendent experience. If you made it to that level, then, finally you would truly be on top of the heap. While everyone admires a MD's wealth and title, no business student stops to ask whether those managing directors are happy people. Let us not even go a step further to contemplate whether they are good and decent people. Robert had seen the answer first hand in his superiors and, unfortunately, within the sort of person he could feel himself becoming.

The pitchbooks had seemed like a way to escape that grueling, hollow climb and cheat the system, but they too failed to set him free. Each big win only temporarily alleviated his anxiety about becoming successful and soon raised the bar for the next goal which again could keep him only momentarily happy. While better than the misery of banking, this was just a different hamster wheel. This phenomenon is not unique to Wall Street. A medical student thinks fulfillment means becoming a doctor; an artist or musician anxiously awaits recognition; and a small town electrician thinks that a little more business would fix everything. When success finally arrives, in short order, we find ourselves empty again and wishing for something more. But, no matter how many times our efforts fail to bring us happiness, we never quit trying. Society even glorifies such pursuits and praises those who "love their jobs" and would gingerly work past retirement. Worse yet, we whip ourselves even harder to "chase our dreams" in a society where the achievement of one's most self-indulgent goals is treated as the height of glory, virtue, and accomplishment. It was this drive which had pushed Robert into his highly competitive profession. No one had forced him to work eighty hours per week for Ronald Lufkin. No one had held a gun to his head. It had been his choice to make a slave of himself. Instead of forging pitchbooks, he could have just simply quit Latham, Schroeder & Holt on any day of the week.

The whip and chain were held in his hands, not Ronald Lufkin's or anybody else's. If there was anyone to blame, it was the man walking this beach alone.

Robert gazed up at the sky, now filled with the morning light coming through the patches of clouds. The water cooled his bare feet with the oncoming waves. Thoughts of the office, their kegerator, their arcade games, and the sophisticated multi-screen stations whispered in his ear and begged him to return to Houston and revel in his success. These material trappings beckoned him to abandon this walk, but his spirit pulled him along for a couple of more steps alongside the crashing waves. Tired and troubled at his core, he rested on the jetty rocks protruding out toward the Gulf of Mexico. About fifteen yards further up the jetty, a fisherman worked a cast net. A pleasure pier in the distance reflected the rays of the sun from its carnival rides and mini-roller coaster. Perhaps the only way to escape the carnival was to refuse to play, but how does any young man resist the almost primal urge to succeed and stand out from the rest, to conqueror and vanquish? Maybe the ocean could tell him the answer. His soul screamed for answers, and he could almost feel it being ripped from his body, drawn by a magnetic force both ethereal and as real as the jetty rocks below him. Its magnetic pull had always been there, but the direction of its will was still unknown to him. As Robert walked back to his car parked on the seawall, flying seagulls flanked him from both sides and traced his every move. They had been watching him for some time, but only now was he paying attention. Robert smiled at them as he climbed into his car and made his way back to Houston.

CHAPTER 27

BUILDING ON A DREAM

Mark's networking focused on smaller accredited investors: doctors, lawyers, dentists, and the like. Nonetheless, piece by piece, Gemini amassed $25 million in assets under management, an enormous amount for someone of his age and limited experience. The fund offered the standard two and twenty fee schedule. Under this structure, Gemini earned 2% of the assets under management each year and 20% of any profits beyond that. Even if the fund remained flat, the team would earn $500,000 per year on the 2% fee alone. Of course, the trouble was that few investors would stick around with flat performance. However, given their less-than-legal tactics, meeting investor expectations was the least of their concerns. Further, unless the market experienced a major crash, they were basically guaranteed upside and another 20% on those returns. Sure, there were overhead costs such as expensive subscription services for FactSet and Bloomberg, but with their low rent in an older building, there was more than enough for them to split.

Gemini's track record had become more valuable than all of their previous trades combined as it served as the marketing tool to bring in more funds. This was the real way to cash in on the fake pitchbooks. On their biggest heist so far, the guys had earned $650,000. With a legal fund, Gemini could earn half a million as a minimum by simply collecting their 2% fee. If they achieved an easy 10% return on the $25 million under management, Gemini would earn another $500,000 for their 20% cut, plus the profit on their own stake in the fund. Being a legal hedge fund manager was the biggest scam of all.

Soon, Mark set his fund-raising goals on larger accounts. Houston had plenty of oil-rich moguls who could single-handedly invest $20 million. Landing even one such investor would mean nearly doubling their assets under management. To capture one of these whales, Mark attended high end charity events like the Wildcatters' Ball and became Houston's latest self-made socialite. While this was the first part of his plan, the next step was climbing the social ladder with an excursion to Dallas where the old oil money invested its wealth. Back in the early twentieth century, the first oil barons to strike it rich went straight to Dallas. This early preference for the city has reverberated through the ages and Dallas is still considered an old money town in Texas while Houston is the oil industry's working town. Unbeknownst to most even living there, the rivalry between the cities is much more entrenched than simply the Cowboys versus the Texans. For these historical reasons, the majority of Texas hedge funds were located in Dallas with only a few notable names in Houston.

The three sat at the same conference table where the SEC had interrogated them only months earlier. Lenny had brought the group together to plan the next major steps for Gemini Capital. Mark poured everyone an ice cold IPA from the kegerator and passed the glasses around the table. He was in his full suit, fresh from a client lunch earlier in the day.

"You guys gotta try this new IPA. It's amazing."

"Cool, thanks," replied Robert.

"Thank you, Mark," said Lenny. "Now, on to something other than the latest IPA from Karbach Brewing. We need to make some big changes. I mean rethink the way that we've been doing everything with Gemini up to this point. I've been thinking about this for a while."

"Really?" said Mark motioning to their fridge full of frosted vodka, their kegerator, huge TV screens, and ping-pong table. "Doesn't look like we've been doing it all wrong to me."

"Yeah, we've done great but who can forget our little incident with the SEC? We just got freakin' lucky. If it wasn't for that, this meeting would be taking place in the jail commissary right now. I'm talking about the next big phase for Gemini," said Lenny. "We can't keep doing leveraged bets with call options – it draws way too much attention. We all already understand that and have taken a break from making them until things cool down. However, even when it's time for the next one, we can't keep making fake pitchbooks every few months."

"Well, what do you suggest, Lenny? That we go fully legit? I mean your trades have done alright, but they're not exactly bringing in the big investors," commented Mark. "No offense, bro. I'm bringing in as many investors as I can, but if our performance doesn't match our promises, it's going to be tough to keep them coming."

"No, you've got a point, and I totally agree, and we're definitely not going legit. Well, not completely anyway. Lately, I've been reading about some of the most successful scams ever on Wall Street and what we can learn from them. Do you guys remember why Bernie Madoff's scam went so well?" asked Lenny.

Mark stared back at him blankly.

Robert chimed in. "Yeah, it was genius. No one suspected him of doing anything wrong because he was consistently beating the market but not by much. He figured out that you don't have to be the guy that produces 30% returns every year. You can make a killing by being the guy who gives investors a 12% return consistently when the market averages 10%. What made it even more genius is that smaller returns in his Ponzi scheme also meant smaller payouts to investors. If your investors are earning huge paper returns, those returns eventually get cashed out, which is a problem for any long-term Ponzi scheme. So, with his scam, which didn't promise ridiculous returns, it took much longer to get caught. Only when the stock market sank and investors began pulling funds regardless of the performance did he get caught."

"Yup, that's right. And I'm not saying that we do a Ponzi scheme. That would be really dumb," stated Lenny. "What I'm saying is that we use Bernie's 12% idea going forward. We just need to beat the market by a small margin. Over the long term, that needs to be our main marketing point with clients – not our huge returns. Don't get me wrong, Mark, you've done an awesome job of selling our big wins to investors and it's been important to get our fund off the ground, but realistically, we can't keep producing those same wins without leveraged options. As our assets under management grow, those sorts of bets will only get more suspicious and difficult to pull off. When we were buying $90,000 in short-term call options, no one noticed it. If we placed a $5 million bet on the same call options, alarm bells will go off at the SEC, and we're already on their shit list. On top of that, we would need new pitchbooks every few months to keep producing the returns, and the more pitchbooks, the higher our chances of getting busted."

Mark took another swig of his beer. "Well, thank you for the kind words about my extraordinary talents Lenny, but what do you suggest?"

"Hey, you deserve it man. Just like Bernie, the real talent is in raising money. Any idiot can create a Ponzi scheme – it takes someone cunning enough to bring in investors to make it work. Bernie built his fund by pulling millions upon millions from synagogues around New York using every connection and acquaintance in the book. In the same way, if we can provide consistent above-market returns and Mark can keep selling our strategy to investors, we've got it made, but our strategy will be even safer and near foolproof."

"Done, dude. Show me the returns, Lenny, and I'll sell it," said Mark confidently. "But I'm still confused what you're getting at with Bernie Madoff. How are we going to consistently beat the market without using the pitchbooks?"

"I was just getting there – hold your horses. Here's the basic game plan. We invest in the energy space to the best of our ability but not in anything too risky. You know, maybe we place our funds into nine really solid companies. Think big names like Pioneer Natural Resources and EOG to give our fund stability. With these nine companies in our portfolio, we try to just meet the average return of the XOP energy index. In a sense, this part of our portfolio plays defense and only tries to track the price of oil. The point is not to be the next market genius – the point is not to lose money with these stock picks. If energy stocks in the market are earning a 10% on average, our portfolio will try to meet that 10% on these nine stocks.

"However, for that tenth pick, we make another pitchbook idea. We won't use call options, but we can still allocate more weight to that stock in the portfolio over the others. So think about it this way: if nine stocks track the average and the tenth stock is a home run, our portfolio will always beat the market average by just a little bit. It's simple math Our gain on any given year might not be huge, but the end result will be just like Bernie. When everyone else is earning an average 10% return, we'll be earning 12%

or 13%, thanks to always having one stock which makes a killing while the rest follow the average. With a pitchbook stock always in our back pocket, we essentially can't lose and at the same time, nothing about our position would attract attention. If the other picks take up eight to ten percent of the portfolio and the pitchbook stock takes up fifteen to twenty percent, nothing looks overly nefarious – it's just a slightly stronger weighting. No call options, no leverage, nothing that draws the SEC's eyes back on us. What's even better is that this reduces the number of pitchbooks. We only need one or two at most per year. In some sense, Wall Street has been doing the same thing for ages. Hedge funds research non-stop, but it's that one stock idea made on an inside tip that makes their year. The only difference with us is that we're not going to wait on that tip – we'll just create it."

"It's pretty smart, man," said Robert.

"Yeah, I like it – it's brilliant, Lenny." Obligatory high-fives went around the table per the team's now regular custom. "Dude, that is F–ing awesome, man!" exclaimed Mark, who went over to the freezer and pulled out a chilled bottle of Belvedere along with a couple of frosted shot glasses to celebrate their new plan. While Mark was already on cloud nine, Robert appeared less enthused. "Why so glum? What's up dude?" said Mark.

"Guys, the plan sounds amazing, but I've actually been meaning to talk with y'all about something as well…I actually also wanted to use this meeting to drop a bombshell…uh, I didn't know that this is what Lenny wanted to talk about today…so uh…it really makes what I'm about to say a lot more awkward, but I hope you guys understand. Man, Lenny, I thought you were gonna talk about getting a new printer or something! You really messed me up here."

"Wwwhhat…what's up man?"

"I've been thinking about a lot of things, and I'm going to have to leave the team."

"What do you mean?" asked Mark in shock. "You don't think the plan will work?"

"No, that's not it. I know that the plan will work. It's fucking genius. You guys are fucking genius. What I mean is that I'm done with this in general…like the whole thing. I'm throwing in the towel. I hate doing this now just as Lenny laid out the new master plan, but seriously, I think I'm done. I've been meaning to talk with you about it for a while, but I just couldn't find the right time. I guess now is as good as ever."

"But, dude, we fucking need you man! You can't just bail on us like that, especially when we're ready to enter like phase two here – you're the one that got us into this in the first place. Dude, you're like our Steve Jobs – we can't do it without you. Didn't you hear Lenny's plan? This is going to be incredible!" exclaimed Mark.

"Yeah, what the hell, Robert?" said Lenny.

"Thanks Mark, I like the Steve Jobs comment, and I appreciate it, and I appreciate everything that you've done for me and everything that we've been through. But it's not true that you need me anymore. You two are the best pitchbook monkeys on the Street, and I'm not good at raising money – I haven't raised one cent for the fund. My job here is done."

"Dude, this is not cool. Look how far we've gotten. This is everything that we dreamed about. Do I need to get you another beer from the kegerator? Cuz, I'll get you another beer. I don't think that you're thinking straight, bro," said Mark.

"Yeah, grab me a beer."

Mark went and refilled everyone's glasses. They clinked them and then proceeded to guzzle down the beers followed by icy vodka shots.

"It's just the whole SEC thing. I don't know man. It freaked me out. I don't think I can do it anymore. I wake up in the middle of the night and can't sleep because I'm worrying about everything all time." He was lying.

The SEC didn't bother him much at this point, and he thought Lenny's plan was damn good, and as safe as any scheme was likely to be. But, like most young men, he had a problem confronting his friends on moral issues and dilemmas. Robert could have told them exactly what was bothering him. In fact, he could talk about his thoughts on the big picture for hours. However, being young and immature and not wanting to insult his friends, he played dumb. "Yeah, I'm serious guys. I don't know…I could handle high pressure and stuff back at the bank, but something with the law just freaks me out. I'm seriously stressing out all the time. Why do you think I've been skipping out at the office all the time? I know that you've noticed."

"I had no idea that it was bothering you that much," said Lenny. "You always seemed so cool and collected in all of the situations that we got our ourselves into. You were our leader, man."

"Robert, quit worrying about everything. The new plan is solid. It's designed to make sure we don't get in trouble again. Didn't you hear Lenny? We'll be doing one pitchbook a year, maybe two at the most," pleaded Mark. "We don't have to do one for like eight months or so, man. We're in good shape now. Don't bail just when things are getting good. Just do one more with us, come on man. You can double your money," urged Mark.

"Naw, dude. I'm sorry to let you down. You're the best, but I can't do it anymore," said Robert, and then he paused. "Look, I think that this has been the best year of my life, and I owe it to you guys, but I'm done." They could see on his face that there was no convincing him. Robert was gone.

"Well, what are you going to do?" Lenny asked.

"I don't know…probably the same thing every washed up investment banker does…you know, maybe I'll start a cupcake shop or write a tell-all book."

"Ha!" said Mark. "You do that, but I'll only come by if they're gluten-free artisanal cupcakes."

"Don't worry Mark. You know they will be. Just for you."

Another round of drinks turned into several more. Before they knew it, the group was grabbing an Uber to the Ginger Man in Rice Village. After perusing the lengthy beer menu, each ordered a round of miscellaneous rare craft beers. They sat at a well-worn wooden bar table and exchanged horror stories of working for Ron, tall tales from college, and recalled their blunders in New York City. As the night wore on, their beer choices became less discriminating. Soon, the long beer list was discarded in favor of Coronas with lime. They had been working on pitchbooks for so long, both real and fake, that they almost didn't realize what good friends they had become. Robert was glad for this night alongside his comrades in arms who had survived the foxholes of investment banking with him. Looking across the table, Robert knew that he would miss Mark and Lenny, but he had to do what he had to do.

The following morning, he came into the office early and packed his stuff into an appropriately titled cardboard banker's box. Usually, you're filling up one of these after getting the boot or moving onto a better job. That wasn't the case here for once. In fact, Robert had no idea what he was doing next, but he did know where he was going. He would go back to see his dad in Laurel. It felt strange looking around the office one last time. He stared at the kegerator. What the hell…they had a kegerator in the office. He turned off the lights and walked out.

CHAPTER 28

CATFISH

Robert pulled up to the hospital in his Ford F-150. The truck had a few years on it now since its purchase following his departure from Gemini Capital. The sides were plastered with mud, grass, and twigs which had caked around the wheels. Robert wore a camou ball cap, khaki pants, and a green polo. His chin was scruffy and unshaven and his curly hair grew wildly without any hair gel to tame it. The hospital was the biggest structure in town, built in 1979 and renovated once in 1998. The second biggest building was the wire factory followed by the high school. He parked his truck in the half empty parking lot and made his way inside. He took off his hat on the way in and waved to the receptionist at the patient check-in. "Hi Judi! How's it going?"

"Hey Robert, good, how you doin'? Bob wanted me to tell you that he's goin' huntin' this weekend and wanted to see if you were comin' out?" replied Judi.

"I'll give him a call. I've got a pretty busy weekend with a friend's wedding on Saturday so I'm not sure if I can make it out," said Robert, walking onward. He side-stepped a group of scrambling nurses and doctors and then swerved out of the way of a rolling hospital bed.

"Hey Doc Owens! Save any lives today?" said Robert to one of the passing physicians.

"Not yet, Robert. It's too early. You fleeced anyone on their bill yet?" replied the doctor with a chuckle as she kept walking down the hall.

"Ouch, Doc, that hurts...that really hurts." He grabbed at his heart with both hands and laughed. His next turn led him to the administrative wing of the hospital. While the rest of the building was at least somewhat aesthetically pleasing thanks to the 1998 renovation, the admin wing remained untouched since 1979, carpets and all. The walls were adorned with terrible motel art and pictures of seagulls with generic motivational phrases underneath them. He turned the corner toward a set of cubicles and stopped at the one with the nametag, "Robert McClure" above it. There was no chance of him getting his own office for another couple of years at the hospital. His job was to keep things running smoothly in the finance group so that the hospital could pay its bills. The doctors were the masters of the universe here. Other than the previously mentioned wire factory, the county hospital was the best job in town, and Robert was glad to have it.

Following a short break immediately after he left the Street, Robert began the hospital job and had quickly been promoted to Manager of Accounts Receivable and Payable. The hospital's finance department had never seen a work ethic like his, which meant showing up on time and occasionally staying late to finish work. During his short tenure, he had rebid several key supply contracts, which saved the hospital an enormous amount of money. He had also reconfigured their receivables system to get cash from the insurance companies an average of nine days earlier than before. His natural business acumen made him a rising star in the small-town health system. Best of all, it was all so easy. For Robert, every day felt like vacation in comparison to investment banking. He tossed his hat and bag on top of his cubicle and fired up his gigantic ten-year-old desktop computer. The lumbering tower of a computer soon showed his old familiar friend on the screen, Excel, except in this case, it was the 2003 version. His list of tasks was very short today, and given that it was Friday he was eager to get out of there.

On the other side of the cubicle, Eric and Dave spoke over a video playing on their screen. They were both recent graduates from Mississippi State University on their first job in accounts receivable, reporting to their manager, Robert McClure.

"What are you guys looking at?" asked Robert. "Did you find another ridiculous hunting compilation on YouTube or are you two perverts staring at the girls of the SEC again?"

"Naw Robert, check this guy out. Have you heard of him?" said Dave.

Robert leaned over the cubicle to see a video on *Bloomberg* news.

He smiled.

There was Mark Edwards, a few years older and dressed in a custom tailored suit and wearing a Rolex that almost blinded the camera. Across from him were Pimm Fox and Erik Schatzker of *Bloomberg*. It had been years since he had seen his old friend.

"His fund beat the S&P 500 and all the main energy indexes four straight years in a row. This guy is a genius!" exclaimed Eric excitedly.

"Let me introduce my next guest, Mark Edwards of Gemini Capital Management!"

Robert always knew that the guys could do it, and he was happy for them.

Pimm Fox began the interview with an open-ended question. "Mark, your fund Gemini Capital Management has been an amazing story. Here you were, a young analyst at an energy investment bank in Houston working insane hours and yet you were able to put together your own ideas and build this fund in your spare time."

"Yes, that's exactly right." Mark spoke with superb confidence which Robert did not recognize from the kid that he once knew. It was impressive. He had grown into his own as a professional. "You know, me and Leonard Lee from Gemini worked day and night coming up with ideas, and we ended up making more money in our personal accounts than from our banking bonuses. When you have that level success with your own trading strategy, it's only a matter of time before you give the bank their walking papers and start your own fund. It was the next logical step." Mark brushed his fingers through his wavy blond hair and smiled at the camera.

"That's an amazing story. You and Lenny have got to be the smartest young energy fund managers on the Street. You've solidly beat the market four years in a row – that's very, very difficult. How do you guys do it? What's your approach to investing?"

"Well Pimm, it's all about picking a solid company and sticking with it. Companies like EOG and Pioneer Natural Resources are always good buys, as are even bigger players like Chevron and Shell." On the screen, the tickers for each stock appeared with their year to date performance. "I think that most people on the Street focus too much on the next quarter, but you have to be more patient. You gotta be a buy and hold forever investor. That's really where you can create the most value for your investors."

"That's fascinating Mark. So, are those your top picks for 2018?"

"Yeah that's right. Buy EOG and PXD and hold onto them. I wouldn't say it's a buy of 2018. I'd say it's a buy opportunity of 2023. These are solid companies, and we're going to hold onto them for an extended period of time. When the companies can no longer extract abnormal profits, then we're going to sell them, but I don't see that happening for a long, long time," responded Mark.

"That is an incredible insight. Thank you again! We just spoke with Mark Edwards from Gemini Capital Management. Join us again next week as we talk with David Einhorn from Greenlight Capital and Bill Ackman from Pershing Square on their latest takes in the market."

Dave closed the Bloomberg video on his screen. "Man, what I would give to work for someone like Mark Edwards. I mean that guy is so smart!"

"Hey Robert! People around the hospital say that you used to work on Wall Street. Is that true?" asked Eric, his eyes growing wide.

"No, it's total bullshit…at least for the most part. I worked in the back office of a bank for a little while. Trust me, it wasn't any more exciting than what you two guys are doing right now." Robert tried to downplay his investment banking past. In little towns, it's best to keep your mouth shut about such things. Folks will either assume that you're full of yourself, or rumors will flow that you're loaded with cash. Either outcome is not good. However, the latter was not completely untrue. Robert still had a nice chunk of the cash left. But after the F-150 and a big deposit on a cabin about fifteen minutes out of town, it wasn't nearly as much as some people thought.

"Man, I don't know Robert. Sounds better than being stuck out here. Those guys are so freakin' lucky, man! What would you do with that type of cash, Eric?"

"First thing – I'd buy a banana yellow Porsche…."

Eric and Dave kept talking while Robert returned to his easy but monotonous work. Around three o'clock, he decided to call it a day. "Hey Eric, Dave. Come on, let's pack it up guys. You did a great job this week. Let's leave early today." As his team celebrated, he shut down his computer.

"Hey Robert. You wanna go out to Jimmy's for a beer after work? We're meeting a couple of people out there?"

"No, I'm good guys. Thanks for the invite and watch yourself on those pool tables. I don't want you borrowing on your next paycheck to pay the rent."

"Robert, Minnesota Fats has nothing on these skills! Come on, Dave. Let's go – first beer is on me."

"Alright, catch you guys on Monday."

Robert walked out of the office and went back to his truck. He put his ball cap back on and hit the highway with his windows down. Within minutes, pine woods surrounded his truck and filled the cab with the fresh and earthy smell of bark and pine needles. The truck made a right on a side road where the pavement soon disappeared and turned into dirt and gravel. A cloud of orange dust trailed behind his truck as he pulled up to his grandpa's land and the lake on it. Robert opened his tailgate and pulled out a couple of fishing rods. Two had floaters on them for the catfish while another had a neon colored bass rig. His dad was just getting off work and would arrive in an hour or so to help man one of those poles. He set the fishing gear next to the water and returned to the truck to retrieve a lawn chair and a cooler, but left his shotgun in the truck. On his first summer out here, Robert again pulverized the cottonmouth moccasin population, and they had not reclaimed their ground since. He cracked open a craft beer from the cooler and cast the two floater rods. With those in place, he began trolling the bass reel along the edges of the bank. The sun was still out and shimmered on the water. The sky was blue with a couple of puffy clouds above, and a light breeze flowed through the trees. After a few casts with no success, Robert tried again, not expecting much as this was far from the optimal time of day for bass fishing. And then suddenly, "Whooosh!"

something pulled on his line – it was big for sure. He smiled, jerked the pole to set the hook, and started reeling it in.

Acknowledgements

First, I would like to thank my parents who spent more time in their life reading textbooks than fiction and I hope that they enjoyed the novel. My wife, who has patiently withstood my rants, whether on chapter structure or the nuisances of formatting and font choices. Thank you to some early readers including Andy Peterson and Vel who let me know the book was on the right track. In addition, a big thank you to the many people that I've worked with in the finance industry who make this business tolerable – you know who you are and if you're not sure, that's a problem isn't it. Lastly, a special thanks to George. May you figure it out without the sleepless nights at an investment bank unless that is what you want.

About the Author

Vedran Vuk graduated with a MS in Finance from Johns Hopkins University and a BBA in Economics from Loyola University of New Orleans. Mr. Vuk has worked in finance for over a decade. He began his career as a mergers and acquisitions investment banking analyst in Houston, Texas. Mr. Vuk has been quoted in publications such as the *Wall Street Journal*, *Investor's Business Daily*, and *Yahoo Finance!* among others.

Contact

If you enjoyed *The Pitchbook*, please leave a review on Amazon.com. If you would like to contact the author, write to ThePitchbook@gmail.com.

Made in the USA
Middletown, DE
30 December 2024

68535870R00170